A TRAILS BO

GREAT
CROSS-COUNTRY
SKI TRAILS

WISCONSIN, MINNESOTA, MICHIGAN, AND ONTARIO

WM. CHAD McGRATH

TRAILS BOOKS
Black Earth, Wisconsin

Library of Congress Catalog Card Number: 2001093463

ISBN: 1-931599-02-5

Copy editor: Laura H. Kearney
Design and production: Sarah White
Map design: Pamela Harden
Cover design: John Huston
Cover photo: Richard Hamilton Smith

Printed in the United States of America by McNaughton & Gunn

06 05 04 03 02 01   6 5 4 3 2 1

Trails Books, a division of Trails Media Group, Inc.
P.O. Box 317 • Black Earth, WI 53515
(800) 236-8088 • e-mail: books@wistrails.com

To four young girls: Leslie Ann, Rebecca, Katherine, and Madeline Tompach.
May they always love snow and accept cold as its companion.

For Martha, a wonderful person who embraced skiing
with the spirit and playfulness she brought to all of us who knew her.
If there's snow beyond, she's skiing on it.

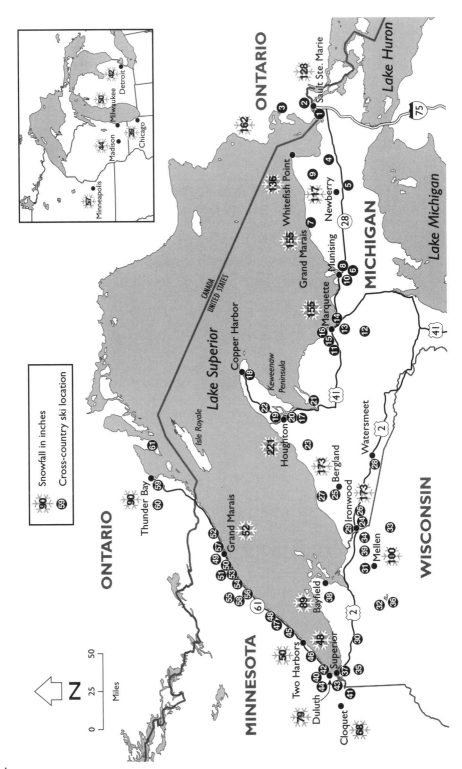

iv

Contents

IV. The Keweenaw Area

V. The Western Upper Peninsula

VI. Northern Wisconsin

VII. The Duluth Area

Introduction

I SPENT AN AMAZING WINTER preparing this book. I was fortunate to have skied more kilometers than many folks ski in a lifetime. I experienced wonderful skiing and equally wonderful vistas, including the ones I encountered while standing on my skis, looking south, north, east, and west at Lake Superior.

There were other wonderful vistas. People ask me my favorite. But favorite is a difficult concept when applied to vistas. Mood is everything, and mood depends on many things: weather, time of day, when I had eaten last, if I was in a hurry, where else I had been that day, if I was alone. I could go on.

My favorite? Sorting through my mental images, I always return to a view of the Sawtooth Mountains, silhouetted by the setting sun. I had skied to the base of Pincushion Mountain, just outside Grand Marais, Minnesota. It was getting late, and I had been skiing fast so that I wouldn't be out in the pitch black of the northern night. My endorphins were surging even before I climbed the quarter mile to the summit. I reached the bare rock knob just before the sun dipped behind the Sawtooths. I saw, for the first time, the saw teeth of the mountains to the southwest. It was amazing, enlightening, and beautiful. As the wind swept past me, over me, I just stood there watching the sun disappear beneath eons-old rock. I was briefly part of it all, melded with nature, complete.

To be sure, there were other impressive vistas: looking down on Duluth-Superior from the west end of the big lake while perched atop Bardons Peak on the Magney-Snively Trail. I could see both the north and south shores recede to the horizon. Another wondrous vista revealed the massive rock outline of the Sleeping Giant stretched out before me, across the horizon on the other side of Marie Louise Lake at Sleeping Giant Provincial Park on Ontario's Sibley Peninsula. There are others: seeing Lake Superior from the northeast at Stokley Creek and from atop King Mountain in Ontario; from the East Vista at the

Porcupine Mountains, peering down at the lakeshore and seeing all the way to Ontonagon and beyond, to the base of Upper Michigan's Keweenaw Peninsula. And there was that incredible wall of rock and the valley below leading to Tettegouche State Park, visible from the Northwoods Ski Trail near Silver Bay, Minnesota. Yes, there were lots of impressive vistas. I have recalled just a few here.

Background of the book. I came up with the concept for this book a couple of years ago, during the low-snow season of 1998–1999. It occurred to me that I'd never seen much information about areas around Lake Superior, areas that I knew received lots of snow—or at least more than other Midwestern ski areas. I had skied several of these places, always enjoying what they had to offer.

Some weather research helped me quantify the concept further, but also helped me realize that annual snowfall is extremely variable. I changed my methodology a bit, from using average annual snowfall depth alone to factoring in a trail's proximity to Lake Superior. As a result, all but two of the trails in this book are within the Lake Superior Basin, as defined by drainage area. One of the nonbasin trails is Rock Lake. It is included because so many people love it, it gets lots of snow, and it is close to the basin. The second outlier is the Mecca trail system, near Mercer, Wisconsin. Mecca, which is within a few miles of Superior's watershed, is my home trail. This fact, plus Mercer's ample average snowfall, made me include it.

Information on snow depth at 17 sites around Lake Superior and at five Midwestern cities is included on the ski trails map on page iv. This information was gleaned from the Midwest Regional Climate Center Web site; the Canadian data was taken from the Environment Canada Web site.

The snowiest place in the climate center's data is Houghton, Michigan, with an average annual snowfall total of 221 inches. Houghton also holds the record snowfall for a single season: 356 inches in 1989. Environment Canada reported that a place near Thunder Bay, Nolalu, received 40.6 inches of snow in a 24-hour period back in March 1975.

Intent of the book. In writing this book it has been my intent that it be more than a travel guide and tool skiers can use to locate and enjoy cross-county trails. My goal has been that the book should also entertain. It is the story of one individual's experiences and adventures while skiing some of the most beautiful trails in the nation.

Each of the 61 tours is unique. They do not necessarily describe an entire trail system. I picked those parts of the system that I felt were scenic, fun skiing. I skied every kilometer of each tour and described what I saw and felt as creatively and accurately as possible. I took notes out on the trail. After all, memory and pencil serve better than memory alone.

I've also included information on nine other ski trails that, for various reasons, I was unable to visit. These trails can be found at the end of several sections in the book.

The book's 10 major sections are presented geographically. They start in the northeast, with Ontario's Stokley Creek. From there we move south and west through the Upper Peninsula, into Wisconsin, around the west end of Lake Superior into Duluth, Minnesota, and up the North Shore, ending with Ontario's Sleeping Giant Provincial Park on the Sibley Peninsula.

The 61 trails, organized alphabetically within each of the sections for ease of use, include a narrative description and a map. The descriptions contain information about directions to the trailhead; grooming, and whether the trail is strideable, skateable, or both; total kilometers in the system and the length of the tour being described; whether there's a fee charged for using the trail; what trailhead facilities exist, if any; and the address and phone number for the trail. Since many trails did not have a Web address, I decided to put such information in a central place. You'll find the list at the end of the book.

Here are a few suggestions for using this book and, more importantly, for ensuring that your ski experiences are as enjoyable and safe as possible.

Trails change. Unlike buildings, ski trails are not monolithic entities. They change, much like the weather. Some wax and wane with people's interest. Some are the creation of one or two individuals; if these people die, or move, or lose interest, the trail deteriorates or ceases to be. Others lose their easements, or get sold and subdivided. Lots of things affect a trail's existence.

Several trails I checked out for this book were like this. The most famous of these is Suicide Bowl, in Ishpeming, Michigan. After many years, this wonderful Nordic skiing area, including several ski jumps and more than 30 kilometers of trail, is no more. A mining company that owns the land will be piling overburden on the site. Grand Portage, in Minnesota, is another formerly thriving trail system, which was essentially nonexistent when I visited it. A charming old trailhead shelter stood near the parking area, but the trails were not groomed, except by snowmobilers, who had taken them over. Inside the shelter were several pairs of forlorn-looking skis and poles. All else was disheveled. In Wisconsin, the old Cedar Trail, from Highway 2 down to Saxon Harbor, isn't groomed anymore. I had planned on skiing this with friends who loved the place. We were all disappointed about its demise. The sad thing is that these things could befall any ski trail. To quote Paul Walker, builder, owner, and groomer of the former Goat Farm Trails near Wautoma, Wisconsin, "A ski trail is an ephemeral thing." At least in part, that's what makes them so precious.

Measuring distance. This is a difficult topic. Americans avoid using the metric system like the plague. Canadians use metric. I've decided to follow the lead of our northern neighbors and use meters and kilometers in this book whenever describing trail distances. One of the reasons is that most trail maps use kilometers.

For another, metric is easier. While out skiing and then while writing this book, I used kilometers, then meters. At first, I converted meters to yards, but it didn't take long until I was thinking in meters. Think fast: How many yards in a quarter mile? Now, how many meters in a quarter kilometer? Since the metric system is based on 10, converting from kilometers to meters (or vice versa) is easy. A quarter kilometer is 250 meters. Have you figured out what a quarter mile is in yards yet?

If you must convert kilometers into miles in order to comprehend distances, there are 1.609 km in a mile. Some people find converting the other way easier: .62 mile is equal to 1 km. Another way to think about it is that 5 km equals approximately 3 miles; 10 km, twice that, is 6 miles; 15 km equals 9 miles; 20 km equals 12 miles. Converting meters into yards is even easier. Just think of a meter as a long yard. The conversion multiplier is 1.1. So, one meter equals 1.1 yard, 100 meters equals 110 yards. And mentally converting meters to kilometers is a lot easier than converting yards to miles. If you don't think in kilometers and meters now, it won't take you long to pick up the system.

I have kept road distances in miles, except when describing such distances in Canada. All elevations are given in feet. All distances, be they road or trail, should be taken as approximate. I did not use a government certified measuring wheel for either effort. Vehicles vary by 10 to 15 percent in their mileage measurements. And my dead reckoning on the trail was sometimes off a bit, too.

Since my first cross-country ski more than 25 years ago, I have loved it as I have no other endeavor. Lucky for me that first experience was on a warm, moonlit night, on an open, forgiving golf course trail. Had someone dragged me off to a scary trail, full of precipitous drops and hairpin, hair-raising turns, I might never have gone out on skis again.

Consider this bit of advice when skiing for the first few times: Don't get involved beyond your level of interest or level of ability. If you're already an experienced skier, don't treat beginners as if they were trail veterans. Yet that's a tough order. Like most skills, skiing must be learned. Some people learn it easily, some have considerable difficulty, some give up. Some folks learn a little and participate at the same level: a little. Others learn just enough so they can have fun, ski five to ten times a year, and look forward to the first skiable snow. And some of us become fanatics. We spend thousands of dollars and hundreds of hours on skiing. We don't just look forward to the first snowfall, we seek it. And spring brings mixed emotions, even sadness, as we watch the last snow disappear.

And so it is today, April 7. A southeast wind rakes the landscape, piling leaves against waning snow banks, pushing birch tops into one another like so many broom heads. The grayness of the day overwhelms all else; the snow is no more, skiing is past. I am sad, afraid that life without snow will be less.

Yet memory tells me there will be green leaves atop graceful trees and bright shiny sun on blue water. Renewal and regrowth will return. And I can always reread these tours. That will help. I hope that you enjoy the book as much as I enjoyed writing it.

Chad McGrath
Springstead, Wisconsin

Acknowledgments

The essence is to travel gracefully rather than arrive.

I have always liked that quote. Yet when writing a book such as this, traveling "gracefully" can be difficult. Arriving becomes all-important. The folks listed below not only helped me arrive but, most important, helped find some of the trails. My thanks.

Phil Leversedge, Paul Sundberg, and Al Hodapp, park managers at Minnesota's Tettegouche, Gooseberry Falls, and Cascade River State Parks.

David Williams, Bear Track Outfitting, Grand Marais, Minnesota.

Jeff and Susan Gecas, owners of the Gun Flint Tavern in Grand Marais, and Deb Bennett, also of the Gun Flint Tavern.

Emilie Good, receptionist, and Becky Bartol, trails administrator, both of the Superior National Forest office near Tofte, Minnesota.

Peter Crooks, Marc Bode, and Chris Hegg, who helped me with information about the Thunder Bay area.

Iris Renolds, who graciously gave me some of her soup, and Jim Dyson, who shared his considerable knowledge of the Sibley Peninsula—both during my visit to Sleeping Giant Provincial Park.

The folks at Duluth Parks and Recreation.

Mary Morgan, parks and recreation administrator for the city of Superior, Wisconsin.

Cecilia Miljevich, of Milje's Trails fame.

Stacy Maki and Dawn Buss, both of the Ottawa National Forest, Stacy in Ironwood, Michigan, and Dawn in Ontonagon, Michigan.

Tracy Barrett, of the Baraga County (Michigan) Tourist and Recreation Association.

Carol Fulsher and Bob Mahaney, who helped me get a handle on the very fluid cross-county skiing situation in the Marquette and Ishpeming area.

Ann Wilson, of the Michigan DNR Upper Peninsula Field Headquarters in Marquette.

Barbara O'Neill, of Marquette Parks and Recreation, who understood my humorous response to their deer population reduction program.

George Herbener, whom I met at Blueberry Ridge near Marquette and who helped me understand my camera.

Laure Tansy, of the Seney National Wildlife Refuge.

Dick Weber, of the St. Ignace District of the Hiawatha National Forest.

John Krzycki, of the Sault Ste. Marie Forest Management Unit, Michigan DNR.

Dean Greenwood, manager and guru of Sault Trails and Recreation, Inc.

Fraser and Elaine Craig, of Stokley Creek, wonderful hosts who made me feel welcome at their skier's Mecca.

Thanks also to Pamela Harden, who has lent her considerable artistic talent (and incredible ability to understand my scribbling) in drawing the maps and other illustrations in this book.

Finally, thanks to my partner, MJ, who helped bridge the chasm in my understanding and manipulation of the Internet. She put together the Web addresses contained at the end of the book.

Cross-Country Skiing Terms

Alpine skiing: Another term for downhill skiing.

diagonal stride: The terms classic, striding, and diagonal all refer to one of cross-country skiing's two basic techniques for propelling oneself down the trail. Movement is accomplished by poling with one arm and kicking down on the snow with the opposite leg and foot. This causes your kick wax (or waxless pattern) to grip the snow, allowing you to push off from that ski and glide forward on the other. Named for concurrent movement and power of diagonally opposite arm and leg. It's called classic because it predates the newer technique of ski skating.

diagonal track: Two parallel ruts in the snow, created for or created by a pair of skis.

double pole: Technique used to propel oneself down the trail. It involves planting both pole tips in the snow near the feet, handles to the side and forward of the head, then bending from the waist while holding arms slightly bent, but ridged at the elbows. As hands pass legs, elbows are unbent until arms are fully extended to the rear, and the top of the torso is parallel with the ground.

glide wax: Substance used on the bottom of skis to eliminate as much friction as possible.

herringbone: Technique used to climb hills too steep for either diagonal or skating. Named for pattern left in snow behind you. Ski tips are rotated left and right making an open "V" with the opening pointing up the hill. One then walks up the hill on the edges of the skis.

kick double pole: Kicking off with one leg, generally in the track, followed quickly by a double pole. Used on flats to add variety, on slight up and down grades for power and speed respectively.

kick wax: Substance used on the bottom of skis to gain friction, allowing skier to grip the snow with skis, and move forward.

klister: Gooey substance that has the same function as kick wax, but works better on ice and in extremely warm conditions.

marathon skate: Technique using a double pole with one ski in the diagonal track and the other used to push off from its edge, as in skate skiing. Used on flats, especially when track is icy and fast.

Nordic skiing: Another term for cross-country skiing.

plow turn: Similar to a snowplow, except that by putting more weight on one ski the skier turns in that direction.

pole throw: Technique involving arm motion that sends poles behind the body. It also involves opening the hands and releasing the grip on the pole so it can momentarily extend fully backward, restrained only by the pole's wrist strap. A basic motion in both diagonal stride and ski skating.

side step: Technique used to climb (or descend) very steep hills. Skier arranges skis horizontally across the hill, then steps up with uphill ski (or down with downhill ski). Skier brings downhill ski up next to higher ski, then repeats process until up the hill. Imagine narrow steps going up the hillside on which you need to place each ski.

skate turn: A step turn, except that a quick kick is applied to the ski edge after unweighting and before lifting the ski, thereby gaining speed. Used around mostly flat corners or corners leading into uphills.

skating lane: Packed snow, without a diagonal track, for skate skiing.

ski skating, skating, skate skiing: One of the two basic cross-country techniques for propelling oneself down the track. Movement is accomplished by poling with both arms while kicking off the edge of one ski. Kick wax is not used. This is what downhill skiers have always done to get somewhere on a flat surface.

snowplow: A downhill technique used to control speed. Skis are arranged into a "V" in which the closed-end points downhill. The knees are held closer together than the feet in order to apply pressure to the inside (uphill) edge of the skis. Master this technique and you will be able to control your speed and feel comfortable with down-hills.

step turn: The quick unweighting, lifting, and replacing (stepping) of the ski in the intended turn direction, followed by the other ski. Used on downhills, where quick, tight turns are required.

telemark turn: A turn in which the uphill ski trails the downhill ski. Both knees are bent, with the trailing ski's knee being bent at a 90-degree angle, thereby raising the heel off the ski. The result is a won-derfully rhythmic motion that cuts graceful arcs down a hill. Only used on downhills (usually alpine) wide enough to make sweeping turns.

track: The part of the trail that cross-country skiers actually ski on as they progress through a system. May have a diagonal track set for diagonal stride, may have a skating lane or may have both, side by side.

V1, V2, V2 Alternate: Three forms of skate skiing, varying only by how and when poling is used. V1 is used up hills and on flats. It involves a near simultaneous double poling on one side (strong side) combined with a kick from the opposite leg. Then the other leg kicks alone, while arms and poles recover, always remaining on the strong side. V2 is used on slight downgrades, flats and easy uphills. It requires poling with each kick. V2 Alternate is used on flats or down easy grades. It is like V2, except the arms do not actually pole with each kick, but with every other. The arms do however completely change sides of the body.

crash: a fall, tumble or unwanted contact with another object or skier. You're not really having fun until you have had at least one of these!

1

Sault Ste. Marie, Ontario, and the Eastern Upper Peninsula

Algonquin Ski Trail

Directions: From the intersection of Three Mile Road and I-75 southwest of Sault Ste. Marie, Michigan, take Three Mile Road west one mile to a T intersection with 20th Avenue West. Go right (north) on 20th another mile to a T intersection with Oak Street. Turn left (west) on Oak, which jogs right a bit and gets renamed 16th Avenue West. The trailhead and parking area are .8 mile, on the left.

Grooming: Most of the trails here are groomed for both diagonal and skating. The grooming is done well and done soon after a snowfall.

Total km: system, 14; this tour, 11; 3.2 lighted

Fee: donation

Trailhead facilities: There is an outhouse.

Contact: Michigan Department of Natural Resources, Sault Ste. Marie, MI 49783; (906) 635-6161.

This is an excellent trail, with good flow and excellent use of the terrain. Ski out from the parking area into a mixed hardwood and conifer forest. The trail is groomed to both sides of some trees in the middle of the trail. This happens frequently and reflects a playfulness associated with the trail and those who care for it. When you reach a bridge over some wetlands, you can cross it if you are striding or follow the trail right if skating. The trail to the right dips down a bit, crosses the frozen wet area, and rejoins the trail on the other side of the bridge.

When you reach Junction 2, bear left, into some spruce and small pine trees. This is a great spot for marathon skating, partly because the skating lane gets a bit narrow. You will cross a snowmobile trail, then the diagonal and skating tracks briefly part company. The snowmobile trail will be right of you during the entire tour. Generally, the snowmobile trail is far enough away so as not to distract from your skiing experience. However, if the wind is from the northwest, you may get some whiffs of exhaust.

The trail follows a ridge forested with spruce, fir, birch, and maple. Then it dips down into and across a boggy area. Tamarack are prevalent here. There's a slight uphill, and you are back on higher ground, at Junction 13, amid jack pine.

Skiing toward Junction 12, note that the topography here is unique. What you are skiing on most of the time are sinuous ridges, no more than a few meters above bogs. The ridges were created long ago, when Lake Superior was much higher. These ridges, which are so well utilized by this trail system, were created by the erosive action of water many thousands of years ago.

When you reach Junction 12, go right. Left is a diagonal-only trail. It's a really fun 1 km ski to the next junction, 10. See how fast you can ski the ridge. There are lots of little ups and downs, twists and turns. The trail designer did a great job of maximizing the quickness with which the trail can be skied. Since there isn't a vertical more than 3 m, you never go anaerobic on a climb, no matter how hard you are skiing. (This, of course, assumes that you are in reasonable aerobic condition.)

If you are skating, when you reach Junction 10, you will have to turn around and ski back the same way. The rest of the trail, through Junctions 8 and 9, is striding only.

When you reach Junction 3, go left. This is called Loop A on the map, and it's a 2.1 km swing through an upland. There are some larger trees here, including white birch and pine. You will encounter the tour's largest tree, a white pine that's a couple feet in diameter. The pine is in the middle of the trail, so it's hard to miss. Here again the trail uses the terrain well, taking advantage of the slightly larger hills and increased room for turns. It's a wonderful cruise. When you reach Junction 2, go left; it's a bit more than .5 km back to the parking area.

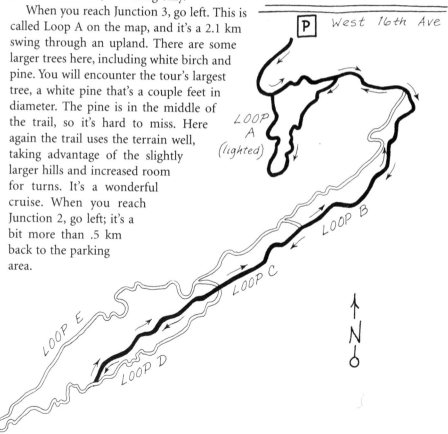

3

Journal: My day started with an 11 km skate ski at Valley Spur, near Newberry. I'd then driven up to Tahquamenon Falls, bushwhacked about 5 km, had a brew at the pub, and headed out for McNearney, where I classic skied about 7 km on a packed but untracked trail. It is now almost 6 p.m., the sun has set, and I am less than excited about skiing here at Algonquin. The only reason I'm going to attempt it is that the first several kilometers are lighted.

Putting on my ski boots for the fourth time is a pain, figuratively and literally. At least I can skate this—the big toe on my right foot would protest another classic ski today. For some reason, it does not like my classic boot and, with every kick, sends painful jabs to my brain. Skating is definitely the technique tonight.

Now that I'm out on the trail this isn't so bad—it never is. The snow is fast, the grooming good, and the trail playful. I especially like the trees in the middle of the trail. This is a great ski. I should time myself coming back in, across the ridges, with their little hills and valleys. Four minutes per kilometer; that's slow! I must be more tired than I realize.

Now that I'm back at the car after this 11 km ski, it's totally dark and the lights never did come on. I don't care; those last couple of kilometers in the dark were fun. My notes are really hard to read, though.

2

Hiawatha Highlands

Directions: From Sault Ste. Marie, Ontario, take Highway 17 north, (also called the Great Northern Road) out of town to Fifth Line East (the number of the "line" goes up as you go north). Go right (east) on Fifth Line East about 1.7 miles to the parking area and lodge on the right.

Grooming: There are three distinct trail areas. Red Pine and associated trails are entirely classic skiing. Crystal Creek and associated trails are largely both skating and striding. Lookout is groomed for both, with the exception of White Pine Extension, which is striding only.

Total km: system, 38 (2 lighted); this tour, 7.5

Fee: Yes, both season passes and day passes are available.

Trailhead facilities: A full-service lodge, including rentals, but no equipment sales, is located at the trailhead. The restaurant serves excellent food.

Contact: Sault Trails and Recreation Inc. (STAR), P.O. Box 580, Sault Ste. Marie, Ontario, Canada, P6A 5N1; (800) 361-1522.

This is a short tour, one that captures only a small piece of all the skiing that's available here. More flavor is available in the Journal section following this tour.

Start across the road from the lodge, in the red pine plantation. Planted in the 1930s, red pines were planted because they are not susceptible to some of the diseases that other pines succumb to, such as blister rust and white pine weevil. They also grow faster on dry, sandy soil than do white pine.

The trail heads out east, but quickly makes a 180-degree loop back west, between rows of red pine. One can deduce that some of the pine have been cut, since there are larger spaces between some of them than others. This thinning helps the remaining pine grow faster and bigger.

It isn't long before the trail takes you out of the planted pines, into natural stands of white pine, fir, and some hardwoods. They get a lot of snow here, so it's likely that everything will be drooping, covered with several feet of snow. If so, the visibility into the woods is poor— only a few feet.

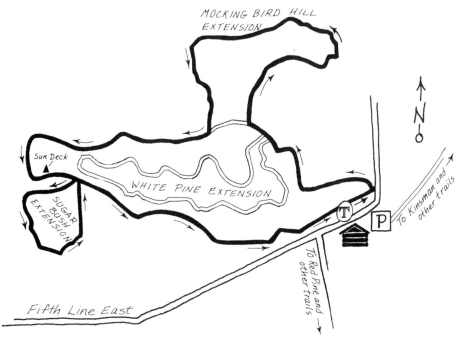

Turn right at the next junction and it isn't far—down and up a couple of moderate hills—until you reach an opening. Before you stretches about 40 acres of open field. Fences weave a tapestry over the snow, and several buildings in the distance lend more substance. This is Mocking Bird Hill Extension Trail. Ski around the loop and look at the farm buildings as you pass close to them. The main log structure was moved to this site from its previous location near Lake Superior. This entire farm complex is run as it would have been in the late 1800s. The church behind the farm was relocated from the village of Goulais River, about 18 miles north.

Enjoy skiing the open field or, if it's windy, hurry back into the forest. Once back in the woods, there's a nice, long downhill grade to the next junction. Go right here, and check out the scattered white pine that grow along the trail. Many of them are multistemmed, starting at six to 10 feet off the ground. Something happened here when these trees were only that tall. That would have been 60, 70, 80 or more years ago. Perhaps a big wind broke the tops off them, or an ice storm cracked the tops off.

As you loop left, rounding the easternmost spot on the Lookout Trail, the woods are more open. There are fewer trees and more light. You will see a "sun deck" on your left. This structure, complete with fire pit, is set up in the thinner woods in order for it to soak up more sun. It can be a pleasant place to rest or picnic.

It's a slide down to the next intersection, this with Sugar Bush Extension. Go right if you can and aren't going too fast. The downhill continues on Sugar Bush, curving right. The hill is challenging because of its length. Once it bottoms out, you will loop gradually back left. There's an especially large, multistemmed white pine on the right, near the trail. You will see many more such pine here as you ski toward the big uphill before the trail reconnects with Lookout.

Go right at the top and it isn't far until you begin seeing odd, green and blue "ribbons" looping between the trees at hip level. Can you figure out what these are? Actually tubing, they are part of a maple sap collection system. Look at how each tree has a small hole with a spigot and short length of tube that connects it with the longer tubes. Come sugaring time, the sap will flow into the tubes, then downhill, via gravity, to a sugaring shack at the base of the hill, along Fifth Line East. The Sault Ste. Marie Region Conservation Authority conducts the sugaring operation so people can see how maple sugar is made.

It isn't very far past the maple festooned with bright colored tubing until you reenter the red pine plantation. It's a pleasant 100 m ski down an arrow-straight, pine-lined alley to the finish of this tour. Your car and the lodge are on the right, across the road.

Journal: As I arrive at Hiawatha there are lots of cars in the parking lot, and a gang of grade-school kids mill about near the lodge. Most of the kids are wearing numbered racing bibs. As I watch, it's clear there is a race going on. It's Thursday, at about 9 a.m. How oddly wonderful, I think. One other piece of information: It's about minus eight degrees Fahrenheit. I can't imagine such a thing happening in the United States.

When I go inside the lodge, there are more kids. I pay my trail fee and head out onto the trail. About half a kilometer into my ski there is another bunch of kids. I stop and talk to the adult at the head of the line of kids, who are single file in the striding track. Her name is Ruth Fletcher, a fifth-grade teacher at Mount View School. She tells me that the classes ski about two or three times a week.

Later, farther down the trail, I pass another long line of kids, all having a great time. As I finally catch and pass the first kid, the head of the pack, I comment to her that she is the jackrabbit of the bunch. She returns a cute, knowing smile. Skiing with kids can be a warming experience on a cold morning. This certainly was.

Stokley Creek Ski Trails

Directions: From Sault Ste. Marie, Ontario, take Highway 17 north out of town about 20 miles to the Stokley Creek sign at the corner of 17 and Old Highway 17. Turn right onto Old 17 and follow the signs to the lodge's parking lot, about 1.7 miles. The short road to the lot is on the right. You will park in the lot and then ski, hike, or get picked up on a snowmobile to travel the last .3 km to the lodge and trailheads.

Grooming: Some trails are groomed for both skating and striding, some just for striding. Dual groomed trails are 13 feet wide, and give you plenty of room for both techniques.

Total km: system, 130; this tour, 18

Fee: Day passes are available, but you should stay the night for the full experience, including the food and feel of the place.

Trailhead facilities: Although a few places along Minnesota's North Shore approach the completeness offered here, nothing really matches it. Besides lodging, the trailside lodge provides a library, sauna, comfortable lounges, waxing area, and, of course, Stokley's legendary food. Guests gather in the "Club House" before supper and munch on hors d'oeuvres such as liver pâté, hummus with assorted crackers, and some delicious cheeses. Meals are served family style or buffet, with plenty of great options.

Contact: Stokley Creek Lodge, RR #1, Goulais River, Ontario, Canada P0S 1E0; (705) 649-3421.

The trail for this tour starts just left of the lodge. It ascends for the first kilometer or so, but the climb feels gradual, even though you are gaining plenty of altitude. This section of the trail's namesake, lovely little Stokley Creek, bubbles alongside the trail much of the climb. There's open water here, even in the dead of winter. Look long enough into one of the open pools and you will see a trout.

Somewhere past halfway up, about 500 m into your ski, you can look over your right shoulder and gasp at the view. There's a mountain. It has all the trappings of a real mountain, a foreground of hills, covered with trees, then a steep cliff face, white with snow, treeless, earth reaching skyward. You have to crane your neck backward to see it. This is King Mountain, which stands nearly 1900 feet above sea level.

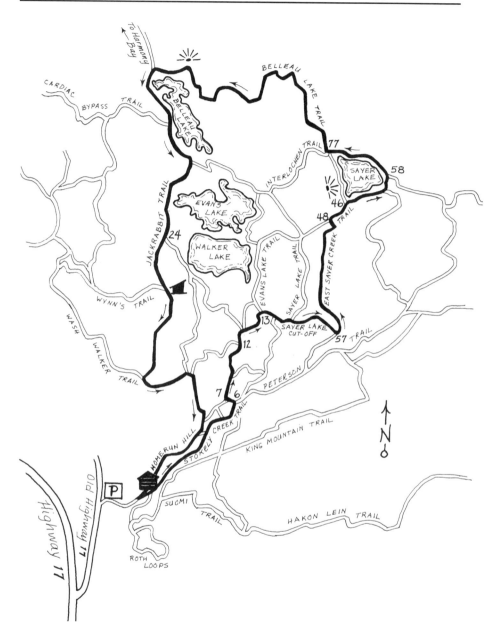

When you reach Junction 6, with Peterson Trail, go left and ski the 100 m or so to Junction 7. Then head right, still climbing. There are some signs posted along here that describe the forest management. They use the word *restoration*. While one can doubt the use of that word for the forestry that's being carried out, the logging has left nothing worse than a parklike look.

Ski on by Junction 12 to Junction 13. Go right and follow the Sayer Lake cutoff through more parklike woods to Junction 57. Go left here and the woods become more diverse, less managed. Sayer Creek is on the left, and there are both conifers and hardwoods around you. There are some especially large yellow birch and nice hemlock, also.

At Junction 48 go right and ski on up to Sayer Lake. The view as you ski up the trail is across the lake. Cedar line the left shore, and beyond is an expansive hardwood hillside. If you stop at the trailside marker that notes Junction 46, you can hear the gurgle of the creek as it drops out of the lake and heads toward Lake Superior. It's one of those places that are hard to leave. When you can, ski right, along the southeastern shore of Sayer Lake, drinking in the view.

Head left at Junction 58, then right at Junction 77. For the next 4 km the trail sweeps up, down, and around hills in remote country. You will pass a giant beaver dam, on the right. If it ever burst, the trail and lots of countryside would be awash.

There are two serious downhill runs in this 4 km stretch. At the top of the second one you will get a view of Lake Superior. It's hard to say what is more exhilarating: the view from the top or the ride down. At the bottom, the trail loops left and begins heading back toward the lodge. The long, sprawling Belleau Lake is below you, on the left.

Just after Junction 24, the trail begins a long, steep climb. This is Jackrabbit Trail, and it includes a hill that's a match for any hill on any cross-country trail anywhere. After climbing for what may seem like an hour, you will crest the hill and start down. The ride is as fast as you let it be. A warming hut is visible on the left, sitting out on a bluff that you whiz by so fast you'll have no idea how you could reach the hut.

One more downhill awaits you. Homerun Hill is fast like the last one, but at least you end up near medical help at the lodge! Have fun!

Journal: What does a Muslim say about a visit to Mecca? I sit here and search for words that describe my experience at Stokley Creek. I could quote one of the first folks I met there, a fortyish skier, thin and fit. He was eating lunch when I asked him what he thought of Stokley. He said, "The place is like heroin, you get a little and then you can't get enough." An accurate, if slightly unsavory, analogy.

4

McNearney Ski Trail

Directions: From the intersection of I-75 and Highway 28, south of Sault Ste. Marie, Michigan, go west on 28 about 30 miles to the intersection with Salt Point (Strongs) Road. This is just east of the village of Strongs Corner, Michigan. Go north and then east on Salt Point Road about 5 miles to the trailhead on the left.

Grooming: The trail is single-track striding.

Total km: system, 15; this tour, 8.2

Fee: none

Trailhead facilities: There is an impressively built scribed-log structure that serves as the trailhead shelter. It contains a potbelly stove and some wood for making a fire.

Contact: Sault Ste. Marie Ranger District, 4000 I-75 Business Spur, Sault Ste. Marie, MI, 49783; (906) 635-5311.

This trail is a good example of what modern forestry practices do to a woodland. I find the parklike look disconcerting and the lack of large trees frustrating. Yet there is some old growth here, and a couple of fun hills.

Start your ski from the parking area into an open field. The area around the trailhead was the site of Camp 4, an early-20th-century logging camp. There is a long straightaway, with some gradual downhills, through an obviously managed hardwood forest.

Go right (straight) at the first junction, and you will be on Big Pine Loop. There is one larger white pine on the right, but it isn't the loop's namesake. The trail here is in a hardwood forest, composed mostly of small (under-12-inch-diameter) trees. You will climb a bit, then make an exciting descent into a black spruce woods. The spruce are densely packed into the wetter valley between hilltops. These hills were once sand dunes along the shoreline of ancient Glacial Lake Algonquin.

Climb a sweeping uphill curve back onto a ridge top. A logging road scars the crest of this ridge, and you cut across it before taking a long, steep ride down into another valley. There are more black spruce here, but as you climb out of the valley, there's a plantation of white spruce on the right. These were planted in the 1960s.

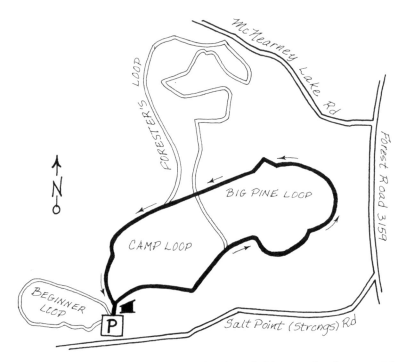

The trail then traces another broad ridge top for the next .5 km. There are a lot of stump-sprouted trees here, the result of a cut done in 1999. Unfortunately, there is hardly a tree over a foot in diameter left standing. The woods are homogeneous and not very interesting.

Fortunately, it isn't long before the trail cuts left and drops off the ridge. The downhill isn't difficult, but can be fast. You have entered an area of larger trees, where two-foot-diameter sugar maple and yellow birch are not uncommon. As you loop around a right curve, a 110-foot-tall white pine is visible off to the right. Although impressive, partly because you have seen so many smaller trees, this pine is still only a young adult among white pine; it can double or triple its size if left alone. Given the intensive forestry along this trail, however, I doubt it has much of a future.

The climb out of the lower land you have been skiing through is gradual. There are lots of small, multistemmed black cherry trees, then the Forester's Loop cuts off to the right. It's an almost 5 km ski, with some difficult hills. Continue straight, and the trail passes the junction where Forester's Loop rejoins it. Just after this junction is a series of four downhill pitches that are lots of fun. Small moguls can develop, making the runouts more challenging.

As the woods thin out, you will ski into an opening about four times as long as it is wide. This means that you are near the last junction. Go right, and the trailhead is about 100 m away.

II

The Munising/ Pictured Rocks/ Newberry Area

Canada Lakes Pathway

Directions: From the intersection of Highways 28 and 403, 1 mile east of the Newberry, take 403 south 1.5 miles to the parking area and trailhead on the right.

Grooming: Sections of the trail are groomed for striding only, and some for both striding and skating.

Total km: system, 13.5; this tour, 12

Fee: donation

Trailhead facilities: none

Contact: Michigan Department of Natural Resources, RR 4, Box 796, Newberry, MI 49868; (906) 293-5131.

This tour will follow the skate groomed main route out to Loop 6 and around it. The trail heads into a red pine plantation that was planted in the late 1950s to early 1960s. The path is wide and flat, with tracks set on either side. It winds through the plantation before narrowing a bit and exiting into a natural woodland composed of white pine, yellow birch, white birch, and some maple, among other trees.

After a junction with Loop 2 that goes right, the trail continues through a thinned hardwood stand. After the next junction, with Loop 3, the trail finally picks up a few hills, although small ones. A hill is visible on the right, then some open areas, and then a view of one of the two Canada Lakes. According to the DNR they aren't much for fishing. They are bog lakes, quite acid and fairly inaccessible.

Stay on the skating trail, and after some respectable climbs—one of which requires some real effort—you will reach Loop 6. Go right to the junction marked 6. The smaller sugar maple here have interesting light-colored, almost white-gray bark. There is very little ridging or grooving, and the color stays light, even on trees as large as 12 inches in diameter.

The trail loops left, climbing and descending some easy hills, curving gracefully through an open forest that was thinned in the late 1990s. The trail here and around most of this loop is very smooth and flows nicely. It's a joy to skate.

Cross the snowmobile trail, ski past small openings that were log-decking areas, and head into an exclusively hardwood forest. Leaves cling to small ironwood trees, filling the understory with a vertical blanket of leaves. Eventually lots of small, Christmas-tree-sized balsam fir pop up in the understory.

A long, gradual 400 m downhill takes you by a hill on the right and into some tall white pine. If there's some wind, this is a good spot to stop and listen to it blow through the pine, high in the air. It's a sound that warms and chills—warming your heart and chilling your bones.

Just before you reach a sign board on the left of the trail, there are a couple of black cherry trees on the same side that have multiple large burls on them. Just past the sign are many small, 9-to-12-inch-diameter yellow birch with lovely gold-to-tan exfoliating bark that glistens in the sun.

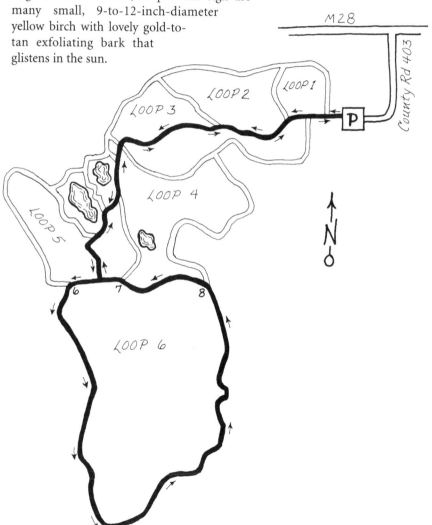

An opening greets you not far from the yellow birch. This is an area where a fire burned hot in the early 1950s. The soil hasn't recovered from having lost most of its organic matter and moisture-holding ability in the fire. Hence, it is a sparsely treed opening. There are scrawny, multistemmed black cherry, some small balsam fir, and small white pine that are sometimes called old field pine because they often come back into fields such as this.

The trail curves up and out of the opening into a dense fir stand. It also tips downward for the next 200 m or so, and makes for an excellent place to skate without poles. Then the forest opens again, and the perimeter is punctuated by tall white pine.

When the trail heads back into the fir, get ready for a climb. The longest climb of the tour starts out up into the hardwood forest about 12 vertical meters, then a couple more, then dropping a couple, and finishing with another 15 m climb up about 4 vertical meters.

The next kilometer or so is really fun. The trail has exceptional flow, winding, dipping, and ascending through dense stands of fir, tall stands of white and jack pine, and even some hemlock, and then past some flagpole-sized aspen.

You will reach Junction 8, which marks where a striding-only trail heads north. Then you'll pass Junction 7, another striding trail that goes north. After crossing yet another fire-created opening, you reach the unnumbered junction where you want to go right, and head back up the trail that you came out to Loop 6 on. There are some nice gradual downhills on the way back, and it will seem faster then the trip out.

Journal: Cruisin' Canada Lakes, skating my way past ice-storm-bent boughs, dodging downed twigs. Fast is better today; I've been striding too many days in a row. I feel released, free, bursting with energy and speed.

Snow-thick branches block my view of the trail ahead, of the woods beside me. And I don't care. I am skating almost effortlessly, down a long, straight stretch of trail, quick pulses of energy fueling uphill bursts. Breath comes in fast, rhythmic pulses, expelling wisps of moisture, ice building on my lashes. Adrenaline and sweat mix on the snow, making a satisfying cocktail, better than most, as good as tequila.

McKeever Hills

Directions: From the intersection of Highway 28 and Forest Highway 13, which is 2 miles southeast of Munising, go south on 13 for approximately 12 miles. The trailhead sign and parking area are on the left.

Grooming: This trail is packed with a snow machine. It is narrow, about the width of two ski poles. There may or not be track set.

Total km: system, 12; this tour, 12

Fee: donation

Trailhead facilities: None, but there is a small general store just north of the trailhead, on the opposite side of the road.

Contact: Hiawatha National Forest, Munising Ranger District, 400 E. Munising Ave., Munising, MI 49862; (906) 387-2512

This is a very lovely ski. There are big trees: pine, hemlock, beech, yellow birch, and sugar maple. There are overlooks, lake vistas, and some outstanding hills. Add this to a well-designed trail that has a wonderful flow, and you have a satisfying ski.

Start from the south end of the parking area. It is a short ski to where the trail divides. If you go right, and then left you will be on a 1 km warm-up loop. It circles around on top of a hill, never changing altitude by more than 2 m. Hence it is an easy ski. Petes Lake is visible on the left as you head out, before you loop back. The trees are mostly maple and beech. Finish the loop along a power line and reconnect with the main trail. Go right, and you are on your way to some exciting skiing.

The next 600 m of trail is called Loggers Run. It is set on an old road, likely one used for logging. Happily, the effects of logging are not apparent on any of this tour; you will see some large specimens. In fact, there are several beech along this section of trail that are nearing two feet in diameter.

Petes Lake is off to the left as you ski down and up a mild grade. Trees block your view much of the time, but there are a couple of tree-less vistas. When you reach a junction, bear left and slide down another gradual hill. There are more conifers here, especially near the lake. Hemlock is the major constituent. There also are some balsam fir

17

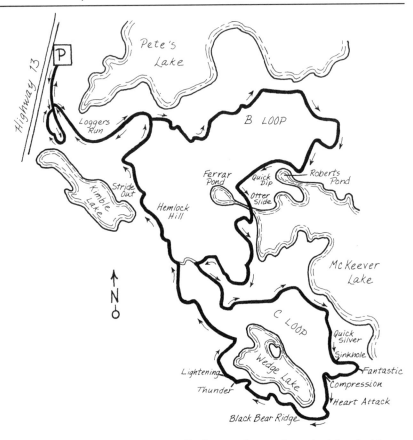

and white spruce. As you climb up and away from the lake, deciduous trees hold sway, especially beech.

About the time you see Petes Lake again, you will encounter the first long, somewhat fast downhill. It isn't technical, so point your skis down it and enjoy. You will notice that the trail begins making more right turns than left. It's looping back south after heading east for about a kilometer while running roughly parallel with Petes Lake. There are two ungroomed trails that connect with the trail you are on. These likely lead to recently logged areas.

After another long, easy downhill, then a bit of a climb, you can see Roberts Pond on the left. It is really an extension of McKeever Lake, which you can see if you peer past the trees beyond Roberts Pond.

It's not far to Quick Dip, an aptly named little downhill that's followed by an uphill. Otter Slide takes you down to a little spit of land that crosses flowing water. The water originates on your right, in Ferrar Pond. It has considerable current as it funnels through the culvert under the trail. There is often open water here, and sometimes, real otter slides.

You will climb up onto a ridge along the west side of McKeever Lake. The lake is visible, but more impressive are the white pine along the ridge. There are lots of them, and they range from 18 to more than 24 inches in diameter, with the tallest ones pushing 100 feet in height. If it's a windy day, make sure you stop for a moment and listen. There's nothing like the sound of air moving through pine boughs 75 feet above you.

There are a couple more hills before you get to the junction with C Loop. The hills are named Go Easy and Whoa, but they are not too difficult, just fun. There is a snowmobile trail that cuts through here and it can cause confusion about what trail you are on, especially when a bubblehead has run onto the cross-country trail. Always look for the blue trail markers on trees. The snowmobile trail has small white arrows.

Turn left at the junction with C Loop. The ski is easy at first, with a few hills, but nothing of note. The trees continue, with some large maple and yellow birch reaching skyward. There is one exceptionally large and lovely yellow birch on the left before you reach the hilly area. You can see the birch from down the trail as you approach it. It's quite tall, and about three feet in diameter. The trunk is hard to see because of a dense stand of small hemlock around it.

When you see the caution sign, it's time to pull your hat down and fasten your jacket. The first hill is named Quick Silver, and it is quick. Next, almost immediately comes Sinkhole, which curves left and is tricky. After a brief respite, you'll slip down Fantastic, which is fairly straight and easy. It's Compression that you need worry about. Although it's not very long, it is steep, and true to its name: It will feel like your body is being pulled into the snow near the bottom. There must be multiple G-forces. If your heart made it by Compression, the next and last downhill for a while, Heart Attack shouldn't be a problem.

Although you may not have noticed, Wedge Lake is now visible on the right. This lovely little backcountry lake is totally undeveloped and full of fish. You will ski along a ridge, perhaps an esker, on the southwest side of the lake. This is called Black Bear Ridge. There's a rustic cabin on the left, but you can't see it from the trail.

You'll ski close to Wedge Lake and then encounter the tour's steepest climb, called Thunder. It is all the more difficult because the trail is groomed very narrow. Herringbone is the technique of choice—the only one that will get you up the hill—but the trail is so narrow that your ski tips dip into the deeper snow. It's a challenging uphill trek.

Lightning is the name of the downhill on the other side of Thunder. It's a steep and fairly long hill. The runout is straight. The rest of the ski to the next junction is through some nice hemlock and yellow birch. It is fairly level.

At the junction, bear left and you will be back on B Loop, headed for the parking area. After you traverse Hemlock Hill, and Stride Out past Kimble Lake on the left, you will find yourself at the junction with Loggers Run. Go left and it's less than a kilometer to the parking area.

Journal: I have made a mistake. I am 1 km into my ski at McKeever Hills and I have no writing instrument. It's a short story. Before I left home I asked MJ if she could figure out how to get the lead into some mechanical pencils I'd bought, used, and run out of lead. She started clicking one of them furiously, and low and behold, lead came out the end. She repeated the miracle with the other pen, and I was satisfied. I had something I could write with on my next trail expedition.

At the McKeever trailhead I put both pens in my pocket and headed out. It's unusual for me to go a kilometer without taking some notes, but today I was cold and wanted to warm up by skiing hard. It's a two-way trail here, and I could take my notes on the way back.

As I tried writing, nothing happened, except for a small hole in the paper where the metal tip of the pencil punched through. There was no lead. Oops! I reached for the other pencil, knowing what was going to happen. Yes, no lead there either.

So, should I go back to the car and find something I could take notes with? I am in a hurry. I have less than an hour and a half of daylight, and about 11 km of difficult, trackless, through-two-inches-of-powder, diagonal skiing ahead. There isn't enough time. I will trust my memory. I have made a mistake, but think I can muddle through.

After just writing this tour, I am happy I didn't have anything to write with. I had a fun ski, unburdened by note taking. And I managed the write-up fine. Thanks, MJ.

Pictured Rocks Trails— Grand Marais

Directions: From Grand Marais, take Highway 77 south about 1.7 miles to Newberg Road. Go west (right) on Newberg Road 1.5 miles to where the plowing stops at the visitor center. The parking area is on the left. The visitor center is not open during the winter.

Grooming: The trails are narrow, single track, striding only.

Total km: system, 16; this tour, 7

Fee: none

Trailhead facilities: none

Contact: Pictured Rocks National Lakeshore, P.O. Box 40, Munising, MI 49862; (906) 387-2607.

As you drive up to the end of the plowed road, you can see treeless, snow-covered dunes rising up past the trees ahead. These trails don't take you onto those dunes, but you can see them from a couple of vantage points. Go southeast from the parking area, which is the wrong direction. But the trail quickly loops back left to the east, then north, crossing the road you just drove here on. Sometimes the banks of snow piled up by the snowplow must be sidestepped down and then back up in order to avoid breaking your skis.

Once across the road, you will ski into a soothing cedar forest, thick enough that there are boughs overhead. This is a nice welcome. A little creek flows through the cedar on the left. When you reach a junction, go left. Ski along a ridge that is on the right, one with big hardwoods reaching heavenward. The trail reaches a wetland opening, lined with full, bushy, open-grown cedar trees. There are also lots of alder and yellow birch.

The trail swings right, up onto that ridge with the big hardwoods, and past a three-foot-diameter sugar maple. Beech become the predominant tree along the ridge before the trail dips down quickly and makes a sharp left turn. The downhill fun continues as you ski over a couple of moguls. You'll get airborne if you're going fast enough.

F Loop joins from the left. A big three-foot-diameter yellow birch sits near this junction. About 20 m farther is the junction with D Loop. You want to continue straight, or slightly left, on F Loop. There's another tricky downhill here, with moguls and another possibility of getting airborne.

When you see an opening on the right, then some buildings, you are nearing the Sable River Gorge. Just past a sign that directs hikers down to the dunes, a look up and forward will take your breath away: Although not a wide view, you will see Lake Superior. Depending on the light, and the ice, you may see a pie-shaped slice of gray with light, white ice flows bobbing in frosty water. Or, if it's a clear, sun-drenched day, you will see bright blue water, with white pieces of ice adrift.

The dunes frame the picture on the left. Stark and white, they rise high above the lake and flow down into the gorge on your left. There are stairs here, and it's worth removing your skis and taking a walk down. The Sable River cascades over several rock ledges here on its way to the lake.

Back on the ski trail, there is a junction with E Loop, just beyond the stairs. Go right and ski the loop counterclockwise. It cuts through a woods of large yellow birch, beech, and sugar maple. There's a big, open area of the park on the right. An old barbed-wire fence loops lazily between leaning wooden posts, testament to early attempts at farming here.

Once you have made the outside of the loop, you will ski up to the tour's largest tree, a yellow birch, next to the trail on the right. It is about 12 feet in circumference, and nearly 100 feet tall. If you look up at it you can see that it's limbless for the first 50 feet. And most amazingly, it is the picture of tree health, with few or no dead limbs. It's a wonderful old tree.

Skiing on, you will see the lake on the right, far in the distance; then you can see the dunes again, just before you get back to the junction near the stairs. Retrace your ski past the stairs, to a junction with F Loop. Go right, then look across a small clearing. You will see a large, single red pine standing above all else. If you feel up to skiing through untracked snow, make a side trip over to the pine. There's another view of the dunes beyond the pine that is worth the trip. Also, just in front of the pine are several striped maple (*Acer pennsylvanica*). These small maple are not common in the area and even less common to the west. They have greenish bark with vertical stripes.

Head back across the open field, the trip easier now that you have skied-in a track. Go right on F and you will ski past some apple trees; this must have been an old homestead. There also are some large alder along the trail and plenty of jack pine.

Go right when you reach C Loop, climb that tricky downhill with the moguls, and bear left at the next junction. There is open parkland

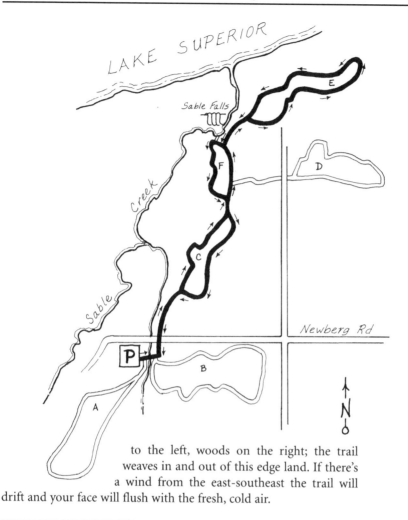

to the left, woods on the right; the trail weaves in and out of this edge land. If there's a wind from the east-southeast the trail will drift and your face will flush with the fresh, cold air.

Journal: My hike down the stairs to see Sable Falls was a challenge. There had been a couple of warm days the week before I visited the park. During the warming, snow on the stairs had sloughed off and down the steps, piling up near the bottom of each tier. When I tried putting my ski boot on the first step, it just slid off. I caught myself on the railing, which was also coated with a thin layer of ice. I finally found a technique that let me descend: I hugged the slippery railing while I placed my feet sideways on each stair. Once near the bottom, the snow was in deep piles, and the problem became different. Finding where the steps were was impossible, so I had to dig my feet into the snow pile, sometimes sinking nearly to my waist.

The reward was the sound and sight of the falls, cascading over ledges. Crystal-clear water played off the rocks and bubbled near the surface, then disappeared underneath the ice and snow. While taking pictures, I stepped off the solid ground onto an ice shelf below one of the cascades. The ice shelf broke with just the slightest pressure, and I lurched back onto the hillside. It would have been a long, cold slide down to the lake.

Pictured Rocks Trails—
Munising

Directions: From the intersection of Highways 28 and 58 near the Pictured Rock National Lakeshore headquarters in Munising, take 58 north, about 2 miles to the parking area and trailhead on the left.

Grooming: This system is groomed for diagonal stride only.

Total km: system, 11; this tour, 9

Fee: none

Trailhead facilities:: none

Contact: Pictured Rocks National Lakeshore, P.O. Box 40, Munising, MI 49862; (906) 387-2607.

From the parking lot, the trail dips down a gradual grade from an opening into the woods. There's a bridge crossing, then you will reach the A-B junction. Go right here, on A. The forest here is deciduous, with lots of maple and some larger beech. The trail follows a shallow ravine on the right, then crosses a snowmobile trail. Stay right at the next junction, which is with C. The trail will pass two spurs that head right, down to another parking area and the end of East City Limits Road. Both of these areas are alternative trailheads.

Once past the last spur, you will be on E. Conifers start populating the forest, with small fir and white pine in the understory. The evergreens make the woods seems warmer, fuller. They seem to belong here. There also are sections of tall white birch—white birch that look less white, more dusky in bark color. Perhaps these are hybrids with the yellow birch.

The trail winds pleasantly through the birch, providing a wonderful, easy flow for your skis across the undulating landscape. When you reach the next junction, with F, go right. It's flat for a ways, then you will encounter your first long downhill. There's a gully on the right and the trail traces its rim. The slide is easy, but the left turn at the bottom is tricky. Stay on F at this left turn (G goes right). The trees are not as large here as they have been, except for some two-foot-diameter aspen that are very close to the trail. If you look through the trees ahead, you can begin seeing Lake Superior and land beyond, which is Grand Island.

The trail stays next to the cliff edge. There are large trees on the right, down the cliff face, and smaller stuff on the left. The trail descends gradually, then crosses a couple of small creeks on bridges that blend with the deep snow, which makes them invisible. Along most of the little creases in the landscape crossed by these bridges, you will see hemlock, some quite large.

There are several trail junctions through here. If you stay right, you will continue along the cliff edge. There is a "Most Difficult" sign before you make a long uphill climb, this tour's first. Once over the top, you will get a good view at right of the island and the lake. Then the downhill will give you a thrill, especially the little hook left near the bottom.

The trail gets close to the edge of the cliff in a couple of places. The first is in a hemlock grove. The view is impressive down the 70 percent grade toward the lake. Then there's a long—400 m or so—relatively flat and straight stretch, great for striding. There are some basswood trees along here, one a three-stemmed stump sprout on the left.

A short dip, about a 2 m vertical drop, and a curve right

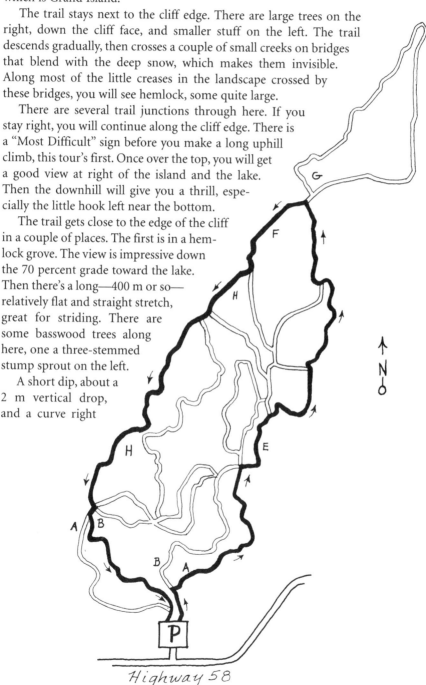

Highway 58

25

bring you to a gully crossing. The trail is narrow, and the crossing is not visible until you are upon it. On the right side—just a pole plant away—is thin air, and a 70-foot drop. Layered rock forms a bowl in the cliff, and a little creek drops over the edge below your feet. It's not possible for you to see the falls from this trail, and, indeed, the creek probably freezes up in the winter.

There are several more quick little downhills that lead to bridge crossings of little creeks farther from the cliff's edge. Then you will curve right, and from near the cliff edge you can look down and into a large, semicircular rock bowl, the rim of which you just skied. Layered rock rises from the bottom of the bowl, recessed near the bottom where it has eroded, but reaching out near the top. Icy stalactites hang from the rock layers, some stretching to the bowl's bottom. Snowshoers sometimes manage the steep slope down into the bowl, and you may see their tracks on the ice below.

From the bowl, ski off into small trees, then into an opening. This opening was the site of a 14-sided barn built in 1912 by early settler Dan Becker. There is an interpretive sign up the trail on the right. The barn was removed in 1975.

Look for the junction with B and climb it into the young deciduous woods. The trail will slope down into another opening, this an old field. You'll ski past some unusual trees: An old apple tree on the left—often with a few apples still clinging to the branches, even in February—and a copse of hawthorn, which are thorny natives that like open areas.

You will climb left, up onto an eskerlike landform. There's a good view of Munising back over your shoulder, and a view of a large crater-shaped depression on the right. You will soon be skiing up the hill on the other side.

Ski down the fairly steep hill, then climb up onto the ridge you could see a minute ago. It's a long climb up into hardwoods and across a snowmobile trail. There are a couple of longer, somewhat difficult downhills here, the last one marked with a caution sign. Loop A joins from the right, then the trail crosses another bridge. After a curve left and a bit of a climb, you will find yourself at the parking area.

Tahquamenon Falls Giant Pines Loop

Directions: What better place to start from than Paradise. Paradise is located on the shores of Whitefish Bay, south of Whitefish Point. Take Highway 123 about 13 miles south and west to Tahquamenon Falls State Park. The park road goes left, or east. Drive into the park to the parking area for the Tahquamenon Falls Brewery and Pub. Who said we left Paradise!

Grooming: Little or none, but it's a short ski in some tall trees and worth the effort.

Total km: system, 6; this tour, 6

Fee: none

Trailhead facilities: The Tahquamenon Falls Brewery and Pub at Camp 33 is a unique, unexpected find in the middle of a state park. Apparently the owner of the land adjacent to the falls sold the property to the DNR, but kept a couple of acres, on which his descendants built a lovely logging camp replica and brew pub. The ale is great; I prefer mine after I ski, but that is up to you.

Contact: Michigan Department of Natural Resources, RR 4, Box 796, Newberry, MI 49868; (906) 293-5131.

Head out from the left of the brewery at the south end of the parking area. The path will be hard-packed snow, no track. This is the same path used by people walking down to see the falls. There is a gradual downhill grade, but it's not enough that you need worry about crashing into the chain-link fence at the edge of the river bluff. Check out the giant white pine just beyond the fence. It's lost most of its top, but the trunk is enormous.

From here you can see some of the river—and that the drop is about 150 feet. Turn right, and head toward the first of three overlooks. The third is best. The river below the falls is open for a few hundred feet, then iced over and snow covered. Above the falls the river is usually entirely free of ice. The falls itself is usually open. There will be some ice formations that freeze out of the spray, but the size of these will depend on how cold it has been.

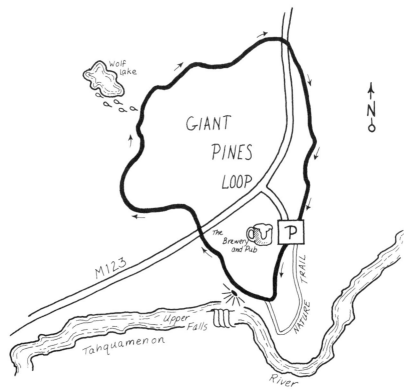

Ski down the trail until you reach the stairs. Take off your skis and walk a bit. There are 94 steps—an easy trek down and up if you're much of a skier! Even less-accomplished skiers find the trek easy. The metal grates are slippery, especially if you have plastic ski-boot soles. Hold onto the railing. Down on the viewing platform, the view upriver is great. But the falls hold most of the interest. The corner of the platform is only a couple of ski-pole lengths away from the top of the falls. There is noise, and there is some spray if the wind is right. These are big falls. They are in fact, the second largest, as measured by volume, east of the Mississippi River. Niagra Falls are the biggest.

The 94-mile-long Tahquamenon River drains a basin of about 900 square miles. The falls drop 48 feet, with a width of almost twice that. The typical low flow over the falls in summer is a little less than 5,000 gallons per second. High flow, in April, is almost 50,000 gallons a second. In a year, 215 billion gallons of water pour over the falls.

When you are ready, climb the 94 stairs and clip your skis back on. There is a trail map board just past the stairs. The trail immediately enters an old growth forest. There's a three-foot-diameter sugar maple, then lots of two-plus-foot-diameter hemlock.

The trail crosses Highway 123, then dips a bit into a hemlock grove. You may see the giant pine before you see the sign for it. The tree towers over everything, and its trunk reminds us that what we think are large trees are only a beginning. This behemoth is 120 feet tall and nearly 15 feet in circumference. The sign says it's only 175 years old, but it might be much older, more than 300 years old. It looks healthy, as though it's in the prime of life. A companion, just down the trail a bit on the opposite side, doesn't look as healthy.

Skiing away from the pines you will see a caution sign, which marks the top of a tiny hill that's nothing to worry about. Large yellow birch join the big hemlock along the trail. You will pass through a low open area, then down another small hill to a picnic bench on the right. After passing a teenaged white pine that's only a couple of feet in diameter, you will reach a junction with the trail that leads to Wolf Lake. Snowshoers use the trail.

Continue on the ski trail, past some really big tip-ups, which are trees that have been blown over and have turned up huge plates of soil and roots at their bases. One along here is the size of a small house. This is one way nature creates the mosaic that allows creatures and plants a chance to succeed. The clearing that the downed tree has made will harbor lots of new growth, which attracts different animals than the old growth you've been skiing through does.

When you reach the snowmobile crossing, you are near Highway 123. The trail can be hard to follow here, but it reenters the woods about 15 m to the right of where it exits. Cross the road and go right; you will see the trail where it heads into the hardwood forest.

This last section of trail is dominated by hardwoods, especially sugar maple and beech. There's one smooth-barked beech tree on the right about half a kilometer from the road. It stands out because it's so large amid lesser trees. There are some hemlock, too, but these are in isolated groves. The trail is essentially flat, with a few bumps. It provides pleasant striding.

There is a nice downhill into the parking area. It's an effortless finish, so you can catch your breath before entering the pub and trying some White Pine Pilsner.

Journal: There's nothing like backcountry skiing. While Tahquamenon Falls isn't really backcountry skiing—there's usually some trail from prior skiers or a snowmobile groomer—it's got a backcountry feel. Such a feel was no more evident than when I bent under a hemlock branch laden with a foot or more of snow. I didn't bend quite far enough, so when I brushed the branch, most of that snow went down the back of my neck, into my shirt, all the way to my waist. Invigorating.

10

Valley Spur Ski Trail

Directions: From the corner of Highways 28 and 94, just south of Munising, take 94 south approximately 6 miles. The trailhead sign is on the right, the parking area on the left.

Grooming: There are about 23 km groomed for skating. That leaves about 20 km that are groomed for diagonal.

Total km: system, 43; this tour, 10

Fee: none

Trailhead facilities: There is a lovely little lodge building at the trailhead, but it is only open on weekends and during the Christmas season. There is an outhouse at the trailhead that's available all the time.

Contact: Hiawatha National Forest, Munising Ranger District, 400 E. Munising Ave., Munising, MI 49862; (906) 387-2512.

These trails are a lot of fun. This tour will take you on some more advanced terrain, which is perhaps the most fun kind. Start from near the shelter. Don't let all the letters on signposts intimidate you. Since this tour is going all the way out to G, that's the letter to follow.

Since A comes first, that's the first trail loop you will be on. It's a very easy loop, and the first part is no exception. The trees along here are typical of the trail: beech, sugar maple, some aspen, and black cherry. There are areas ahead on this tour with large-diameter trees.

When you reach the first junction, go right and stay with G. Then bear right two more times. At the next junction, A goes right and you go left. The trail begins going uphill almost immediately after this junction. The grade isn't too steep, but it's steady. And it keeps going up, for about half a kilometer. This is the hill lovingly referred to as Stairway to Heaven. There are some large black cherry trees along the way. The hill you are climbing is part of a complex of ridges that form the backbone of this trail. You will ski part way down and up them several more times in the next hour. The junction with E and C is at the top of the hill. You want to go more or less straight, on E.

It's only a short ski on E before you encounter Boomer, a respectable downhill run. As with virtually all that follow, this downhill zips down, then curves right to a climb back up onto the ridge. Once back on the ridge, the trail loops in and out of big maple and cherry.

The intersection with F precedes another downhill, this one named Bigfoot's Revenge. It is a long downhill, one that isn't entirely visible from the top. In fact, most of the downhill isn't visible from the top. The trail twists and turns several times before you finally hit a level. There are a couple more dips and climbs before you climb back up the ridge. The trail follows the ridge for a while, and you can see the lowland off toward Lake Superior if you look through the trees on the left.

Another little climb and you arrive at the top of Catapult. This hill is likely named for the severe hook to the right just beyond the hill's bottom. The idea is that you will be catapulted around the hook. However, this will only happen on really slick snow or ice. Most of the time you'll have lots of room for slowing up before the corner.

This time you will not climb all the way to the ridge top. But there will be another downhill, this the first of three in a row, all named Lemans. If you look to the right at the end of the runout from Lemans number one, you will see a three-stemmed black cherry tree. Each stem is more than 20 inches in diameter. What's more amazing is the size of the stump that it sprouted from. That tree, cut perhaps a hundred years ago, was more than three feet in diameter.

The next Lemans is easy, straight but steep, just like number one. Before you reach the downhill, look right and behind you. These ridges look layered, almost like old shorelines, which they may be. Glacial Lake Algonquin was much larger than Lake Superior, and there are beach ridges even farther south than Valley Spur.

Lemans number three is less steep than the first two, but longer. There's a climb in between each of the Lemans hills. After the last Lemans, it's a short 30 m stride to the top of Slingshot. Launch yourself down it, and be ready for a bit of a curve.

Now it's time to stride and then herringbone up onto the ridge again. The trail takes advantage of a notch in the ridge. It's still a long climb, not unlike Stairway to Heaven. About a soon as you reach the top, there's a drop, this one called Skier's Delight. And it is a delightful little hill, steep, but short.

The trail then parallels a high ridge on the left. You also can see the skating trail, Y, off to the left, below the ridge. It isn't long before the trail begins climbing that ridge. The skating trail climbs through the same ridge notch as G, your trail. It is a steep climb, and herringbone is a must. Once at the top, look back. You can't see too much because the notch is narrow, but seeing how steep your climb was will give you a feeling of accomplishment.

Once over the ridge top, it's downhill, into some balsam fir and red pine. The trail passes through an open gate, then runs on a road

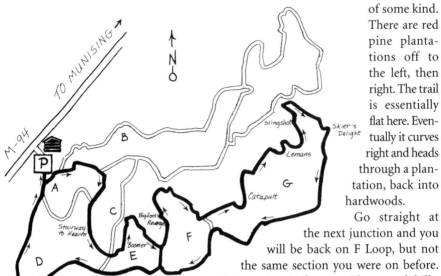

of some kind. There are red pine plantations off to the left, then right. The trail is essentially flat here. Eventually it curves right and heads through a plantation, back into hardwoods.

Go straight at the next junction and you will be back on F Loop, but not the same section you were on before. This section is flatter, with no real hills.

Bear left at the junction of E, and just past the junction you will see a big white pine on the left. It's close to the trail, and you can look up at its double leader. The pine is less than nine feet in circumference. A similar double leader pine was the national champion. It grew in the Porcupine Mountains and was more than 18 feet in circumference before it was toppled in a massive flood along the Little Carp River in 1985.

At the junction with D, bear left again. There's about a kilometer of gentle ups and downs before you hit Heaven, the long downhill off the ridge. If you start double poling when you see the skate trail, you should just about make the junction with A without needing to stride. Once you are there, it's less than 100 m back to the parking area. You have been to heaven and back.

Journal: I discovered something today. It's a bit embarrassing. After I skied at the Munising Pictured Rocks trail, I noticed that my toes were unusually cold. The air temperature was only in the mid-teens, so my toes shouldn't have been so cold. When I took my ski boot off, I felt my toes and they were sort of wet. I wondered how my socks had gotten wet, but dismissed it and drove to my next ski, at Valley Spur. My toes didn't get cold this time, but they were wet when I removed my boots.

Then the explanation dawned on me. I'd skied with those boots for the last couple of weeks and I had never taken them out of the car. There was two weeks' worth—more than 140 km worth—of sweat in those boots. Sweat that had frozen and thawed ten, maybe twelve times. Sweat that had never evaporated because it was too cold.

Like I said, it's embarrassing.

III

The Marquette Area

11

Al Quaal Recreation Area

Directions: From the corner of Deer Lake Road (which is directly across from the National Ski Hall of Fame and Museum in Ishpeming) and Highway 41, take Deer Lake Road north .3 mile to Prairie Street, which is the middlemost of three streets at the intersection. Take Prairie another .2 mile and the recreation area is straight ahead.

Grooming: A wide area is packed, then a track set in the middle. The placement of the track makes skating without messing up the track impossible. It's a good place for striding or, better yet, practicing your marathon skate.

Total km: system, 1.5; this tour, 1.5

Fee: A local pass is required.

Trailhead facilities: There is a nifty shelter (lodge) located down the street, near the entrance. It has lots of wooden tables, and a lovely wooden floor. There is snack food available. The shelter serves the real attraction here, the toboggan run.

The run begins at a little house on top of a hill behind the shelter. The toboggan sits on a short, tablelike contraption. When everyone is seated and secure, the table gets tipped downward, and the toboggan slips off into an iced runway between a couple of two-by-sixes. The grade isn't really all that steep, but the toboggan really gets moving on the 1,500-foot-long slide. When that table dips and the toboggan shoots out of the building, riders let out some blood-curdling screams. When they get to the bottom, they dismount and climb back up the hill. They even get some exercise.

Contact: City of Ishpeming, Parks Department, 100 E. Division, Ishpeming, MI 49849; (906) 486-6181.

Although this is a short trail, it still makes a nice, quick ski. The trail starts beyond the little ski tow house at the end of the parking area. It might be tempting to sluice down the slope, but the towrope only works on weekends. The trail enters a deep, conifer-studded forest. Since this area gets tons of snow, the effect is as if everything is frosted. The trail is about three ski lengths wide.

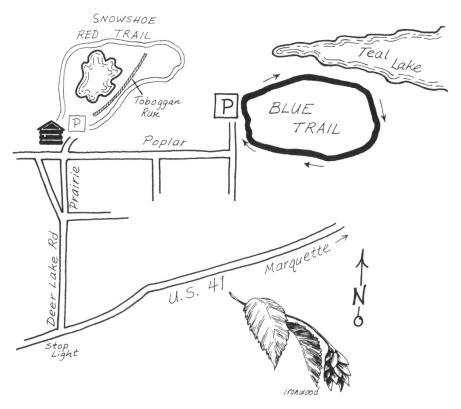

Far below on the left is the westernmost end of massive Teal Lake. The ravine looks as though it should shelter a river. The trail takes you down at first, then climbs and curves right, away from the lake. The conifers thin out a bit as the trail gets higher, but there are some large white pine. You may see an ungroomed trail that sometimes has ski tracks from bushwhackers. This is the old 3 km trail. It's been discontinued with the building of a new subdivision to the east.

Follow the groomed trail as it loops up and right. You will pass where the old trail rejoins your trail. The balsam fir are really thick here. Then almost suddenly, you are in a maple-oak woods. There are a couple of large red oak on the left. The smaller trees here are ironwood, a shade-tolerant species.

After a brief ski on a flat trail, the track tips downward, and you are off on the last 50 m of trail, all down. The parking area is on the left.

Anderson Lake Ski Pathway

Directions: From the intersections of Highways 35 and 557 west of Gwinn, take 557 south approximately 5 miles to the parking area on the right.

Grooming: The trail is groomed for striding only.

Total km: system, 7; this tour, 7

Fee: donation

Trailhead facilities: none

Contact: Gwinn Forest Management Unit, 410 W. Highway M-35, Gwinn, MI 49841; (906) 346-9201.

The first few hundred meters of this trail is on unplowed park road, hence, the trail is wide, and the groomer sets two tracks, one on each side of the road. The forest is a mix of deciduous trees such as maple and oak, along with some conifers, such as balsam fir and pine. Although the road heads to Anderson Lake and the campground, you won't see either because the trail ducks right into the woods and off the road. You will see Flacks Lakes (there are two of them) on the right as you ski down the wide road toward the campground.

Once off the road, the trail is narrow, about the width of a snowmobile groomer. You'll encounter your first downhill soon after you leave the road. It's a straight, easy affair, but sitzmarks at the bottom can cause problems.

The woods are different for a while after the downhill. It's densely packed with balsam fir and there are tall white pine above the fir. Snowshoe hare like it here because there's lots of cover; there are usually plenty of tracks. You will pass the trail's largest white birch on the left as you climb from the bottom of one small hill.

When you reach Junction 5, go left and you will be on Loop 2. Your first serious downhill is just ahead. It is straight, but long enough that you'll build up some speed. If the sun is out, and it's a warmer day—especially in March—you will feel the slowing effect of sun-warmed snow as you zip down this and the next hill. The third of these downhills takes you into a cedar swamp. The cedar have a brown tinge in winter, and their coloring stands out as you ski toward them.

On the other side of the cedar the trail climbs steeply, then

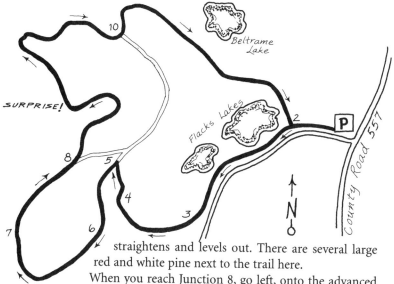

straightens and levels out. There are several large red and white pine next to the trail here.

When you reach Junction 8, go left, onto the advanced Loop, 3. Initially, there's nothing advanced about it. You will ski through a notable stand of white pine with tall, straight trunks reaching high overhead. Then there's a striding climb up a long hill and out of the older, nicer woods into a young forest of multi-stemmed maple and small pine. There are only scattered large pine here. A long, easy downhill lets you glide past an early 1980s clear-cut that's pure aspen.

Once you leave the aspen, you will climb a bit, then encounter a split in the trail. The easier downhill is to the left, the harder one to the right. What makes the right one harder is not so much the hill itself—which is pretty straight—but the 90-plus-degree turn at the bottom. Since this trail is narrowly groomed, there isn't much space for snowplowing, so it's difficult to control your downhill speed. Luckily there's a runout straight ahead at the turn. There's also a humorous surprise mounted on a tree at the bottom of the hill.

Once around the corner at the bottom of the hill, you will gradually climb up into a pretty red pine forest—not a plantation, but one that sprouted naturally. After a ski through some aspen you will encounter another downhill. The hill isn't too bad, but the sharp right corner at the bottom would give even an Olympian trouble.

After the difficult right turn, the trail slopes downward, on a long, gradual incline to Junction 10. The forest type changes back to the dense fir understory, with a big pine overstory, as it was through the middle of this ski. Make a hard left at Junction 10 and enjoy the flat to slightly downhill trail that loops past one of Flacks Lakes. Ski out onto the lake if you like. Shortly after the lake you will come to Junction 2, which you passed on your way up the park road near the beginning of this ski. Go left, and the parking area is only 200 m away.

13

Blueberry Ridge Pathway

Directions: From the corner of Highways 480 and 553, 6 miles south of Marquette, go south on 553 about .2 mile to the parking area on the left.

Grooming: The trails are diagonal-only on the Crossroads, Husky, and Spartan Loops. The rest of the system is groomed for both diagonal and skating techniques. It is groomed well, and often.

Total km: system, 18; this tour, 12; lighted loop, 2.7

Fee: donation

Trailhead facilities: There are well-kept outhouses.

Contact: Michigan Department of Natural Resources, Upper Peninsula Field Headquarters, 1990 U.S. 41 S., Marquette, MI 49855; (906) 228-6561.

The trail begins just right of the trailhead sign. It is essentially flat for the first kilometer, until just before the junction with Husky Loop, where a nice, easy downhill will actually take you by the junction. Most of the forest on the Crossroads Loop is young white, jack pine and oak. Fire has played a role in the forest here, hence some of the fire-regenerated jack pine.

Past the junction with Husky Loop the trail stays about the same, with some easy hills, both up and down. When you see the "Expert Only" sign, you are at the trail's junction with Spartan Loop. Spartan is rated "expert" because of a couple of steep downhills. While they are indeed steep, they are not very long.

The forest changes a bit past the Spartan junction: There are more large red and white pine in the canopy. Indeed, barring fire, wind, or logging, they will form a supercanopy here in 50 or so years.

After a short downhill, and a mild climb up Highway 480 is visible on the left. Loop around and you'll reach a sign that reads, "Caution, Steep Hill." The hill is indeed steep, sort of a double-dip with the grade easing up in the middle. Then there is a series of smaller hills followed by a short but steep downhill, with a hook left at the bottom. Watch out for sitzmarks at this hook. Some folks don't quite make the turn and fall down rather than hit the trees on the outside of the curve. Seems like a reasonable compromise.

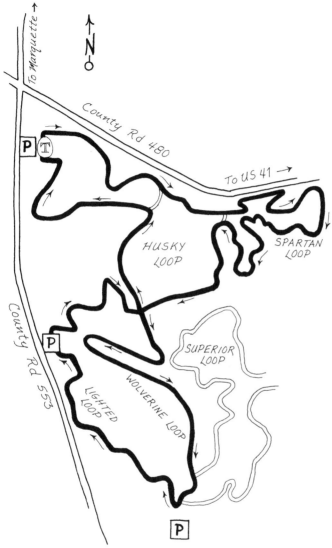

More small hills lead you to a trail sign that doesn't really mark anything, but assures you that this is still Spartan Loop. You will climb a bit after the sign, into large white and then red pine. A herringbone climb takes you to a relatively flat area of the trail and past a stand of 30-year-old aspen—one of the few such stands on this trail. Don't look back at the aspen as you cruise by, because there's a tricky down-hill with a left curve ahead. It is a nice gradual downhill curve, but your speed can send you out of the track if you don't angle your edges and assume the coma position. (Shift your weight so you automati-cally roll onto your edges.)

The downhill run ends at the trail junction with Husky Loop. Husky is flat for .5 km or so, then tilts down gradually, causing an increase in your speed. A curve right at the end of the long downhill can be difficult—the imprints of bodies in the deep snow on the outside of the curve prove that.

There's another flat section, then a long climb up to the junction with Wolverine Loop. A bench here gets used more than most since the climb is long and requires some splayed-ski herringbone technique.

Turn left at the junction and you will notice a change in the trail. It's become wider. Skating is OK on Wolverine, which is groomed for both techniques. The grade is level, or slightly downhill, and the trail takes you into an open area with some small pine. A long, sweeping curve almost reverses your direction. Where this curve straightens out, look left, and about two ski lengths into the woods you will see a stump with a two-stemmed white birch growing out of it. It's unusual for white birch to grow from stumps.

For the next kilometer or so the trail bobs and weaves with easy hills and turns, through pine and aspen forest. There are a lot of jack pine here, and along most of the rest of the trail. Fire swept through this area years ago, leaving perfect conditions for jack pine regeneration.

You will pass the entrance and exit to and from the Superior and Wildcat Loops. These are great trails, with some steep climbs and drops, not unlike those you encountered on Spartan. After passing the exit from these two trails, you will arrive at an alternate parking area, and the beginning of the lighted loop. At the next junction bear left. The woods here are full of jack pine, favored by the fire discussed earlier. Eventually you will notice Highway 553 on the left, as the trail comes quite close to it.

When you sweep by the next parking area, you will notice an outhouse on the left. Loop right, across an old road and to a steep downhill. There is a bypass of this hill, but since the hill is straight and not at all technical, go for it.

At the bottom of the hill you may notice some dead jack pine on the right. These may be victims of a small wildfire. It's only about 400 m to the junction with Husky Loop. You passed here before. Make a left and notice that the trail is narrow again, this is diagonal-only territory.

It's about 1.5 km back to the trailhead. It's mostly flat, with a couple of small hills. You may notice one section of trail that is forested with the ubiquitous jack pine, but also dotted with small white birch. The contrast between the almost black jack pine trunks and the white of the birch is subtly beautiful.

National Ski Hall of Fame and Museum

The National Ski Hall of Fame and Museum building screams skiing. As you approach it on Highway 41 in Ishpeming, Michigan, the first thing that strikes you is the arched spine that supports the atrium entrance. It looks for all the world like a ski jump! It's said that the hall of fame's officials once offered a free cup of coffee to any jumper who'd give it a try. A trio of former Ishpeming Olympians figured they could clear the four-lane highway out front and land in a parking lot across the street. No one ever collected the coffee.

Both the American and Canadian flags fly outside the building. The hall acknowledges the importance of both countries to the sport of skiing. The hall is on the Circle Lake Superior route, and lots of Canadians visit.

The National Ski Hall of Fame and Museum was established in 1954, and it moved to its impressive new 1.5-million-dollar building in 1992. Its bright glass-enclosed atrium lobby invites visitors inside. A four-story-high arch sweeping past an elegant stained glass window greets all who enter.

A broad hallway exits the atrium. Plaques with the names of benefactors decorate the walls. There's a classroom where you can view a video highlighting skiing history. It makes no mention of the different types of skiing. Indeed, the Hall of Fame seems to downplay the differences between alpine and nordic skiing. According to one of the hall's officials, "The sport started out as one and the same. The first winter Olympics were only Nordic. We just treat the subject as it developed."

Opposite the classroom, on other side of the Hall, is the Roland Palmedo Library, which contains one of the largest collections of ski-related material in the United States. A goal of the Hall is to become the country's number-one repository for such information.

At its far end the hallway opens into a room that repeats the atrium arch seven times. Silk banners mimic mountains as the beams recede to meet the back wall, 62 feet above. This larger room houses the actual hall of fame: pictures and brief biographies of more than 300 prominent members of the skiing community.

The museum's displays occupy an area behind the Hall and on an open second-floor deck. One of the most impressive exhibits is of two life-sized 13th-century Birkebeiners carrying an infant king across the Norwegian plateau between Rena and Lillehammer. Their skis are scroll-tipped, wide, wood boards. In addition to the infant, they tote an enormous broad ax, a four-meter-long spear, and a big, round metal shield. It's a great display that brings alive a bit of Norway's history.

Ski freaks will love the assortment of old skis on display. There's a Finnish racing ski, circa 1920, and a "prairie ski" that's almost five meters long! Waxless-ski enthusiasts and detractors alike will enjoy the waxless-ski exhibit, with five different types of such skis displayed. As if to prove that nothing really changes, the exhibit copy says, "Early waxes involved everything from fish livers to jam jar paraffin." Maybe you should try some fish livers on your next ski outing.

It's safe to say that most skiers have never heard of Osterdal. This late-18th-century blend of equipment and technique was practiced in Norway and Sweden. According to the display, "It featured one short, fur covered ski about 4-6' long and one long ground ski often twice that length. The short ski, called the Andor, was used to push off." Imagine how strange that looked—sort of like riding a modern day scooter, but on skis instead of wheels.

The museum is packed with interesting skiing items and is well worth a look. As the introductory video says, "Skiing is: speed, grace, serious, serious fun, terror, exhilaration, and joy." Anyone disagree?

Directions: The hall is located on the south side of Highway 41 in the middle of Ishpeming, Michigan.

Fee: Yes, daily admission or memberships available.

Contact: P.O. Box 191, Ishpeming, Michigan 498449; (906) 485-6323.

14

Kawbawgam Ski Trail

Directions: From the corner of Highways 41 and 28 south of Marquette, take 28 east 5 miles to Kawbawgam Road. Go right (south) on Kawbawgam Road .25 mile to the parking area and trailhead on the left.

Grooming: The trail is groomed for diagonal stride. The first couple of kilometers are double tracked.

Total km: system, 6; this tour, 6

Fee: none

Trailhead facilities: none

Contact: Chocolay Township, 5010 U.S. Highway 41 S., Marquette, MI 49855; (906) 249-1448.

This trail was inaugurated in 2001, so it's quite new. There are plans to redesign the first kilometer or so and expand the trail so it heads farther east along Lake Le Vasseur.

If you don't recognize a jack pine you will by the end of this tour. Lake Superior is less than a mile north of the trailhead, and the area that this trail traverses was beachfront (even lake bottom) a few thousand years ago. In recent times, fire and dry, sandy soil have predisposed the site to vegetation that can tolerate such harsh conditions. Jack pine is the tree that can grow here—and grow it does.

Start the tour from the parking area. The first 1.9 km of trail is straight, flat, and easy. The jack pine are small, head-high and slightly larger. They are also scattered, not dense. There was a fire here in the late 1970s, which is why the jack pine are so prevalent. Jack pine cones don't open and release their seed until temperatures rise above 110 degrees Fahrenheit. So it's fire that jump-starts the reseeding of jack pine.

The trail cuts right, crosses a snowmobile trail and then enters some slightly older and bigger jack pine. These trees are as much as 10 inches in diameter, and are generally denser than the little ones encountered earlier. The topography also changes a bit, becoming slightly hilly. These are old sand dunes. Although not big, the way the trail curves around and over them, the dunes make for some tricky skiing.

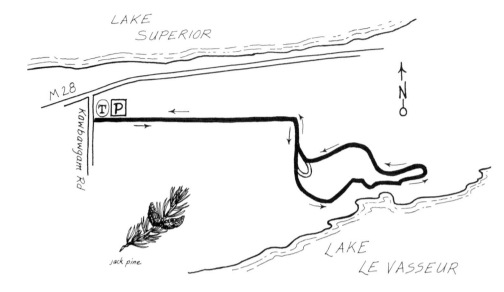

jack pine

When you reach an open area, which is a summer road, look right and you will see a sign and the boat landing at Lake Le Vasseur. Although the trail may not be groomed down to the landing, ski on down. The lake looks more like a wetland, with a small dam, a creek below, and cattail-filled lowland above. This used to be called Mud Lake, and even with the flood-control dam, the water's shallow.

Head back up to the trail and go right, down off the roadway. The trail gradually climbs up on top of a ridge that runs the length of the lake and former creek bed. It's a pleasant ski along this undulating ridge until you reach a downhill that takes you off the high ground. The hill is neither steep nor is it long, yet the left turn at the bottom is not a reasonable one and so can't be made by staying in the track. You will need to step turn, or head off into the untracked snow between the jack pine.

The jack pine continue, ever more thickly packed together. You will pass a partially open field on the right. As you loop around the field, the jack pine along the trail thin out and you reach a junction where you should go right. This is the trail you came out on. Ski across the snowmobile trail and head down the straight stretch toward the parking lot. And don't forget what a jack pine looks like!

Kivela Road Trail

Directions: From the intersection of Highway 41 and Baldwin/North Road in Negaunee, go north on North Road (Baldwin becomes North Road within a few blocks after turning off of Highway 41). Approximately 2.5 miles to Kivela Road. Go right on Kivela Road less than .3 mile. The park and trailhead are on the left.

Grooming: This is a narrow trail, groomed for striding only.

Total km: system, 4.5; this tour, 4

Fee: none

Trailhead facilities: There is a cinder-block outhouse.

Contact: Negaunee Township, 42 Highway M-35, Negaunee, MI 49866; (906) 475-7869.

This trail is not very long, and therein lies its only fault. It's a fun little trail that you will wish there was more of. Start at the north end of the parking lot. The trail takes you around the outside perimeter of the baseball diamond's outfield fence. Somewhere near right-center field, the trail veers left into the woods. There may be some brush and low tree limbs along this trail that could hit you in the face, so be aware.

Not more than 10 m into the woods you will see a large, three-foot-diameter white pine next to the trail on the right. This venerable old giant has limbs almost down to the ground. It would make a great climbing tree or a spot from which to watch wildlife pass by. As you ski farther, you will notice other large white pine around you, but more about them later. There are also plenty of fir, birch and maple, although it's the pine—both white and jack—that impress.

At the first junction go right (a left will take you back to near the trailhead), and you will have skied the easy, beginner, Blue Loop. Going right leads you to the trail's first "Steep Hill" sign. With this and the two ensuing "Steep Hill" signs, they should read, "Tricky Hill." None are really that steep. On this occasion, the trail makes a couple of hairpin turns as it winds down a moderate grade. Because the trail is narrow, there isn't much room for error or to maneuver your skis.

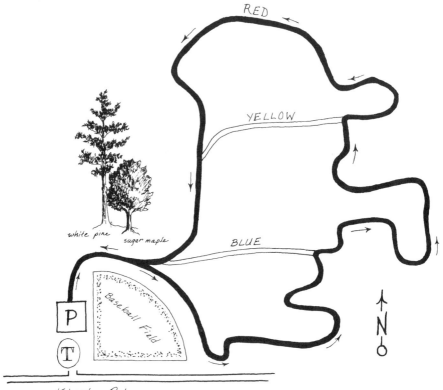

As you climb up from the bottom of a hairpin hill, note the over two-foot-diameter white birch on the right. It's a magnificent specimen of this type of tree, and one that belies the commonly held idea that birch never get very big and are short lived.

The trail continues gradually uphill past the birch. This is a good place for looking up at the treetops and noticing how tall the white pine really are here. They tower over the understory of fir, birch, and maple. If you look at the trunk of one of the pine near the ground you will notice that they are only about 15 to 20 inches in diameter—not giants by any stretch of the imagination. These pine are good examples of what will develop into supercanopy pines. Over the next hundred years or so—baring intervention by man or wind—these pine will continue growing, getting up to and above 100 feet tall. The trees under them will also grow, but they will thin out a bit. Eventually there will be two stories of trees here.

When you see the next "Steep Hill" sign, remember that it isn't the steepness that will get you, it's the T intersection at the bottom! The Yellow Loop goes left here, and you may also choose to because that's the easiest way to turn to avoid going off into the thick woods at the head of the T. Turn around and head right on the Red Loop.

It's a short 40 meters or so to where the trail enters a two-acre wetland opening. The naked spires of dead spruce pierce the ski above the wetland area. Perhaps some beaver flooded this little patch of land, killing the trees. The trees around the opening are thick and lush, with a couple of the ever-present sentry white pine lording over the scene.

You will ski up a bit, away from the opening. The land dips on the right, and as the trail loops left, you will begin seeing a 20-foot-tall rock wall on the left. As you ski along the wall, it becomes higher and higher, eventually rising about 40 feet above the trail. There are also some ice falls hanging off the bare rock face along the way. These can be quite lovely, depending on the temperature, time of year and moisture in the soil. There is one place you can climb up into a notch in the wall. It looks like a trail goes through here in the summer, but it isn't groomed for skiing.

The final "Steep Hill" sign awaits near the end of the rock wall. You will ski past the end of that wall, then sweep down a curve into a half-acre opening that marks the beginning of a long, 20-to-30-meter-wide lane between planted fir and red pine. A few adventuresome cherry trees have colonized the opening.

You will see a trail join from the left. This is where the cutoff for Yellow Loop rejoins the trail. From here it's only about 400 m back to the ball field and parking area. Since the trail is short, it can be fun to head back out the way you came in and cut over on the Yellow Loop. That way you get to make the left turn at the T intersection and keep going.

Journal: I almost didn't ski the Kivela Road Trail, thinking it was not long enough and probably unremarkable. When I arrived at a treeless, ball-field trailhead, I was even less eager.

But once I saw that big white pine near the start, I felt better. Then there were all the tall pine, pine becoming supercanopy. The rock wall was the clincher. As I saw the end of the trail I felt sad, wanted more, and knew this trail was going into this book.

16

Marquette City Fit Strip

Directions:	From the corner of Highway 41 and Business 41 near the Holiday Inn in Marquette, take Business 41 about 1 mile to Seymour Street. Take Seymour left .2 mile to the T intersection. Turn left and go .2 mile to the parking area where the road ends.
Grooming:	The outside loop is striding only; inside loops are groomed for both striding and diagonal.
Total km:	system, 3.5; this tour, 3.2
Fee:	donation
Trailhead facilities:	Sort of. The day I skied here there was a chemical toilet in the parking lot, but it was tipped over into a snowbank. It looked as if the snowplow had gotten carried away.
Contact:	Marquette Parks and Recreation, 300 W. Baraga, Marquette, MI 49855; (906) 228-0460.

This is a unique ski trail. It sits in the middle of a residential/business neighborhood. It's an oasis really. The pines are big, and the trail lots of fun.

Start out to the left from the trailhead sign. There are two trails here, an outer one that is classic only and an inner one for either technique. Let's ski the classic first. Tall pines grace the trail from the beginning. In the summer this is a fitness trail; the various stations look odd in the winter, buried under three feet of snow.

The trail parallels a road on the left, and you can see apartments on the other side of the road. There are some easy hills, up and down, then you come to a knoll that overlooks a drop in the trail and an oriental, bonsai-looking red pine next to the trail below. You drop down, past the pine, and scoot up the next hill, then glide down past more big red pine.

There isn't a junction, but you will see the inside loop on your right. You need to stay left, and you will ski into a dense conifer stand comprised of large white and red pine, plus some jack pine. There are smaller hemlock in the understory, which makes for dark, primeval-looking woods.

The trail crosses a little creek, then traces the creek bed before crossing back over and climbing. There are houses visible on the left. One has a tall wood fence between it and this wonderful wood lot.

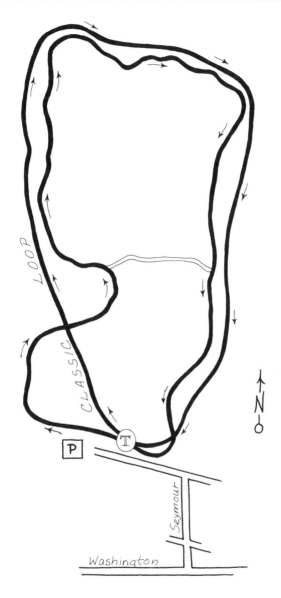

Why would you want a visual barrier that blocks your view of this place?

You will ski past a giant old white pine on the right. A close look once you are by it reveals that there's been a fire set near its base. The charred bark is black and ugly. Yet the tree looks healthy. Big pine such as these—their thick bark insulating the living tissue underneath—are built to withstand fire.

The trail takes you out into an open area and traces the edge of a cemetery to the left. The openness provides a nice contrast with the forest you've been skiing in. Once the trail loops back right and into the woods, it's just 30 m back to the trailhead.

The inside loop is more challenging than the outside one. Start out the same way, but take the first left. There are some gentle hills, then a herringbone climb up a ridge followed by a double-dip downhill on the other side. Another herringbone hill brings you to where the outside and inside trails almost meet.

Stay right and ski to a little hilltop with a nice-sized white pine on the right and a red pine of equal size on the left. There's a steep 3 m drop off this hill and then a right-curving run through perhaps the loveliest section of big pines.

Some easy hills and more curves find you in an area of smaller pine, oak, and maple. Then you are near the open area and cemetery. A brief ski through more oak and maple brings you back to the trailhead.

Journal: There's a guy skiing here who is obviously working out, probably training for something, perhaps the Birkie. He's lapped me twice now as I ski the outside loop, taking notes and enjoying the scenery. I wonder if he sees the big trees, the wonderful little creek bed, the cemetery. Skiing fast can be an end in itself, but the trade-off is that you don't experience some of the wonder that's always out here. I hope he realizes what's here, and can appreciate the beauty of this place.

Deer and Teal Lake Loops

Directions: From the corner of Highway 41 and Deer Lake Road (which is directly across from the National Ski Hall of Fame in Ishpeming), take Deer Lake Road north .3 mile to Prairie Street, the middlemost of three streets at the intersection. Take Prairie Street another .2 mile; the recreation area is straight ahead. (These are the same directions as those for the Al Quaal Recreation Area trail.)

Grooming: Trails will be groomed for skating and striding.

Total km: approximately 18

Fee: donation

Trailhead facilities: A shelter located near the entrance to the recreation area has lots of wood tables and a lovely wood floor. Snack food is available. There are plans to build a trailhead shelter closer to the actual ski trails, east of the toboggan run.

Contact: Superiorland Ski Club, P.O. Box 864, Marquette, MI 49855. Phone the Lake Superior Community Partnership (Ishpeming-Negaunee-Marquette Area Chambers of Commerce) at (888) 578-6489.

As this book goes to press, ski trails in the Ishpeming-Negaunee-Marquette area are in transition. At least 4 of the 13 trails listed in the Marquette County 2000–2001 cross-country skiing brochure won't exist as trails in 2001–2002. Most notable of these are the SUNTRAC Trails, (Superior Nordic Training and Recreation Area, and individually called the Hill Street Classic and Suicide Bowl trails). These two long-time mainstays among the area's famed ski trails are about to disappear. It seems that Cleveland Cliffs, the mining company that owns the land that the trails use, is going to put mine overburden on the area. The same is true for the Tilden Township Trails (formerly National Mine Trails).

And now, here's the good news. It is likely that two new trails will be in place for the 2001–2002 skiing season. Designed by John Morton, a nationally recognized ski trail designer, the Deer and Teal Lake Loops will utilize some magnificent real estate on the north side of both lakes. The Deer Lake Loop will traverse old growth and afford exceptional views of the lake. Teal Lake Loop will utilize more rugged terrain and should be a challenging ski. Parts of both trails will likely be included in the Noquemanon Ski Marathon course. In the past, the Noquemanon course, which covers 53 km between Ishpeming and Marquette, has not been open to skiing, except during the race. In addition to the Teal and Deer Lake Loops,

51

there are plans to keep the last 15-20 km groomed for the 2001–2002 season.

What all this transition means is that cross-country skiing in Marquette County has a bright future. But before you plan your ski trip there, give the Lake Superior Community Partnership a call and find out what's new and fun.

Presque Isle Park Ski Trails

Directions: From any street in Marquette, drive to the lakefront (east), turn left (north), and follow Lakeshore Boulevard along the lake up to Presque Isle Park.

Grooming: The trail is groomed for both skating and striding.

Total km: 5

Fee: none

Trailhead facilities: There is a log cabin pavilion that's open on the weekend. Coffee and hot chocolate are on the house.

Contact: Marquette Parks and Recreation, 401 E. Fair Street, Marquette, MI 49855, (906) 228-0460.

This is a cool place, figuratively and literally. Sometimes the wind tears at your clothing while you are taking in the wonderful views of Lake Superior. But that's a small price for the beautiful surroundings.

In planning my trip to the area, I had decided that Presque Isle would be my first ski in Marquette. I had run on the road circling the island in the summer and had ridden my bike here during a triathalon. I knew it was a lovely place and figured the lake in winter would make it even more beautiful.

When I reached the parking area, I was greeted by some yellow ribbons and homemade signs that said the park was closed. Puzzled, I called the Parks and Recreation Department on my cell phone. The poor guy who answered must have taken many calls about the closure, some of them apparently not nice. He was businesslike but terse. He let me know that the park was closed because sharpshooters had been called in to thin the burgeoning deer herd. The situation had caused quite a controversy in Marquette. Making matters worse, it took the shooters a lot longer to do the job than anticipated. I can't help wondering where the deer were hiding on the little island.

IV

The Keweenaw Area

Chassell Classic Ski Trail

Directions:	The trailhead is located in the village of Chassell, which is on Highway 41 about 6 miles south of Houghton. Look for the sign that points west to the Chassell Heritage Center, which is one block west of 41 on the north end of town. Parking is located just to the east of the large old schoolhouse that the Heritage Center occupies.
Grooming:	This is a classic-only trail. It is groomed frequently.
Total km:	system, 9; this tour, 9; 1 lighted
Fee:	donation
Trailhead facilities:	There is a warming hut near the ice rink, which sits behind the old school and is hard to see from the trailhead. The hut is not always open.
Contact:	Keweenaw Tourism Council, (800) 338-7982.

After traveling around outside the right field fence of the local ballpark, the trail enters the woods, climbs a couple of small hills, and cuts into a lovely little hemlock stand. There's a modest stream and gully on the left.

About the time you settle into the tracks and develop some a feel for the trail, you'll see a caution sign, and accelerate into a left turn. Up ahead, bright orange fencing guards the right side of a little bridge that spans the small creek you've been paralleling. The downhill to the bridge isn't difficult, but be cautious. Tangling your ski tips in the fencing would be an embarrassment!

After skiing through the woods for a while, you'll enter a field. There are houses in the distance. The trail loops back into the woods after about 100 m and winds through a maple woods, which has been used as a sugar bush for many years. Note the collapsed buildings that served as sap boiling shelters.

Once out of the sugar bush, the trail cuts across another field (the same one actually, just farther west). Note the large poles sticking out of the snow. These are here so the groomer doesn't loose the trail. Remember: Winter can bring 300 inches of snow here.

Shortly after reentering the woods, the trail crosses a snowmobile trail, then reaches an intersection. If you go left you will be headed back to the trailhead. Turn right and you're off on the Paradise Loop.

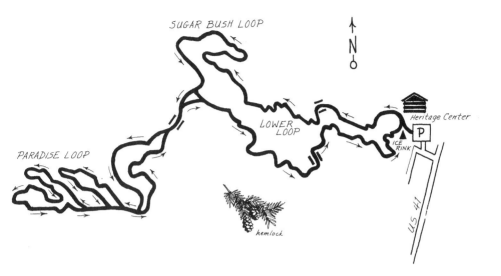

A wide section of trail, which is double tracked, takes you to a down-hill and another bridge crossing. After a small climb the trail splits and is single track again. Go right and ski through an old field, which is slowly reverting to trees. Someone is helping the field revert, and soon you ski through the first of many conifer windbreaks and plantations. Four rows of 10-foot-high white pine make this planting look like a living fence.

The trail loops gently around this field, tracing a slight rise that looks like a tiny esker. The view from this ridge is oddly beautiful. Small trees, including white pine, cherry, oak, and alder, dot the undulating ground, all overwhelmed by white. If it's windy, it will be harder to appreciate the landscape, and you may just want to get back into the trees.

And as you progress farther, you find more and more trees—almost all planted by someone—in rows. There are some larger spruce and pine, plus plenty of smaller trees such as birch and maple that have seeded in on their own.

When you enter a dense spruce stand where the trail is hugged by warming, snow-laden branches, you are near the turn-around loop. Several houses along Paradise Road are visible from the trail here. Look for the snowmobile with the tracking equipment attached.

Headed back to the trailhead now, you will notice that the trail is straighter. After three sections of double track, you will reach a junction you were at after leaving the sugar bush and crossing the open field. Just ski straight ahead at this junction and get ready for some fun. This section of trail is rated intermediate and is hillier than what you've done so far. There are a couple of long downhill runs that are particularly welcome after lots of flatland. The caution sign at the top of one of the hills is nothing to get excited about. The hill is tame.

The trail crosses another bridge, this one over a cute hemlock-sheltered gorge. It seems as though the trail continues downhill for quite a ways. Then there's a short climb and a sweeping downhill to the left. This is arguably the most difficult downhill on the trail. The most difficult uphill is right at the end, past the skating rink; it's a herringbone-only pitch. But you can skip it by taking off your boards and walking around the rink, back to the parking area.

Journal: It's early in the skiing year, December 11, and I haven't skied much yet. Starting at Chassell is a good idea: only 9 km of classic trail, and nothing too difficult. Except, there are a couple of inches of new snow in the tracks, and besides being new, it's also cold, around three degrees Fahrenheit. New and cold, plus loose and untracked can make for slow skiing. And it did. It took me two hours to ski 9 km— twice what it would usually. My excuse? I had to take notes. It's always good to have an excuse.

Copper Harbor Pathway

Directions: From anywhere south (all the way down to Miami, Florida), take Highway 41 north to Michigan 26. At this T intersection (Lake Superior is very evident to the north) turn right and head into the little village of Copper Harbor. (Highway 41 continues on east half a mile to Fort Wilkins State Park, where it ends, after about a 2,000-mile journey.) Make a right turn at the sign for Fanny Hooe Resort and follow the road about .3 mile to where it ends in a snowmobile trail. Be careful not to drive on the snowmobile trail—you will get stuck—and don't park too near the end of the plowed road or you may have a snowmobiler for a hood ornament when you return.

Grooming: There is some track set here, but it is not a high priority for the folks who do it. If you travel to the Estivant Pines, there is no grooming done inside this Michigan Natural Area. Be prepared for a backcountry-type ski. Take provisions, a compass, and extra safety equipment. Let someone know where you are going and when you will be back. You might also pack your snowshoes in case there's been a lot of snow and no grooming.

Total km: system, approximately 26; this tour, 7

Fee: none

Trailhead facilities: None. There is a grocery store in Copper Harbor, but very little else is open in the winter.

Contact: Fort Wilkins State Park, (906) 289-4215; or Keweenaw Tourism Council, (800) 338-7982.

I once saw a postcard that showed a road sign that read, "End of the Earth . . . 8 miles. Copper Harbor . . . 10 miles." Whenever I go to Copper Harbor, I think about that card. And if it's winter, I am sure I'll see the actual road sign along Highway 41 as I drive north through a canopy of snow-dripping pines that literally encloses the highway.

The ski trails here have that end-of-the-earth feel, too. They are remote, sometimes windswept, and set upon an incredible amount of snow—normally 200 to 300 inches a season. There is real danger in accidently getting off the packed trail. Think about it. How many inches tall are you? Now how many inches of snow did you just read is normal here? Get it? You'll disappear. If you're lucky, your hat will float on top of the snow long enough so your buddies can pull you out!

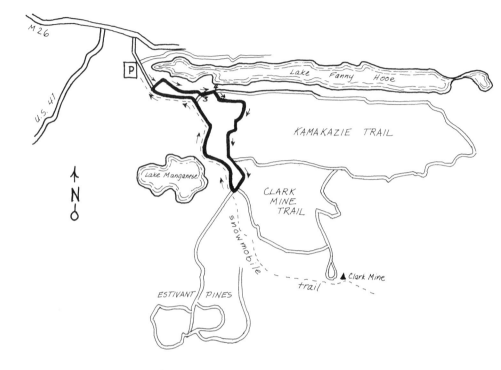

A good way to get a feel for the trails is to start out on the Green Trail. It begins where the road maintenance ends, on the left side of the road. The first 100 or so meters may be plowed, but you will see where the trail goes off to the left along the south shore of Fanny Hooe Lake. There are several openings in the thick conifers that allow a good look at the lake, which is undeveloped and lovely. As the thin, perhaps 100-m-wide ribbon of land that separates it from Lake Superior erodes, some day someone will be looking at Superior from these vantage points.

Just past the largest of these openings is a stand of large, up-to-15-inch-diameter white cedar on the left. Cedar are not rare, but bigger ones are because they grow slowly. Seedlings are rare, too, thanks to an overly abundant deer herd.

The trail climbs up to a clearing where you will find a sign post with the number 3 on it. Bear left and you will cross a bridge. Stop and hear the water below gurgling under the ice. After a short ski, you arrive at another signpost with the number 4 on it. It's time for some real climbing. Go right and you will encounter a 75 m uphill pitch that no kick wax on earth will conquer. Because the trail is narrow and set at odd angles to the hillside, even herringbone technique is difficult. If it seems too much, turn back, because after an all-too-brief section of relative flat, there's another uphill longer than the first.

Eventually the trail levels out and winds through some dense conifers. You will reach a low headwall, perhaps five feet high. Herringbone up it and angle right. This is probably an old narrow-gage railroad bed. As the trail traverses a more open area, you can see what looks like a lake off to the right, but which is actually the Grant Township landfill.

When you reach the next signpost (at the snowmobile crossing) you need to decide if you are heading on to the Estivant Pines, or taking the snowmobile trail to the right and home. You also could head back the way you came, but those two uphill pitches would be murder going the other way.

I accidentally went the wrong way here, taking a trail up the hill to the left, and then out toward Clark Mine. There hadn't been any grooming and the park folks hadn't put all the trail signs in yet (this was early December). The sign that marked the route to the Estivant Pines wasn't present, and I got lost back in the woods somewhere beyond the mine. I eventually figured out something was amiss and followed my tracks back out—otherwise I might still be wandering around the Keweenaw!

If you see the Estivant Pines, drop me a line and let me know how they look.

Maasto Hiihto

Directions: Take Highway M-203 west out of Hancock about 1 mile to Birch Street. There is a sign on the corner of Birch and M-203 that points down Birch toward the Houghton County Fairgrounds. Go north (right) on Birch about .7 miles, almost to the dead end, then turn left. You will see the trailhead sign ahead and to the right.

Grooming: A big old track truck does a nice job, almost daily, of packing and setting track. Most of the system is groomed for both skiing techniques, but there is also some classic-only trail out by the Lookout.

Total km: system, 21, plus another 7, called Churning Rapids, that are connected; this tour, 10

Fee: donation

Trailhead facilities: none

Contact: Keweenaw Nordic Ski Club, P.O. Box 564, Hancock, MI 49930; (906) 482-2784.

Set on the edge of a light industrial-sports complex conglomeration with an excess of chain-link fence, the trailhead area does not impress. But don't worry: The trail leaves this area immediately and covers some very neat real estate.

To get started, walk through the narrow opening in the chain-link fence, clip on your skis, and head out St. Urho's Loop, which is to the right. The trail cuts a straight line through mixed and scattered birch and popple for the first couple hundred meters. Then it turns right and begins a long, gradual climb. If you look off to the left, you can see why the trail turned: A deep gorge holds Swedetown Creek far below. Although there are too many branches for a good look, it's obvious that the gorge is deep. And you're going down there on this tour.

Carefully ski across the snowmobile trail, and then climb some more. The trail crosses under an overhead power line and over an old railroad grade. The trees here are mostly white pine, also called old field pine because of their proclivity to seed into old fields. The pine make for a tight, cozy feeling along this section of trail.

The next intersection is with the Railroad Ravine Trail. It's .3 km long and drops all the way down to the creek, where it crosses a bridge and connects with the Dam Hill Trail. It is very steep! Continuing on St. Urho's Loop, you'll cross under the power line again, then enjoy

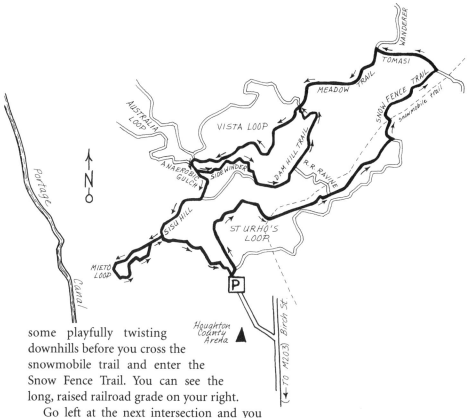

some playfully twisting downhills before you cross the snowmobile trail and enter the Snow Fence Trail. You can see the long, raised railroad grade on your right.

Go left at the next intersection and you will quickly see a long, wide downhill and a sweeping uphill beyond. At the bottom is Swedetown Creek. Swoop on down and gather as much speed as you can because the uphill is just as long. Actually, it's a good spot for practicing your V1 technique. Maybe you should do the hill two or three times.

The hilltop intersection marks the joining of four trails: the Tomasi, which you came up the hill on; the Wanderer, which cuts off to the right; an unnamed, ungroomed striding trail that goes straight; and Meadow Trail, which is to the left—the direction you want to go.

Meadow Trail hugs the woods on the left. Beyond the trees is the ever-present gorge. There's a field on the right. This can be a windy spot. It's only about 300 windy meters from the intersection to where the trail ducks back into the woods, near the intersection with Dam Hill Trail. Dam Hill is one way, coming up from the gorge, so continue on Meadow, which becomes the Vista Loop. The woods are exclusively deciduous, with lots of hard maple and red oak. There are many stump sprouts, which are multistemmed trees that grow out from a stump after a tree is cut down.

Soon the trail tips gently downward, and if you look left, you can see across the Portage Canal. Both are signs that you are close to the next intersection. Head left and begin a gradual descent to the junction between Sidewinder and Anaerobic Gulch. Go left on Sidewinder. Appropriately named, Sidewinder is cut into the side of the gorge and winds down like a snake. It drops, then levels off, then drops again—four times. There's really never a precipitous dip, but if the track is fast, beware. And also be careful when you shoot out onto the connecting trail, Dam Hill.

Dam Hill is incorrectly named. It should be Damn Hill. At first the trail presents only mild ups and downs. When you reach the intersection with Railroad Ravine Trail, take a look up at where it comes from. You have seen where Railroad Ravine leaves St. Urho's Loop, and it looks more forbidding from down here.

Dam Hill begins its climb after this intersection. It is mild at first, but gets increasingly steeper. Make it all the way up to the next intersection without stopping to suck air and you deserve a pat on the back.

You have been through that next intersection before. It's where the woods begin after the Meadow Trail and the path gets rechristened Vista Loop. Ski Vista again and round the corner toward Sidewinder, but this time bear right onto Anaerobic Gulch. Be ready for the hard right turn, and then become one with the speed. The hill is long, straight, and fast. Mercifully, the junction with River Trail is not a T; instead, you can merge, just as you would on an expressway. And your speed may approach that of an RV.

Now it's time to climb Sisu Hill, which is a two-pitch affair: a long first pitch and a short, steeper second one. It isn't as difficult as Dam Hill. At the top of Sisu Hill go right and you are off on another downhill adventure. Mieto Loop is only .9 km long; it will take you about a minute to do the first half. The climb back up can take five or six minutes, maybe 10. Once back to the top of Sisu Hill, bear right, and it's a mere 300 m back to the parking lot.

Journal: Sometimes people assume that because I ski a lot I don't fall down. Those people should have been watching as I took on Anaerobic Gulch. The trail hadn't been groomed after the last four inches of snow and at least three skiers had proceeded me down the hill, although I'd been alone on the trail all morning. I started down with some caution, not knowing what was before me. The hill has a 90-degree right turn near the top, so you can't see what's down below.

I succeeded in making the turn, which involved weighting my right ski while still managing to drag and turn my left one under the snow. Suddenly, I realized that there was one enormous sitzmark dead ahead. There wasn't time or ability to miss it, and before I could register much at all, I was tumbling. Something about snow splashing on your face feels good. There really were only two tumbles: head, heels, shoulder, side, stop. I took inventory, like you do after a fall. None of my parts were damaged, although an old left shoulder separation let me know it hadn't liked the reenactment. None of my equipment was damaged. But there was some injury. My ego was bruised.

Michigan Tech Trails

Directions: From Highway 41, approximately 2 miles south of downtown Houghton, turn south on MacInnes Drive, which becomes Sharon Avenue within a couple of blocks and winds to the west. When you see the Michigan Tech football stadium on the right, look for the next road south (left). If you see baseball fields on the left, you've gone too far. Head down this unnamed, dead-end road about a quarter mile, to the end, and you will see the trailhead and parking area.

Grooming: It's OK to stride or skate these trails. It's difficult to imagine, but these trails are groomed using nothing more than a snow machine and a drag, plus some track-setting equipment. The day I skied here, a guy on a snowmobile pulling something so buried in snow that I couldn't tell what it was, whipped by me. He didn't look happy. Grooming here could be better with better equipment, but it is usually adequate.

Total km: system, 10; this tour, 10

Fee: none

Trailhead facilities: none

Contact: Keweenaw Tourism Council, (800) 338-7982.

We're going to start this ski with the easy Upper Loop, so named because it stays on top of the hill overlooking Sharon Avenue and the rest of the city. From the parking area, stride or skate off to the right. The inviting, wide trail snakes over mostly flat terrain, amid some pleasant old-growth red oak. You can catch a glimpse of the ball fields mentioned in the directions if you look off to the right as you negotiate a couple of easy corners half a kilometer into your ski.

You will then ski by a small wetland on your left, followed by a cut-over corridor on top of a buried gas pipeline. As the trail turns left you will encounter your first little climbs and descents. Then you will see another ball field on the right and some buildings that are part of the Houghton High School complex. Sometimes snow blows off the ball field and creates wonderfully folded cornices of snow just a little ways up an embankment from the trail.

Once the school is behind you, the trail straightens out and looks as if it might be following an old railroad bed. When you make a slight

63

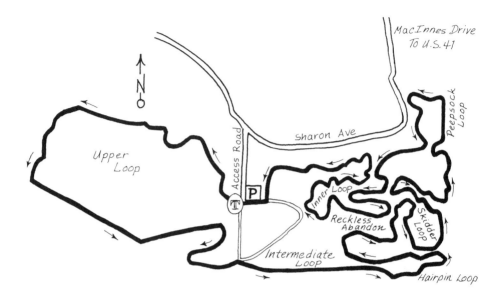

left turn, be ready for a pleasant free ride down a long, gradual hillside. A right turn then takes you into a pine plantation. Another jog right and then a left finds the trail in a stand of pure black ash trees. While they are not very big, their bark and limb texture paint an uncommonly uniform picture on the sky and snow.

When you reach a major junction take the rightmost trail, the Intermediate Loop. This will parallel that gas pipeline for about half a kilometer and then form another junction. If you go left you will stay on the intermediate loop. Going right is more fun.

If you went right, you have entered Hairpin Loop. While the next four loops are rated expert or advanced, unless it's icy or you are really uncomfortable with downhill, left turns, they are not too imposing. Hairpin is really just one moderate downhill with a tight turn at the bottom. Control your speed on the way down and you will have no trouble.

After you climb back up from the Hairpin turn, you will have an option of taking a cutoff or turning right onto Reckless Abandon, another little downhill run with a turn or two. When you reach Skidder Loop you again can take a cutoff that goes straight, or turn right and do Skidder, which is even tamer than the first two loops. When you finish Skidder, or if you take the cutoff, you will see a sign that reads, "Holy Wah!" This marks the steepest descent on the entire trail, but it is only 25 m long and not very difficult.

Continuing past Holy Wah! you are in for the most difficult downhill turn of the tour. There is a "Sharp Turn" sign for warning, but be sure to control your speed before you get to the sign. The turn is very sharp and is situated where the trail still heads downhill. The trail is also narrow here.

Once you negotiate this difficult turn the trail is mostly uphill until you reach the Peepsock Loop, which requires another right turn to enter. This is the easiest of the loops and will take you downhill, along a spur road off Sharon Avenue, then parallel with it until you reach a junction with the "Inner Loop."

Inner Loop can be grueling. It consists of a series of short hills and twists that make it difficult to get into a rhythm. There is one nice downhill run before you get near Sharon Avenue again, but then the last .5 km or so is mostly uphill. When you reach a T intersection, turn right. You are only 150 m from the parking area and the end of this tour.

Journal: I'm driving in the Upper Peninsula. It has snowed about six inches overnight and the road amazes me. It is covered with hard-packed snow. There is some evidence that sand—or something like it—has been spread on the road's surface, but most of it has blown off onto the shoulders. Yet here I am traveling at 60 mph. It doesn't seem slippery. Perhaps it's the minus-five degree temperature. As cross-country skiers well know, snow doesn't slip well when it's so cold. Or maybe that sandlike stuff is really magic Finnish traction dust, spread by Yoopers driving rusty old trucks, so they can quickly get to their favorite sauna.

21

Pinery Lakes Trail

Directions: From the intersection of Broad and Main Streets in downtown L'Anse, take Main Street east 1.8 miles to Indian Cemetery Road. Go right on Indian Cemetery Road and drive 2.1 miles to the parking area on the right.

Grooming: The trail brochure says the system is groomed for both skating and diagonal. This trail is better if skied diagonal because it isn't really wide enough everywhere for skating without trashing the diagonal track. Besides, this kind of ski trail is a classic anyway.

Total km: system, 8; this tour, 8

Fee: donation

Trailhead facilities: none

Contact: Baraga County Tourist and Recreation Association, 755 E. Broad St., L'Anse, MI 49946; (906) 524-7444.

This trail is a sleeper. The pines here are spectacular, not so much for their size as their preponderance. Acre after acre of virtually pure, naturally occurring red pine are rare. Plus, skiing the trail is fun.

The trail starts from the southwest corner of the parking area. It enters the pine woods and runs gently downhill for about 100 m. Then there's another short, easy downhill pitch, followed by yet another. All along here are pine, big ones to little ones. The little ones are an unusual sight because pine do not self-seed well, so the amount of new, under-10-foot-tall pine here is amazing.

As the trail curves left, you can see some larger jack pine up on the ridge farther left. Then you come to the first junction, marked with a number 1. If you go left, you will miss some of the best hills on the trail. Go right and climb a little ridge. There is an open area on the left that is part of Pinery Lake.

The trail snakes it way along near the lake, with some playful dips and climbs. It then comes to an area on the right that has been clear-cut. Thankfully the trail never really enters the slashed area. Two large (more than two feet in diameter) white pine stand between the cut and the trail. I wonder how many such pine were sawed down.

The trail curves left, away from the cut, and dips into a marshy area. When it climbs onto higher ground again, you find yourself in a maple woods. The pine are gone for a moment. It isn't long until the trail drops steeply down to a bridge at the south end of the lake. The pine are back, both bigger and smaller ones.

Across the bridge is a steep uphill. It's the steepest of the tour, and you regain most of that altitude you lost on the first three downhills. Once at the top, you are in a jack pine woods. Until now most of the trees have been white and red pine. These jack pine have unique bark. It varies a lot from one tree to another. Some have bark that looks flaky, with thin, plate-like pieces that are tinged a tan color. Others have bark that is very dark, almost black, with a texture that is ridged or furrowed.

It's a wonderfully curvy ski through this area, until you reach a steep downhill. Scout this downhill a little. There's a small hemlock tree on the right, its branches hanging low over the track. Although the hill is short, it's steep enough that there is some compression at the bottom. Be ready for it. Oh, there's also

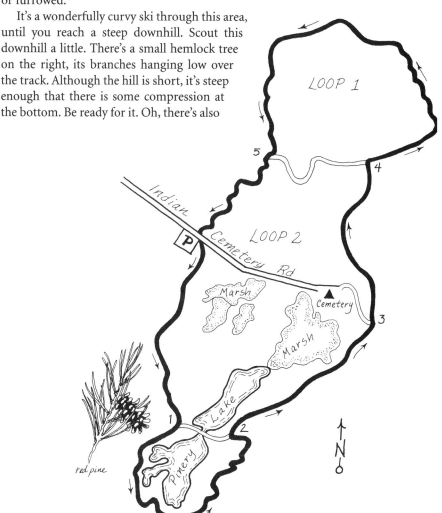

a hook to the right at the bottom that you cannot see from the top. Have fun!

If you liked that hill, then the next one will make you even happier. It starts easily enough, but just when you have built up some speed, it starts curving left. Then it curves some more, until you are almost headed back the way you came. It makes one more jog, this time back to the right, and curves you back to the next junction, number 2.

Go right and ski into an another stand of red pine. Notice that there is nary a plant sticking up from the snow under these pine. They are so dense that almost no light shines on the forest floor here, so nothing much grows. As you ski on, you can see more red pine, but they are joined by white and jack. It's a magnificent pine stand.

You will see an open area on the left, which is a marsh, north of Pinery Lake. There are some small white and even red pine trying to grow near the edges of the bog, even though it's quite wet. When the trail curves left, along the bog margin, notice another pure stand of red pine on the right. The densely packed, reddish-brown stems all reach straight up, a vertical tapestry of color, texture, and line.

When you cross a snowmobile trail, the next trail sign is on the left. It's marked with the number 3, and lets you know you are close to the Indian cemetery. Continue on down the trail until you reach the second driveway. Then take a side trip down the road that is to the left. You will see the cemetery on the left. If the snow isn't too deep, you can see the Spirit Houses that are built over the graves to accommodate the spirit of the deceased. Often arrows, clothing, and other items were placed in the houses in order to help the spirit on its four-day journey to the spirit world. There are headstones in the cemetery that date to the 1840s. A plaque talks of the "Chippewa Nation . . . casting nets in Keweenaw Bay in the 1660s." This is a sacred spot. Stand for a moment and experience it.

When you are ready, ski back up the road to the trail. Climb over the plowed bank and ski off into an aspen woods. The trail takes you to a low spot where there are lots of different kinds of trees: yellow birch, basswood, hemlock, maple, and red oak. Then you'll ski into a younger woods, obviously the recipient of some recent "management."

When you reach trail marker number 4, you can head left, and it's about half a kilometer to marker 5. The ski is through a fairly open area along a recently active logging road. If you choose to head right, you will ski through a nice stand of mixed northern hardwoods. As the trail curves left, you can see more hemlock, which gradually get bigger and more prevalent. Sadly, some were marked with paint when I skied here. Mead Paper owns the land along the trail here and plans on cutting many of the hemlock. It seems they want hardwoods, and will convert this lovely woods into something far less interesting and less ecologically vital than it is now.

You will ski out of the paper-company land and into an area with even bigger yellow birch and red oak. There are also some more two-foot-diameter white pine here. There is a long, gradual downhill, a great place for kick-double polling. When you see the opening on the left, trail marker number 5 is just ahead. Go right here, and it's a pleasantly winding, slightly downhill stride back to the parking area.

Journal: At trail marker number 3 I took the snowmobile trail left, figuring I'd find the Indian cemetery. I found a driveway, and then the ski trail, which I continued down for 50 or so meters before turning around and retracing my path back to marker 3. During my excursion I heard a dog barking. There were a couple of houses at the end of the driveway, and I figured the dog lived there. But as always, I looked for the dog, a bit concerned that it might be loose and unfriendly.

I made it back to the trail marker, and continued on the trail. It was only 30 m to the driveway, which I crossed, and then I was skiing on a bit of trail I had just been on—near where the dog had been barking.

Suddenly, I topped a little rise in the trail and saw it. A large, black dog crouched in the trail 20 m ahead. It was still. I stopped. My heart raced. Adrenalin poured into my bloodstream. It was fight or flight. I looked around, saw a big old jack pine with forearm-sized, dead lower limbs, and I reached over and snapped one off at the tree's trunk, surprising myself with my strength. It became my right pole as I started toward the dog. He had not moved. He just glowered at me, silently, menacingly.

It was time I said something. Still skiing, slowly toward him, I quietly said, "Nice dog." How are you?" This is all it took for him to leap up and start running toward me. I noticed his tail was wagging. By the time he reached me I was pretty sure he wasn't going to eat my skis, and, indeed, he just circled me, tail still wagging, then dropped into the track behind me. I proceeded to the next driveway, then down it to the cemetery. Fido got bored while I was reading headstones and left.

Swedetown Trails

Directions: From the corner of Highway 41 and Swedetown Road just south of Calumet, take Swedetown Road west about 1 mile to the T intersection with Osceola Road. Turn right on Osceola, and you will see the Swedetown sign and entrance road immediately to your left.

Grooming: Trails are well-groomed. Most of the trails are wide enough that they are groomed for both diagonal stride and skating. There are a couple of striding-only trails.

Total km: system, 30; this tour, 8; approximately 5 lighted

Fee: yes

Trailhead facilities: There is a two-story chalet with bathrooms, snack bar and other amenities. It is not always open during the week.

Contact: Chalet, (906) 337-1170; or Keweenaw Tourism Council, (800) 338-7982.

Swedetown is home to The Great Bear Chase ski marathon held close to the middle of March each year. Prodigious amounts of winter snow make the late date possible, and indeed it is one of the last Midwestern races each year. I decided to ski and describe the Red Trail for this book. It is rated most difficult, but unless the trail is icy or otherwise very fast, the trail is better rated intermediate.

Head out from the chalet on the wide main trail. It's a bit of a climb at first, then things even out. Stay left and look for the Red Trail sign at the first junction. After turning left, there's an easy downhill almost immediately. The next .5 km or so will find you negotiating a number of quick little hills—bumps almost. The trail twists and turns a bit while traveling through stands of small white pine intermixed with birch.

When you reach the next junction, with Blue Trail, bear left into a corridor formed by somewhat larger white pine. It's only a couple hundred meters until you reach a four-way intersection. If you go left, you're headed out on the 5 km Green Trail, an easy ski. To continue on with the Red Trail, go straight. A longer downhill will give you a thrill. Then you'll ski by an opening to the left. Wind sometimes piles a little snow here. A climb is next, about the same distance uphill as you just traveled down.

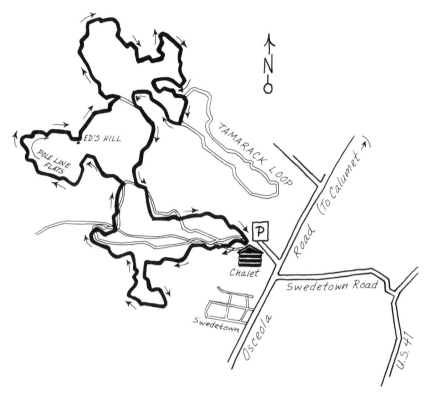

The trail splits after this climb. If hills bother you, go left so you will bypass the next one. If you go straight, the hill you'll encounter is not much bigger than the one you just climbed.

A triangular junction awaits near the top of the next hill. There's a signboard posted on a big red oak tree, which sits near the apex of the triangle. Head left, and you will go under some power lines. Note that the trees here are almost all red oak. The locals call the next kilometer or so of trail, Pole Line Flats.

Just after you cross back under the power lines, get ready for an uphill climb, then a nice downhill as a reward, followed by yet another uphill pitch—this one pretty steep.

You may be winded, but you will arrive at a sign that proclaims, "Ed's you are here hill." Go left at the sign and you will enjoy the longest downhill run thus far. The trail then enters a cedar swamp for about 300 m. Sometimes there are deer tracks here when they are absent everywhere else. It can also be wet early and late in the season (see "Journal" at end of this description).

A short climb will get you back to higher ground. Go left at the T intersection. The woods here are different from those on the other side of the swamp—they're bushier, with smaller trees. The trail follows a low ridge, with some lowland plants such as speckled alder on each side.

With a pleasant abruptness, the trail enters a red pine plantation. The trees are of some size—10 to 15 inches in diameter—and their orderly ranks are in stark contrast to the other trees you've skied near today.

Eventually the trail partially exits the plantation and heads in an almost straight line toward a horizon that is punctuated by upright, narrow spires of columnar poplar trees, probably a cultivar named Lombardy.

Before you get to the poplars, the trail curves right, around some more red pine. It then begins a long, gradual climb. When the climb ends, there's a decision to make: Go left across a little cutoff and miss a quick downhill, or go for it. If you do the downhill, there'll be a corresponding uphill before you get back to the cutoff.

The trail winds and undulates for about a kilometer before you reach another intersection where a trail comes in from the left. This is the trail that you joined at the top of the swamp. Had you gone right instead of left you'd have been here much sooner, but you would have missed a couple of kilometers of fun.

About 600 m more and you will reach a T intersection with the lighted loop. Go left and it's less that a kilometer back to the chalet.

Journal: My nose is bleeding! Blood stains the back of my terry-cloth glove as I swipe it across my face, trying to remove the snow that stuck there when I fell. Yuck! Nobody likes blood on their good ski gloves. Then I have a very brief panic attack, over-whelmed by thoughts of some serious nose bleeds last year, one of which sent me to the emergency room. I need to know if there is a lot of blood, as there was then, so I check by tipping my head down and shaking it. I figure if there's a problem I will see crimson snow beneath me. Whew—just white, no blood. So I touch my nose with my glove again, again getting my glove bloody. I want a mirror, and if not that, my fanny pack with the first aid kit, which I have left in the car. Bright.

Do you want to know what happened? You see, I was skiing through this cedar swamp below Ed's Hill. It hadn't been groomed yet this year because it hadn't frozen sufficiently to get the groomer through. Because I'm a conscientious guy, I felt I had to get through so I could write accurately about the Red Trail. Things were going swimmingly—no water, not even any wet spots—when suddenly my left ski slipped backward and down, way down, which caused me to fall to my knees. So as not to let my foot—or worse, my knees—get submerged, I reacted quickly and yanked my left leg forward and up, which, because I was sort of on my hands and knees, propelled my ski tip into my face, with bloody consequences for my right nostril.

Once the pain subsided, and I had assured myself I wasn't going to bleed to death there on the Red Trail, I laughed. My nose is bleeding. Indeed, maybe next time I'll take the Blue Trail.

Twin Lakes State Park

Directions:	From the corner of Highway M-26 and Poyhonen Road in Twin Lakes, go northwest on Poyhonen Road 50 yards to the DNR offices. Turn right at the first driveway and go around to the back of the buildings. There is a ski trail sign and trailhead to your right.
Grooming:	Single track diagonal striding. The trail is narrow and intimate by today's standards. The volunteer groomers do a nice job.
Total km:	system, 9; this tour, 9
Fee:	none
Trailhead facilities:	None, but there's a resort and minimart across M-26.
Contact:	Twin Lakes State Park, (906) 288-3321; or Keweenaw Tourism Council, (800) 338-7982.

Twin Lakes State Park ski trail offers a lot in a small package. Its narrow single track groomed trail harkens back to before the days of ski trail superhighways, with 12-foot-wide paths cleared so skate skiers and striders can live together in peace. We also need trails like this, where the trees feel close and the woods are almost unblemished by the trail.

Start this ski from the parking area behind the DNR office. There are some larger hemlocks intermixed with spruce and maple along the first 200 m of trail. Find one of the larger spruce near the trail and cast a glance upward. The spire goes on, up and up. These are some tall trees.

When you reach the first junction, you will have passed most of the conifers and entered a mostly deciduous northern hardwoods forest. One difference between these woods and many in the Upper Peninsula, is that they haven't been cut since the early 1950s, and then only lightly. So there are some large-diameter trees. (If you want to see some really big trees, in an area that's never been cut, visit the Porcupine Mountains trails; see page 87.)

Bear right at the first junction, climb a gentle hill, then enjoy the ride down the other side. Highway M-26 is off on the right, and you will notice it if a big truck rumbles by. Just before the trail cuts left, away from the road, there's a sign on the right informing you about

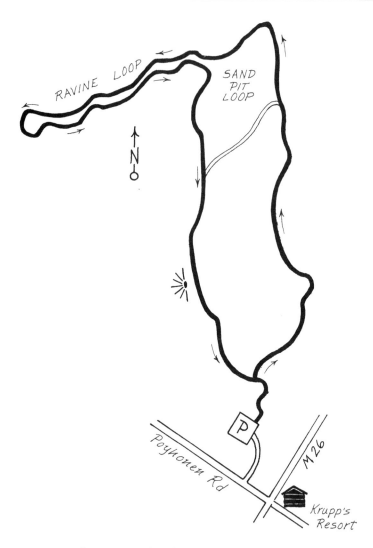

past forestry practices (summarized above) in these woods. If there is a lot of snow, more than three feet, the sign may be buried.

Enjoy the woods. There are some big sugar maples here and there, lovely trees limbless for 60 feet then holding out hefty branches, stiffly, at impossible angles. Add a thick coat of snow, clinging as lake-effect snow does, and you have a unique overhead canopy.

The next trailside sign mentions that a clear-cut occurred at this spot "several years ago," but the woods here don't really look that different. But as you proceed, there gradually will be fewer of the larger trees around you.

About 100 m before the next intersection, another sign tells you about the Military Road, cut in the 1850s from Green Bay to Copper

Harbor. You are skiing on a section of that road, and it is easily visible as you ski along it up to the intersection that marks the beginning of the Sand Pit Loop.

Go right on the Sand Pit Loop, and you will immediately notice an open area as you slide down a nice, straight hill. The woods here are decidedly less impressive, with lots of stump-sprouted maple, all less than 10 inches in diameter.

You will climb a minor hill and come to the intersection with the Ravine Loop. Bear right and you will pick up one of the two set tracks that take you about a kilometer (one way). When you see the "Steep Hill" sign, don't fret; there are worse downhills on trails rated easy. As you regain the altitude lost on the downhill, you will see a deep ravine on either side of the trail. There is something of a vista to the right, hills tracing the horizon a couple miles away. If you want to, ski carefully off-trail to the left where there is an opening and you can peer down into the ravine on that side. Somehow deer manage to negotiate the steep hillside and walk up and down it, crossing the trail while traveling from one deep sanctuary to the other.

The Ravine Trail makes an abrupt circle and then returns back the way it came. You will reach the intersection with Sand Pit Loop and go right, past where the Superior Loop rejoins the trail. The trail is rather flat and uneventful, but look to the right and you will eventually see Lake Superior. On many days, it can be difficult to tell the lake from the horizon. On other days, this being lake-effect-snow country, you can't see a thing because it's snowing so hard.

Just after the trail crosses the snowmobile trail again, look left and you will see the trail's largest yellow birch tree. It is almost three feet in diameter, and must have been pretty big when these woods were last logged. When you start seeing more conifers again, you are near the junction with the spur trail that takes you back to the parking lot. Bear right, and it's only 150 m.

Journal: I am tired. I've just eaten a grilled chicken sandwich and fries, drank a big Coke, and driven the 25 miles from Houghton. I am on my way home after three days of skiing in the Keweenaw. But since the Twin Lakes trails weren't groomed on my way north, I need to ski them now. I don't want to. It's only four degrees out, and as I drive into the parking area I hope that the trails still aren't groomed. They are. I reluctantly take off my mukluks, don my ski boots, coat, gloves, and hat, grab my skis, and head out. I am cold for the first two minutes. Grouchy too. But by the time I reach the first trail sign, I'm into it, enjoying the lovely trees, new snow, and finely groomed trail. The rhythm of skiing and the wonder of the woods have captured me. Again.

Old Grade Ski Trail

Directions:	From Mass City, which is southeast of Ontonagon, take Highway 38 about 7 miles east to Forest Road 1960, which goes right (south). The trailhead is .1 mile on the left.
Grooming:	The trail is groomed about once a week and is a striding trail.
Total km:	6.5
Fee:	none
Trailhead facilities:	none
Contact:	Ottawa National Forest, Ontonagon Ranger District, 1209 Rockland Rd., Ontonagon, MI 49953; (906) 884-2411.

I was unable to ski this trail, but it sounds interesting. Part of the trail is set upon a late-1800s-era railroad grade that was used for logging. The trail traverses some pine plantations and areas of hardwoods. The cutoff trail, which is approximately 3 km, skirts the edge of Courtney Lake.

V

The Western Upper Peninsula

ABR Trails

Directions: From the intersection of Highway 2 and Lake Street in Ironwood, take Lake Street south to Frenchtown Road. Go left on Frenchtown Road, which becomes South Range Road. When South Range Road makes a T intersection with West Pioneer Road, ABR will be straight ahead.

Grooming: These are some of the best-groomed trails anywhere. Co-owner Eric Anderson hosts grooming clinics for folks from all across the country with such responsibilities. There are 27 km of striding-only trails and 13 km of dual-groomed trails.

Total km: system, 40; this tour, 5-plus

Fee: yes

Trailhead facilities: There is a trailhead shelter with toilets, and a wax room. ABR (the acronym for Active Backwoods Retreats) also rents equipment and sells snacks and beverages. The place is a complete Nordic center, save perhaps for equipment sales. There is also a sauna available, plus a trailside cabin you can rent.

Contact: ABR, E-5299 W. Pioneer Rd., Ironwood, MI 49938; (906) 932-3502.

If you're looking for early snow, the kind that lets you ski in late November—early November some years—ABR is the place. There are two things required for good early skiing: One is obviously, some snow, and two is a place that grooms its trails well. An accomplished groomer with the right equipment and a well-manicured trail can make even a couple inches of snow skiable. Because of its location in the Lake Superior snow belt, ABR averages 10 inches of snow in November. In 2000, they had 10 inches on October 6! Given Mother Nature's cooperation, ABR owners Dave and Eric Anderson take good care of the rest.

All the trails begin just south of the parking area and warming cabin. There's a .6 km, nearly flat Oval Loop that traces the edge of an open field. This is a great spot to warm up, get your rusty ski legs limber, or show off your technique to parking-lot bystanders. It's also a great place for little kids or for first-time-on-skis adults.

A right turn about .2 km from the parking lot puts you on the 5.5 km River Trail. It provides access to all the other trails here, and once

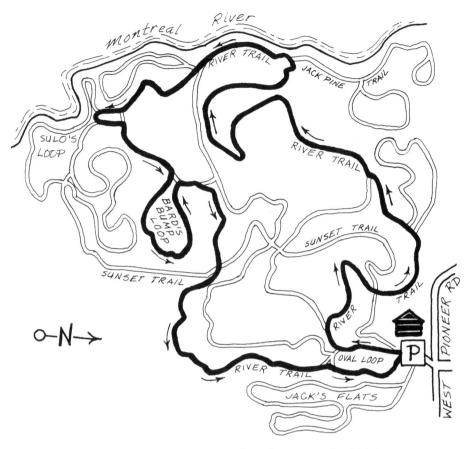

begun is the minimum distance you can skate ski. Easy Trail, which is for diagonal striding only, exits River Trail shortly after the Oval Loop. Easy Trail is 3.5 km long and incorporates parts of the River Trail.

If you stay on River Trail, you will get a view back toward the warming cabin and parking area, then ski right past the home of Dave and Helen Anderson. Just past the house you will encounter your first real downhill of the ski thus far. Then you will pass the entrance to Popple Plunge, a steep downhill cascade that can be nasty if the snow is icy. Check it out if you'd like, but you can also choose to pass it by and just continue on River Trail.

Your next decision comes as you get to Pit Point Loop, an excursion of 1.1 km that incorporates a serious downhill, off of Pit Point. The hill is not long but it's steep, and because of a curve in the trail near the top of Pit Point you can't see the end of the downhill run.

The next trail option past the junction of Pit Point Loop and River Trail is Jack Pine Trail, a 3 km, striding-only trail that leads to an abandoned farmstead and takes in some lovely river views on the way.

River Trail bears left at the junction with Jack Pine, and for about half a kilometer skirts the banks of the Montreal River. This is one of the prettiest stretches of trail in the system. Wisconsin is on the other side of the river.

Past its meander along the Montreal, River Trail eventually breaks out into a clearing. If you bear right onto Sulo's Loop you will travel an additional 3.8 km. Sulo's is an easy trek if you choose it. Bard's Bump Loop is your next option, again a right turn. Bard's is .7 km and packs a fairly steep, but not technically difficult, up-and-down hill.

Your final trail decision, if you are striding, is Ice Falls Trail, which exits left off River Trail. Ice Falls is noted for its ice formations, which hang off Blueberry Bluff on the right. These can be quite lovely. Ice Falls ends at the south end of Oval Loop, as does River Trail. One of the most fun downhills of the entire trail comes just before River Trail connects with Oval Loop. Let the momentum take you out onto the loop and halfway back to the parking lot. It's a scream.

Journal: I'm skiing on the Jack Pine Trail here at ABR. This striding-only trail is narrow and winding, tracing the banks of the Montreal River. Not many miles downstream is Saxon Falls, a magnificent waterfall that I've hiked across in the early spring. As I hear the river gurgling off to my left, it reminds me of that falls, frozen stiff, anxious for spring, running under the snow pack. While this current ski is not dangerous, the memory of past excursions reminds me that it is the little bit of danger that is one of the attractions of being cold and sliding on slippery snow.

Bergland Ski Trail

Directions: From the intersection of Highways 28 and 64 in Bergland, go north on 64 approximately 1 mile to Bergland Road. Go left (west) on Bergland. Continue about a quarter mile and the parking area/trailhead is on the left.

Grooming: The trail is groomed for diagonal stride and is packed by one pass of a snowmobile and grooming machine. It's narrow.

Total km: system, 4.7; this tour, 3.9

Fee: none

Trailhead facilities: none

Contact: Ottawa National Forest, E-6248, Highway 2, Ironwood, MI 49938; (906) 932-1330.

D on't be discouraged by the bland topography and scenery as the trail leaves the parking area. The aspen stand isn't pretty. It's the result of a clear-cut back in the mid-1970s. The trail leaves the aspen after the first .5 km or so, and enters a lovely woods.

By the time you reach a junction, where you should bear right, there are a lot of conifers around you. The bigger hemlock are up to 18 inches in diameter. Equally impressive and more unusual is the hemlock regeneration. In most North Woods places, hemlock is not regrowing. It seeds in and germinates fine, but the plethora of deer throughout the last decades has munched down most hemlock seedlings before they get a chance to become trees. Not so here. The feathery fronds of five- and six-foot-tall trees rise proudly above the snow, bringing a distinctly different texture to the understory.

After the junction, the trail bumps over hummocks and twists around obstacles, gradually leaving the conifers behind. You can see a hillside ahead, and as you begin the easy ascent look at the trees around you. There are wonderful specimens of several species, including sugar maple, yellow birch, basswood, red oak, black ash, and one really large white ash on the right near the bottom of the hill.

You will reach a junction with the more difficult trail that goes right. When the snow is too deep, this trail is not groomed, so head left, staying on the inside, easy loop. Ahead is a pleasing, 100 m slide diagonally across the face of the ridge you have been slowly climbing.

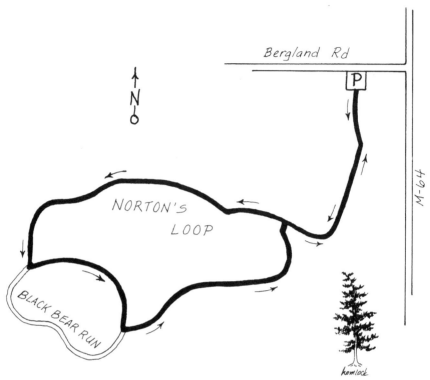

The trail designer did a nice job of providing just enough descent, but not so much that you develop too much speed.

There's a short stretch of flats, then the trail dips again, past the junction where the more difficult loop rejoins it. You cross a little creek, then continue down next to it. The trail has several hummocks in it here and if you get going fast enough you'll catch some air (that's downhill slang for "airborne") off one or two of them. Relax, let it happen, and you'll be surprised at how easy it is. Maybe this is how ski jumpers get their start?

When the ravine ends, the trail curves right and passes a big old hemlock that's been tipped over in a windstorm; it has a partner on the other side of the trail that didn't tip. Both are more than two feet in diameter. Look right and you will see a steep hillside. Snow sometimes falls off the hemlock, where it collects in big lumps. The hillside is so steep that the snow lumps roll downhill, toward the trail, making little avalanches.

You will see a 10-inch-diameter maple on the right that has a yellow sign which reads "Bearing Tree." The sign is posted near a section corner but doesn't contain any information about its location. Ski ahead past the bearing tree and you'll arrive at the first junction you reached earlier on this tour. Go right and you will be skiing back toward the parking area on the trail you skied to get here.

Journal: Little trails like Bergland are a phenomenon. Their histories all vary, but have one common thread: someone who cares about them and spends a lot of his or her spare time grooming and maintaining them.

Bergland has Bill Witt. He's a Michigan State Trooper by profession. Witt's been grooming Bergland since 1996. He got involved with the trail because he's a skier and lives nearby. He uses Forest Service equipment, an old Polaris Indy snowmobile, and a 25-year-old, homemade track setter.

Witt skis the trail a lot, and tells me he's seen coyote, fisher, and even black bear while striding the trail. Bergland is a surprising little system, well worth a try. But don't get caught passing recklessly or exceeding the speed limit, Witt might just nab you.

Milje's Ski Trails

Directions: From the intersection of Highways 2 and 519 in downtown Wakefield, Michigan, take 519 south about 2 miles. You will see the sign and parking area for Milje's Cross Country Trails on the right.

Grooming: Trails are groomed for diagonal stride only.

Total km: system, 9.4; this tour, 9.4

Fee: donation

Trailhead facilities: While not at the trailhead, there is a cute cabin less than a kilometer down the trail from the parking area. It has a wood stove that can turn the place into a veritable sauna. There's carpet on the floor, comfortable furniture, and the makings for coffee, tea, and hot chocolate. And there are usually some cookies on the table. There is also an outhouse, out of sight, beyond the cabin.

Contact: Cecilia Miljevich, 205 Smith St., Wakefield, MI 49968; (906) 229-5267.

It's not often that you ski a trail with a history that's entwined with a family in the way this one is. Rollie Miljevich created it in 1980, on a suggestion from his wife, Cecilia. According to Cecilia, Rollie had been out skiing on a nearby trail and was frustrated with its sharp, almost impossible downhill turns. When he came home and complained about "skiing in brush," Cecilia made her suggestion. Since the family owned land nearby and since Rollie was a bulldozer operator, all that was needed was motivation. Rollie had plenty of that—and he made sure there were no difficult turns.

From the parking area ski off toward the camp, which is within a kilometer. Bear right past the buildings and then again at the junction just beyond. The woods around you are young. Rollie was a logger by trade, and that, combined with a major windstorm around the Fourth of July 1999, left few big trees standing.

Something you will see on no other ski trail are signs that are written in both English and Finnish (someone called it "Finglish"). One of the first you will see is, "Lil Py Lil I Ko Up Da Hill." The hill you climb here is hardly noticeable. After you start a long, very easy downhill, there's another sign that's easier to read: "Dixie's Run."

Go straight at the junction where the trail makes an X with itself. It loops down into a northern conifer forest, then climbs back out,

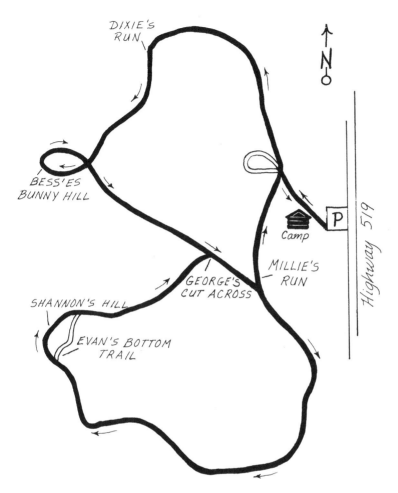

crosses over itself, and dips gradually into a big open area where many trees were blown down in the Fourth of July storm. Here we find a sign that tells us: "Finland 8,000 miles." An arrow below the sign seems to point southwest.

When you reach George's Cut Across, continue straight and climb the little hill to a junction that says Dorothy's Run. Follow Dorothy to the right and you'll cruise down another small hill, past a shattered hemlock stump on the right. There are many tipped-over aspen here, too, all testament to the ferocity of that July storm.

Once you see the sign for Helen's Scenic Area, you are well within the conifer forest that covers the west side of this trail system. There was less wind damage here because the area is lower and a bit protected. You will still see one large spruce that blew over. There are some larger, upright cedar and spruce, and one big black ash near the end of the conifers, just before you ski up and out into the deciduous woods.

Now it's time for a climb, perhaps the trail's longest, although no climb on this trail is arduous. A sign tells you that this is Shannon's Hill. You may opt out of the hill and travel Evan's Bottom Trail if you like. (I took Shannon's Hill—Evan's Bottom didn't sound very appealing.) Notice the four-stemmed black cherry tree just left of where the trail divides.

Shannon's Hill involves a short climb up and a nice easy run down. There is quite a bit more hill visible above you before you start your downhill run. It could have been incorporated into the run, but remember: Rollie's goal was to keep the trail simple, and skiers out of the brush.

Stride on down the trail until you encounter George's Cut Across again. Then bear right and ski over the area you've already been on to Dorothy's Run, but this time go left, to Millie's Run. Actually, you will climb a bit before you reach the run. It will take you into a clearing and a curve right, where you will join the short trail that you came out on from the cabin.

Make sure you check out the cabin before you leave. Write something in the visitor book. Have a cookie. And throw another log on the fire for the next skier. Lastly, thank Rollie and Cecilia for letting you share their trail and a bit of their family history. Rollie's death in February 1999 has left care of his trail to others. Cecilia is working at making sure it stays groomed . . . and that the cookie container is well-stocked.

Journal: I met Cecilia Miljevich the day I skied Milje's. I had called the number on the trail map because I wanted to make sure the trail was skiable. Cecilia answered and invited me over to her home, where she gave me some materials on both the trail and her husband, Rollie. She's an impressive lady, who'd been through a lot, having lost a husband and then much of his woods to a storm six months later. Nonetheless, she was gracious and giving of herself.

Later that day, as I started out onto Cecilia's trail, I met her again, skiing in from her cabin with a friend. She remembered me, and wished me good luck with my book. I will always remember her.

Porcupine Mountains Wilderness State Park

Directions: From the corner of Highways 64 and 107 east of Silver City, head west through town, across the Iron River and into the park. It's approximately 3.5 miles from the corner to the ski hill and Nordic area entrance and parking lot on the left. The road is only plowed a quarter mile beyond the turn, so you can't get too lost.

Grooming: The park has developed some of the best grooming anywhere. The groomers are accomplished at their work and do a great job. Most of the system is groomed for diagonal only, with two sets of parallel tracks laid on each side of the trail. The Nonesuch and River Trails are skateable; only one track is set, making the other half of the trail the skating lane.

Total km: system, 42; this tour, 17

Fee: Yes, which includes use of the downhill-area lifts.

Trailhead facilities: There is a pleasant lodge with extensive food service; tables beside a window wall overlooking the downhill slopes; ski rental; and equipment, wax, and other cross-country accouterments sales.

Contact: Porcupine Mountains Wilderness State Park, 412 S. Boundary Rd., Ontonagon, MI 49953; (906) 885-5275.

This is a long tour, the longest in this book. I love this place, and couldn't just do a little of the trail. You can cut the distance in half by taking the downhill lift up the hill and going either right or left, following the tour that way. This is also a tour with more than 700 feet of altitude change.

Start from the parking lot or the lodge and head east (left from the parking lot). You are on Nonesuch Trail. According to park literature, this trail follows the route of the old Nonesuch Mine tram road. You enter the dense, deciduous woods at the end of the parking area. The trail is level for the first couple hundred meters, then begins a descent that takes you down about 40 meters of vertical in less than a kilometer. It's a pleasant downhill, not too steep and without difficult turns. There are often lots of deer in the area. There also are plenty of seeps along the trail's edge, where water melts the snow from underneath, creating a deep snow bowl with bare earth at the bottom.

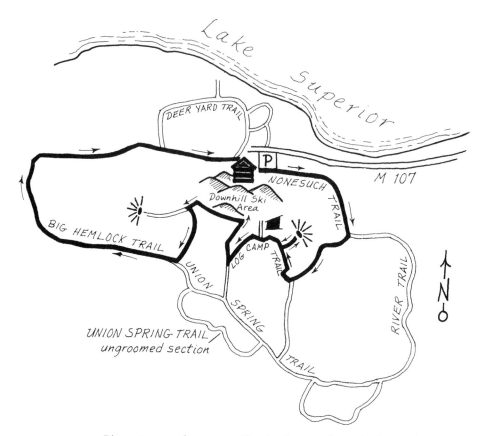

Bigger trees and more conifers begin near the end of your downhill run. There is also a sign on the right that reads, "Nonsuch Tram Road, built in 1881."

The trail begins its long, upward tilt just after the sign. The trees around you are nothing short of awe inspiring. There are many hemlock, yellow birch, and sugar maple that measure between two and three feet in diameter. In fact, the average-sized tree is well over a foot in diameter.

When you reach the junction with River Trail, go right and continue climbing. You will see a giant cedar just past the junction on the right side of the trail. It's been blown into another cedar, so it leans sideways. It is almost three feet in diameter and hundreds of years old.

You will stride on up into younger woods: sugar maple, basswood, aspen, and some red oak. You will note that when you look left you see nothing but treetops. Look right and you see the uphill slope. You are gaining altitude. When you reach the next junction, you will have gone from just under 800 feet elevation at the last junction, with River Trail, to almost 1,100 feet at this junction, with Log Camp Trail.

Turn right onto Log Camp, and continue your climb. The trail turns right in about 60 m, then levels out and even dips a bit—your first downhill pitch in about 2 km. Your rest is short-lived, because the trail turns back left and up the hill again. As it finally levels off, you find yourself in a woods of both red and sugar maple, plus increasing numbers of red oak. If you look right, through the trees, you will see a white line in the distance. This may seem as if it should be Lake Superior, but it isn't.

The junction with East Vista Trail is just ahead. Turn right and head out the quarter of a kilometer to the vista. The view is wonderful: Lake Superior is in front of you. It may be ice free or completely frozen, depending on the winter weather. As you look right, you can see Highway 107 hugging the shoreline below. Treetops blend together far below, where you were just a short time ago; it may surprise you how far you have climbed. It's no small accomplishment. Further off to the right and in the distance is the old mine at White Pine. The smokestack and buildings look out of place here. Left of the buildings, toward the lake, there is a vast, treeless area. This is the white that you saw through the trees from back on the trail. It is a large area of tailings ponds: water and waste generated by the White Pine Mine. Its proximity to Lake Superior is frightening.

Head back down the trail you came here on and go left at the junction. There is a log shelter, complete with windows, about half a kilometer away. There is even an outdoor toilet. Just past the shelter is a trail that leads right, and a sign that reads, "To Alpine Area." It's a short ski over to a downhill run called Hidden Valley. Another sign indicates that it's a quarter mile to the lodge, down the alpine slope. If you are a good skier, you can head back to the lodge. But let's head back to the trail that will take us around the mountain.

Go right at the shelter and it's a fairly level 1 km to the next junction. Go right there, back up to the alpine area. You will climb out of the smaller trees you have been in for quite a while, and be amid wonderful big old hemlock, basswood, and red oak. Once you reach the downhill slopes, stay left. Make sure you check out the views of the lake and the scary downhill drops on some of the runs. You are at about 1,500 feet elevation. Ski along the woods on the left edge of the hilltop opening, and you will find where the cross-country trail reenters the woods. If you miss the entrance, you will be headed downhill on Sunset Run. At least it's rated easy.

The trail takes you through a small stand of big hemlock, then to a junction. If you go right, you will take the 1–km trip to West Vista, which overlooks some of the park's interior. There's a long climb involved. Go left, and after about 100 meters of level-to-uphill skiing, you are on your way down off the mountaintop. The run is almost a kilometer long, and most of the pitch is moderately steep. There is speed involved, but you can always snowplow. The junction at the bottom of the run is a T, so make sure your speed is under control by the time you reach it.

Go right, and you are on your way around the back of the mountain. Although there are brief uphills, most of the time you are on the level or headed downhill. A notable landmark is the wall of hemlock that becomes clearly visible as you ski toward it through smaller deciduous trees. The dark, almost foreboding wall was created at around the time that the park came into being. Loggers were cutting in the area you are skiing through. When they quit, the clear definition between logged and unlogged area was left for all of us to ponder. Ski on into the deep, dark hemlock, and enjoy their shelter, mystery, and depth. Be thankful that these soft needled, big old trees still stand. Oh, and be careful of the first, quick little downhill with a tight right turn just inside the wall.

The next tree wonder you see is a grove of giant white pine. Storms have cast a couple of these trees to the ground and lightning has ripped others. These trees are more than 100 feet tall. There's one dead pine, on the left a few meters off the trail, that was a two-stemmed tree. The left stem broke off years ago, and the remaining spire sticks up 90 feet or more into the sky. The trunk on that tree is over 12 feet in circumference. Even in death these trees are testament to nature and her magnificent accomplishments.

After the pines, the trail continues its gradual downward tilt until you pick up some speed and cross a little creek. Early in the season the trail uses a small bridge, but when enough snow has fallen, they groom right over the creek bed.

There's a little climb after the creek, then a downhill followed by a caution sign posted on a tree. This means you are about to drop the final 200 feet to Highway 107, which is a snowmobile trail this time of year. It's a fast downhill, with a sharp right turn at the bottom. The trail parallels the snowmobile trail for about 700 m, then cuts back into the woods.

It is fairly level here and all the way back past the junction with Deer Yard Trail. Then you lose another 200 feet of altitude as you approach the downhill area. It's a fun, easy downhill that gets you in the mood for hobnobbing with downhillers back in the lodge.

If you aren't too worn out from your tour, head up on one of the lifts, and enjoy the mostly downhill skiing coming back off the top of the mountain. You can go left off the lift and retrace your uphill tour, taking Log Camp to River to Nonesuch Trail. Have fun!

Journal: I have skied the Porkies (the local name given the Porcupine Mountains) for years. They just get better. This year new grooming techniques and equipment created the best skiing I have ever had here. There is a palpable difference skiing the Porkies and skiing anywhere else. Since trees make up most of the vegetation visible on a ski trail, it makes sense that the more magnificent and grand the trees, the more magnificent and grand the scenery. Most people are used to seeing trees. And they see some fairly large ones in yards and other semiurban areas such as parks and schools. But rarely do people see big trees in the forest. Odd, isn't it? We are used to large, venerable old trees in residential neighborhoods, around places where people play and work, but once out in the forest, where trees dominate the landscape, we rarely see a really big one.

We get used to forests of adolescent trees. Forests made up of trees often less than half or even a quarter of the size they can easily attain. Why? Because the age of trees on most of our forest land is determined by economics. We harvest our trees at young ages because we can't or won't wait until they mature. There's economic incentive to do so: Paper and other fiber producing companies want pulp, particularly from aspen. So they convert the woods to aspen by clear-cutting it every 30 years or so. Or they plant ("reforest") the denuded landscape with red pine. Pine plantations are monocultures, rather like your yard's lawn, just taller. Not much lives there.

The Porcupine Mountains afford us the opportunity to see what a Midwestern forest can look like, feel like, smell like. The trees you ski through here are hundreds of years old. They are twice the height of most of the forest trees you see anywhere else, because they are older. They harbor wonderful varieties of wildlife and plant life. And they soothe your soul in a way no managed forest can.

Retreat here sometime, drink from this oasis in an otherwise overharvested, chain-saw, buncher-feller abused forestscape. And take a bit of it back home with you. Tell others about it. Together maybe we can begin creating places like it, not for ourselves—it takes hundreds of years once a place has been cut—but for our descendants, and for a world that will need these places even more than ours does now.

Here are a few facts about Porcupine Mountains Wilderness State Park. The park encompasses 60,000 acres. Saying that another way, the park is almost 100 square miles in area. With approximately 27,000 acres of virgin timber—particularly eastern hemlock—it is one of the largest virgin forests in the eastern United States. Concerned individuals fought hard in the Michigan legislature against logging interests to establish the park in 1944. Loggers were cutting in the proposed park area until the very last minute before the law creating the park was signed.

The park was to be a "forest museum." It has become much more than that. Thousands of hikers, campers, fishermen and fisherwomen, hunters, and wintersports lovers visit the area each year. It's also an area where scientists come to study an ecosystem and its parts that are less disturbed by humans than most other eastern U.S. locations.

Come to the Porkies and experience both the tangible and spiritual rewards offered by a truly big woods near a big lake.

28

Watersmeet Ski Trails

Directions:	From the intersection of Highways 45 and 2 in Watersmeet, go west on 2 about 2 miles. Sylvania Outfitters and the trailhead are on the left.
Grooming:	These trails are all diagonal only.
Total km:	system, 12; this tour, 7
Fee:	donation
Trailhead facilities:	Sylvania Outfitters rents equipment and sells some ski-related items. Snack-type items also are available. Bob Zelinski, the owner, is quite an interesting guy, so make sure you introduce yourself.
Contact:	Sylvania Outfitters, W. U.S. Highway 2, Watersmeet, MI 49969; (906) 358-4766.

Theoretically, rain that falls here in the parking lot flows north, eventually into Lake Superior. Rain that falls just a couple of miles south and east of here eventually flows to the Gulf of Mexico. Start this ski by flowing to the right of the buildings located behind the parking area. A large hemlock tree (its diameter is more than two feet) stands near the beginning of the trail. It's the biggest one you will see on this tour.

The trail here is set with two striding tracks, a nice touch if you are skiing with a friend. It is also a two-way trail. The woods are mostly deciduous: maple, basswood, and aspen. You will ski across a treeless pipeline right-of-way, then back into the woods. There are some interesting, steep-sided hills visible on your right. These look like kames, a knob of land formed when water-carrying sediment drained through a hole in the glacier.

Soon the woods change, with hemlock, spruce, and balsam fir pre-dominating near the trail, giving it a tunnel effect. The trail skirts a big hill on the right, climbing up and around it, also leaving the conifers behind. There's a large, two-stemmed basswood on the left before you make a slight downhill run to a junction.

Bear left at the junction and in about 50 meters you will meet the first significant downhill of this tour. Called Ruff Hill, this run is named for the moguls that often appear. It isn't too tough, but will stimulate you after your mostly flat ski to it. It isn't far to Runout Hill,

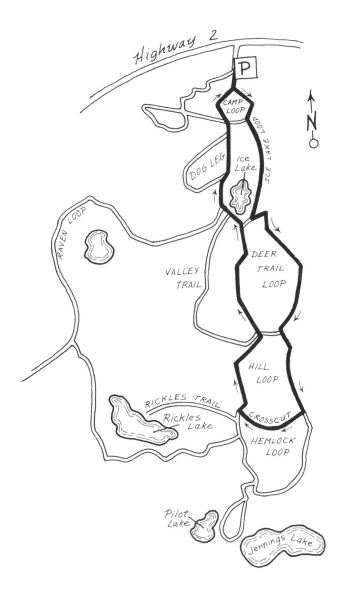

which is a longer run with a bit of a right curve near the bottom.

The trail takes you past a bog on the left, then dips down farther until it climbs a hill, leaving the bog. There's one more significant downhill, with a left curve, before you reach the next junction, number 6.

Go left, and you are on what's called Hill Loop. You will climb up, into hardwoods again. The grade is up for a long way, then you will see the next junction. Go right here on what's called Crosscut. There's a large, open bog on the left that you can see as you climb up a long hill. Actually, Crosscut is mostly—about half a kilometer of it— uphill. When you reach the next junction, you want to go right; going left takes you out on Hemlock Loop. It's a nice ski and adds almost 3 km. The rub is that you must ski Crosscut again. You decide.

Having turned right, you will enjoy a couple of long, gradual runs through a maple woods. These runs are easy if the snow is soft, and fast if it's icy. Although there are no turns as such, the trail does snake through the trees, making riding in the track more challenging.

You will ski into a hemlock grove with a little bog lake on the right. When you reach Junction 7, go left, onto Deer Trail Loop. There are some larger trees along Deer Trail, including a two-foot-diameter yellow birch on the right, and a three-stemmed black cherry on the left. The trail heads roller-coaster-like up and down some hills before reaching Junction 5. Go left to Junction 4, then left again, up a long hill that is a divided one way. Watch the arrows; skiers may be rocketing downhill at you and you wouldn't want to be in the way.

From the top of the divided highway hill, there's a wonderful downhill slide through a forest of gray-barked maple. You will cross the pipeline again, then wind your way back to the parking lot.

Wolverine Nordic Trails

Directions: From the intersection of Highways 51 and 2, take Highway 2 east approximately 3 miles to Section 12 Road. Turn left on Section 12 Road and go 1.2 miles north to the intersection with Sunset Road. Turn right on Sunset and go .5 mile to the Wolverine entrance on the right.

Grooming: Wolverine is conscientiously groomed. A single striding track is set on one side of the trail, and the rest is rolled and left for skate skiing. Hence, both styles are encouraged. Although permitted, skating feels a bit cramped here, as the trail isn't quite wide enough and one ski invariably slides into the groomed track.

Total km: system, 17; this tour, 15

Fee: donation

Trailhead facilities: There is a shelter at the Sunset Road trailhead, complete with small changing rooms, benches, and tables. There are also pop and hot chocolate machines. Other goodies are sometimes for sale, when local club members are offering them. Wolverine also boasts a ski jump, although it is not in routine operation. Trek and Trail located on Highway 2 in Ironwood can provide wax, rentals, or any other things you may need for your ski outing. It's their phone number listed below.

Contact: Wolverine Ski Club, 350 W. Midland Ave., Ironwood, MI 49938; (906) 932-5858.

This ski trail is located in a very hilly area, but the trail never gets too difficult. Although portions are rated "most difficult" on the trail's official map, unless it's icy they are probably only of intermediate difficulty, or "more difficult." There are some very distant, scenic views, and the trail connects with Big Powderhorn Mountain Downhill Ski Area. There's an inexpensive, one-ride lift ticket available if you want to experience the downhill one time.

Wolverine offers four loops. The 7 km Powderhorn, 5 km Wolverine, and a short warm-up loop are all accessed directly from the Sunset Road parking area. Ottawa Loop is accessed directly from the parking area behind Grandview Hospital, just off Highway 2.

The warm-up loop is right of the shelter. At a couple of kilometers, this is a good place for checking your kick wax, or just warming up a little. It also makes for a wonderful short family ski. And for those of

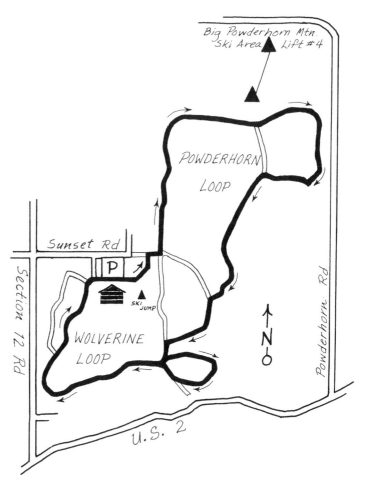

you who skijor (ski behind a dog or two pulling you with a tug line), this is a great loop.

Both the Wolverine and the Powderhorn Loops take off to the left (east) of the shelter. This tour will take you out the Powderhorn Loop, onto the Wolverine Loop, then for a quick trip around the 3 km Ottawa Loop before finishing on the Wolverine.

From the shelter the trail climbs a hill and parallels Sunset Road. Then you'll swoop downhill past Sunset Road's dead end. Once past the road, there's a three-way junction; take the Powderhorn Loop to the left. A long, sweeping climb is ahead. If your grip is good, you can stride the first half or so. If you're skating, you should be able to V1 right up to the top. Near the top you'll notice that the trail widens. This is a summer road that leads to the top of the Big Powderhorn ski hill.

Your next landmark is a cleared area, the first of three linear scars across the forest that mark buried pipelines. Their one redeeming aesthetic value is that they supply a line of sight that allows you to see off into the distance. Look east and you can see other hills of the Gogebic Range.

Skiing north again, past the next two clearings, you'll encounter your first yellow caution sign tacked to a tree. Unless it's icy, don't sweat it, the hill is easy. After a little climb, you'll encounter the second pipeline, and shortly after you'll begin to see things in the distance, through the trees. You are nearing the top of Big Powerhorn Mountain, and the Big Powderhorn Downhill Ski Area.

As the trail snakes closer to the treeless mountaintop, you can begin seeing chairlifts. If it's a busy day on the hill, you'll hear the heavy machinery groaning as it labors carrying hundreds of folks up the hill. Just think, you got here with muscle power! If you're interested, you can ski down the big hill, get a special, one-time lift ticket, and ride back up.

Continuing on your tour, follow the trail, which briefly skirts the edge of a downhill run before it heads back into the woods. But don't miss the view. Looking north you can see a line of hills running east-west. In about the middle of those hills is one with an enormous ski jump sticking out from it. This is Copper Peak and the jump is the Copper Peak Ski Flying Tower. It's 469 feet long, and reaches about 300 feet high above the top of the hill. People actually jump off the end of it and fly more than 500 feet through the air. The jump, which is about 10 miles north of you, can be reached easily by car on Black River Road, which goes north from Highway 2 about three miles east.

Back to cross-country skiing. Once you've reentered the woods, the trail winds its way around the backside of the ski hill until it hits a junction. Powderhorn Cut-off goes right. If you take it you will miss some of the fun at the top of Big Powderhorn Mountain, so go left.

You'll leave the woods one more time, ski around a lakelike depression and find yourself once more on top of the ski hill. The trail takes you down the ski hill about 200 meters before it turns right. There's a large blue sign with a cross-country skier on it that points the way. Don't get carried away practicing your telemarking, or you may miss the turn. Once you're off the ski hill you're on a straight, wide summer road that gradually takes you farther downhill, across Snow Summit Road and into the woods.

When you turn off the wider trail and head back into the woods, look on the right because you will see the biggest tree on this entire trail. It is near the trail, and it's a three-foot-diameter basswood tree.

After some twisting and turning, the trail crosses another road and traces one of those pipelines for several hundred slightly uphill meters. You'll turn left off the pipeline at the junction with the Powderhorn Cut-off.

For the next kilometer or so the trail follows a valley. You'll pass a woodland swamp on the right and cross over a little creek several times.

The next junction is with the Wolverine Loop. Continue on to the left and you will notice that there are treeless, snow-covered bluff tops off to your left; you're slowly climbing out of the valley you've been in. When you see a hillside ahead and off to your right you are near another junction. The hill straight ahead is Wolverine. Go left at the junction, climb up for about a 100 meters and then enjoy the ride down to the next junction, this with the Ottawa Loop and the Grandview Hospital Trailhead.

The Ottawa Loop is not quite 3 km in length. Its first 300 m or so are a gradual downhill. Then the trail is mostly flat, and cuts through an alder swamp. It passes by the Ottawa National Forest headquarters buildings, then loops back toward the hospital. It rejoins the trail near the hospital trailhead. Go right, and climb back up to the Wolverine Loop, then go left. You will climb some more and then encounter two downhills with caution signs. Neither is much to worry about, unless it's icy.

When you loop out into an open, west-facing field there's a nice view. If it's windy the track will be blown over. Once in the field the trail pitches downward a bit, and then a bit more. There's no tree for a caution sign, but this is a tricky spot. You'll pick up speed, round a bend, and then enter the brushy wood's edge at considerable speed. If you stay upright, your momentum will carry you well into the woods. From here it's an easy 1 km ski through the woods back to the shelter. There are a couple of fun downhills and one junction with the warm-up loop, but nothing to worry about.

Dressing for Cold Weather

The secret to staying warm while cross-country skiing (or doing anything strenuous outside in the cold) is layering. When we exercise, our body heats up. Eventually we perspire. Once wet, our body loses heat exponentially faster than when it's dry. That's great on the beach, but lousy on the snow. Taking off layers of clothing as we warm up, before we break into a sweat, is the solution.

Another secret is to use nonabsorbent fibers next to your skin. There are many brand names on the market and several different fabrics. All are variations on the theme started by a generic fabric called polypropylene. Polypro, as it's called, is a plastic polymer of propylene that will not absorb water. There are newer fabrics today that are soft and feel better next to your ski than polypropylene. As with many things, the more expensive brands are often better. I'd suggest you experiment with different fabrics and brands until you find the one you like best.

Another boon to skiers has been the development of Lycra and similar stretch fabrics. Yes, they look good on the right body, but they also support, breathe, and block wind, without adding weight or bulk.

If you prefer natural fabrics, stick with wool, which retains much of its insulating capacity even when wet. Silk is another fabric that some people use next to their skin. I find it feels cold and clammy, but there are folks who love it. Your worst choice is cotton because when cotton gets wet—from sweat or melting snow—it is almost useless as an insulator.

The final layer, wind pants and/or jacket, should be a lightweight windbreaker of some type. The best windbreakers are made from fabric that breathes, allowing moisture to escape, without allowing moisture through. Gore-tex was one of the first and remains one of the best. But there are many other brands out there that work well, and some that do not. Experiment and find out what you like.

VI

Northern Wisconsin

30

Brule River State Forest
Afterhours Ski Trail

Directions: From where Highway 2 crosses the Brule River just west of Brule, Wisconsin, travel farther west about a quarter mile and turn left at Afterhours Road. The trailhead is on the left.

Grooming: The trail is wide. It is usually well-maintained and groomed for both diagonal stride and skating.

Total km: system, 13, plus another 2 or 3 if you include the "Alternate Trail," three arrow-straight roadways to the south and west of most of the trail system; this tour, 10

Fee: Yes, daily and annual passes are available.

Trailhead facilities: There is an approximately 12-by-14-foot warming shelter at the trailhead. Although generally austere, the building offers something that I know of in no other trailhead building: two heat lamps mounted in the ceiling that afford warmth to a chilled and/or wet skier. There was a lovely young lady standing under the lights the day I skied Afterhours. She had locked the keys in her Suburban, gone out and skied, and then couldn't get in the vehicle on her return. She kept warm under the heat lamps while she waited for the locksmith.

Contact: Brule River State Forest, 6250 S. Ranger Rd., Brule, WI 54820; (715) 372-5678.

Since we are near the Bois Brule River, a famous, wonderful, playful stream, our goal on this tour is to see the river, and ski along it. Take the leftmost trail from the parking area. The woods are unimpressive, mostly small white pine and aspen. The trail dips, then climbs before you bear right. The trail climbs a bit, gradually but steadily to another junction, appropriately called "Hilltop Junction." The trail becomes very wide, and after a jog left, very straight. This is a great spot to practice technique. It's flat and straight, with few distractions.

It's about 300 m to a junction where River Trail goes left. The woods beyond the junction look full of soft evergreens. These smallish trees are Norway spruce. More about Norway spruce later.

Soon after you bear left onto River Trail there is a wonderful, long, gradual downhill. This is nature's way of telling you that you are

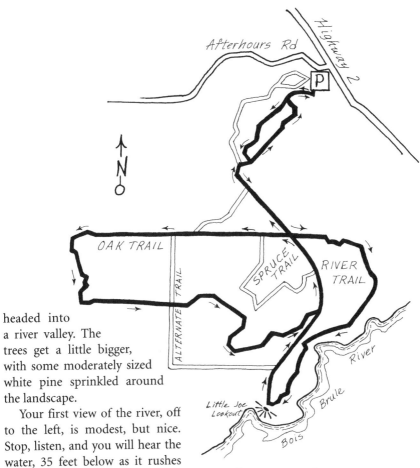

headed into
a river valley. The
trees get a little bigger,
with some moderately sized
white pine sprinkled around
the landscape.

Your first view of the river, off
to the left, is modest, but nice.
Stop, listen, and you will hear the
water, 35 feet below as it rushes
toward its meeting with Lake Superior, still 15 or so miles away.
Where you get your first glimpse of the river there are several large,
old scotch pine near the trail on the left. These nonnative pine are
notable for rust-colored bark on the upper half of their trunks. One
wonders how nonnative pine are so common here.

Ski on, and you'll cruise down another easy hill and past several
river overlooks before reaching Little Joe Lookout. There's a sign
posted on a tree near where the spur trail leads to the lookout. The
sign tells you that there had been a railroad trestle across the river at
this spot back in the 1890s. It also says that Little Joe was a river guide
who swamped his boat and got rather wet near this place while fer-
rying some client's belongings on the river. If you ski left at the sign
you will quickly arrive at the lookout. Although there may have been
a railroad trestle here in 1890, there is absolutely no hint of it today
beneath the snow. The river is 20 m below, audible as it rushes north.

Back on the trail it's only 200 m to the next junction, with the "Alternate Trail"; don't go left unless you want to ski in a straight line for quite a ways. This section of the River Trail traverses the old railroad grade that led to the former bridge across the river. If you look at each side of the trail you will see that the trail is elevated a couple feet above the level of the rest of the land. When the trail curves left, look right. You can see that the old railroad bed continued straight here, then curved to the right. If you twist your neck farther right, you can see a bluff on the other side of the river.

Continue on until you reach Main Junction. This is where the River Trail ends. You were here before, when you started out on River Trail. If you go right you will retrace your ski tracks. Our tour takes us left, past an outhouse on the right, and into a stand of small aspen, also on the right. You will be on Spruce Trail briefly, then on the agonizingly straight Alternate Trail for a couple hundred meters.

Oak Trail is also rather straight and flat, but it offers a change of scene as it turns left and crosses an isthmus between two larger wetland areas. Once across the wetlands, the trail turns left again and proceeds back up a little hump in the trail and through upland. Then there is a long, straight downhill. At the bottom of the hill, near where your runout ends, look left and you can see some large Norway spruce. You will know they are Norway spruce by both their nine-inch-long cones, which hang conspicuously from the higher branches, and by the extremely droopy branchlets. These are among the biggest Norway spruce in the area, and since this type of spruce is not native, these trees may be the parents of the thousands of other such trees you've been seeing along the trail.

For the next half kilometer or so the trail crosses several small ravines that cut across the landscape as they drop down into the Brule River valley. This makes for a nice roller-coaster-like ski.

Turn left at the next junction, and you will be skiing back over trail you have skied before. You will pass Main Junction and then Hilltop Junction, where you should bare right. Less than 100 meters farther you will reach yet another junction. Skiing out, you came up from the trail on the left.

If you want some downhill fun, go right here and get ready to slide. The hill starts a little way past the junction and takes you down toward the river valley in a fairly straightaway fashion. Then there is a sharp left turn and the bottom drops out. This is a great way to end the tour, with a fast, slightly tricky downhill. The hill's runout takes you to a junction. Turn right and you are only a few minutes away from the trailhead.

Copper Falls State Park

Directions:	From the intersection of Highways 13 and 169 just north of Mellen, Wisconsin, take 169 about 2 miles to the turnoff for Copper Falls State Park, which is on the left.
Grooming:	The trails are groomed for diagonal striding only.
Total km:	system, 22; this tour, 6
Fee:	Park vehicle sticker required
Trailhead facilities:	none
Contact:	Copper Falls State Park, RR 1, Box 17AA, Mellen, WI 54546; (715) 274-5123.

This is a tour of some fine waterfalls and river gorges. Start out into a red pine plantation at the end of the parking lot. Climb a bit, then curve left, past a giant old three-stemmed basswood on your right. Go straight at the junction with Vahtera Loop. After a short downhill you will see a hemlock grove on the left.

Soon you will be skiing through a white pine plantation. White pine plantations—unlike red pine plantations—are uncommon. Red pine seem to have been preferred for reforestation because they have fewer pest problems. Paper companies love red pine. There are several small hills in this section of trail, but nothing is very difficult.

When you reach a split-rail fence, behind which are a couple of outhouses used by summer visitors, you are near the Bad River and Brownstone Falls. The ski trail does not go close enough to the river bluff for you to get a good view, so, when you see snowshoe tracks heading off left, ski down them—carefully. You will reach a river over-look within 30 m. A sign proclaims, "Brownstone Falls." The falls are really on the Tyler Forks of the Bad River, which flows in from the right. Directly below is the boiling confluence of the Bad River, just below Brownstone Falls, and the Tyler Forks of the Bad River. Depending on how cold it's been and how much water is flowing, you may see mostly ice, or you may see lots of foaming, crashing water.

Ski back to the real ski trail and go left. The trail parallels Tyler Forks before it heads across on a bridge. There's a little downhill at the turn onto the bridge that can be tricky. Once across the bridge, the trail turns left and traces a path up the other side of the river, into

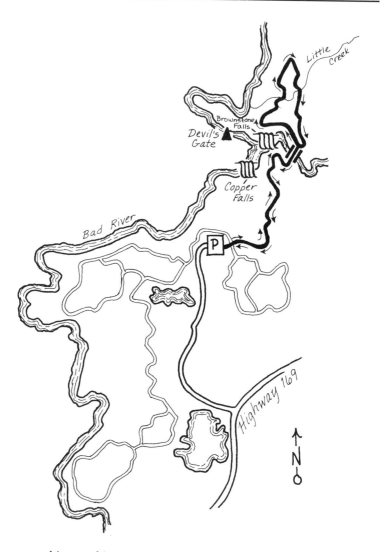

some bigger white pine. When you reach the stairway down to a viewing platform, take off your skis and walk. The view here isn't a good as before, but you can see up Tyler Forks, and what are called the Cascades. These are usually frozen solid in winter.

Climb back up the stairs, clip your skis back on, and continue your tour. The trail climbs a bit, then stays alongside, but away from the river gorge. When it begins looping right, past a sheltered bench, you will see a snowshoe path that heads straight ahead. It's only about .5 km down it to Devil's Gate, a narrowing in the river that creates rapids. Because of the downhill before you get there, it's best you take off your skis.

After you explore Devil's Gate, continue down the ski trail. A sign will tell you that the trail dead ends in one half mile. Then another sign lets you know that the ski trail loops back. Reassured, continue on, down a little dip, over Little Creek, and then back up hill on the other side.

You will pass a large cedar immediately next to the trail on the left. Woodpeckers have carved holes in its trunk, but the tree looks healthy. As the trail rounds its northern most curve and heads back south, there's a significant downhill. Then you will climb some more, and then drop suddenly down to Little Creek. Climb up the opposite bank, there's only one more quick downhill before you reconnect with the loop you came out on. Cross the bridge and reverse the route that got you here.

Journal: Before I begin skiing at Copper Falls a ranger lets me know that about half the ski trails are closed, due to logging. I get angry but don't outwardly react. I decide to see what's going on before I complain.

Out on the trail, it's immediately apparent that there's been a big wind here recently. Many trees are tipped over and others that were broken off 10 or 15 feet above the ground. I'm glad I kept my mouth shut.

Drummond Ski Trail

Directions: From the intersection of Highway 63 and County M in Cable, take 63 north 8 miles to Forest Road 213. Turn right on 213; the trailhead is about 1 mile on the left.

Grooming: The trail is diagonal only.

Total km: system, 20; this tour, 12

Fee: Forest Service vehicle fee required

Trailhead facilities: none

Contact: Washburn Ranger District, 113 E. Bayfield St., P.O. Box 578, Washburn, WI 54891; (715) 373-2667.

This is a great ski trail. It offers about 20 km of unduplicated trail, laid out in loops. The trails are one-way, except the central trail, named Boulevard, which accesses all loops and is two-way. Boulevard is double tracked, making skiing with a friend comfortable and conversation easy.

We are going to ski about 12 km, from the parking area on Forest Road 213 to another point farther south and east on the same road and then back again via one of the loops, Jackrabbit.

Heading out on Boulevard, which is the only option, the trail is double tracked and fairly flat. Within a few tenths of a kilometer Racetrack cuts off to the right. It offers some small hills and rejoins Boulevard in 1.2 km. Continuing down Boulevard, you will note that there are some large white pine along the trail. These giants, some three feet in diameter, are as much as 180 years old.

Antler, a trail that heads off to the left shortly after Racetrack, is a short 3.2 km loop, with moderately hilly terrain.

At the next junction, Jackrabbit heads left. We will ski it on our return. For now, go straight. You will soon pass out of the pines into an almost entirely deciduous woods. Then there are a couple of moderate climbs, the first good test of your wax on this trip.

When you arrive at the next junction, bear left. This is actually a segment of the famous North Country Trail that, when complete, will be 3,200 miles long—extending from New York to North Dakota—and the longest such hiking trail in the United States. The difference

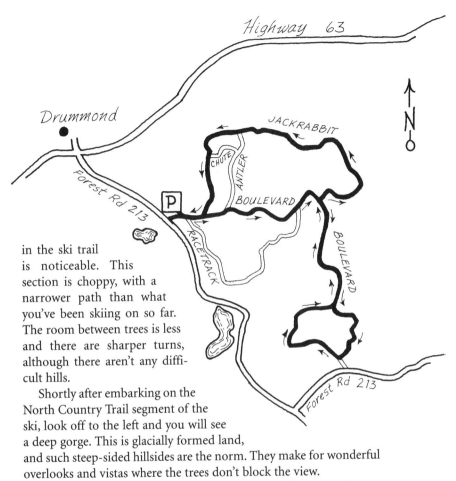

in the ski trail
is noticeable. This
section is choppy, with a
narrower path than what
you've been skiing on so far.
The room between trees is less
and there are sharper turns,
although there aren't any difficult hills.

Shortly after embarking on the
North Country Trail segment of the
ski, look off to the left and you will see
a deep gorge. This is glacially formed land,
and such steep-sided hillsides are the norm. They make for wonderful
overlooks and vistas where the trees don't block the view.

At the next junction you can turn left and head down to Forest
Road 213 or go right and complete the loop back to Boulevard. It's
about .2 km to the road, all downhill. The trail's often not groomed,
and is pitted by previous skier's mistakes. It's not an easy ski, but if
you need a thrill, go for it.

If you go right and ski back to Boulevard the skiing is on a wider,
less twisting path, having left the North Country Trail. Once back on
Boulevard, you'll go down the two uphill pitches you had to climb
before. There's nothing really tricky about the descents, unless
someone else has fallen and messed up the track.

When you get to the next junction right, it will be with Jackrabbit.
Go right, and enjoy the longer hills and more rolling topography.
When you see the caution sign on a tree about a kilometer from the
junction, don't worry, the upcoming downhill is really gentle. From
the sign it's about 4 km back to the parking lot.

When you get to a junction with double track, that's Boulevard and you want to go right. The parking lot is just .5 km away.

Journal: Skiing the Boulevard to North Country to Jackrabbit route with a friend I discover how fast she is on her new striding skis. As usual, I didn't clean the wax off the skis from my last outing, so the Swix Purple that's hiding under some newly applied Blue just isn't getting the job done in this newly fallen, 15-degree snow. Of course, the problem isn't entirely equipment. Barb is an Elite Wave skier in the Birkie, and she's faster than I am even if the equipment is equal. Today she's practicing her double-pole technique. I'm discovering that one of her double poles is about equal to one of my kick double poles.

When we reach the North Country segment of our ski, I finally can relax a bit because the tight turns and little moguls slow her down. But by the time we reach the junction with Jackrabbit, I'm sucking air again, and resign myself to the distance Barb begins putting between us.

I've sort of settled into a more leisurely pace when snow starts pelting me. It's one of those snowstorms that make it impossible to see. Not only is the air filled with flakes, my eyes are bombarded with them, and they quickly turn into tiny icicles hanging from my lashes. As I slide down a moderate hill, I can't see the track, or much of anything else. Mercifully, Barb stops to let me catch up, and as I approach, she laughs and asks if I'd like to use her sunglasses. "No thanks," I respond, "I kind of like not being able to see, it makes an easy trail more challenging."

As the snow builds up in the track, my Swix Purple grabs ever more of it, caking the bottom of my skis with a snow layer that slows me down so much I have to pole downhill! What a good excuse! When we finish, I make sure Barb sees the layer of snow on the bottom of my ski. Why else would I have been so far behind? Indeed.

Mecca Ski Trails

Directions: From the corner of Highway 51 and County J in downtown Mercer, go south on 51 about 1 mile to Beachway Road. Turn right on Beachway and go .1 mile to the junction with Mercer Lake Circle. Bear left on Mercer Lake Circle. Keep the cemetery on your right and continue straight to the dead end (no pun intended), about .9 mile. There are signs for the ski trail at all junctions. When you see the sewage treatment plant (cemetery, sewage treatment plant, this trail may have a public relations problem!) drive into the parking lot, and the trailhead is to the left.

Grooming: Mecca is groomed for both skating and striding, although some of the Homestead Loop and Spruce Hills Loop are diagonal only.

Total km: system, 16; this tour, 6

Fee: donation

Trailhead facilities: There are no facilities at the trailhead, but there is a shelter, with wood stove and outhouse, on the trail.

Contact: Mecca Cross-Country Ski Club, P.O. Box 76, Mercer, WI 54547; (715) 476-2389.

This is a classic ski tour. Stride out from the parking area across an open field. It's only a hundred meters to the woods, and most of that is slightly downhill. The forest here is comprised of smaller trees, both deciduous and coniferous. An interesting component near the beginning is Scotch pine. This nonnative pine must have been planted nearby, because the small trees next to the trail are naturalized—that is, they have grown from seed cast by parents that grew in the area. Larger trees develop interesting rust-colored bark on older limbs and trunk.

You will ski past the Scotch pine and some balsam fir into the ever-present aspen, then to the first trail junction. Go left here and you'll encounter two small downhills and one climb up to the next junction. From this junction it's about 10 meters to the top of a downhill called Waterfalls. While the hill is short, it is quite steep, and there's some compression at the bottom. If you can maintain your speed down the hill, you won't need to exert any effort going up the next little hill—you will glide there.

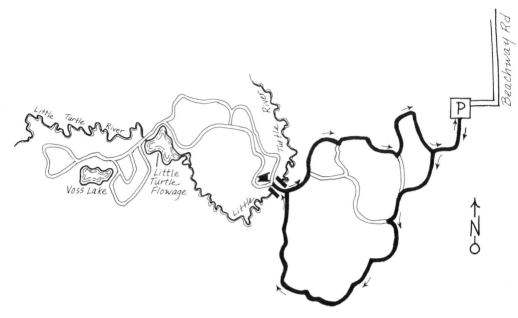

The next couple of hills are small and lots of fun, with nice curves and easy runouts. You will make your first real climb, then reach another junction, where you should go left. After a couple hundred meters of mostly flat skiing, you will reach The Chute, a triple pitch downhill that isn't very long. A bit of a left curve after the second pitch can be tricky.

After the downhill, the trail takes you through a mix of aspen and birch, with balsam fir and spruce growing underneath. Then there's a sudden change: You are skiing into and through red pine. It is difficult to tell if these are planted or naturally seeded red pine, but it is a plantation. The trail is nicely designed and winds in and out of the rows, through areas where the pine have been thinned. It makes for a pretty and fun stride.

Your nose may tell you before your eyes that you are approaching a snowmobile trail. This is a busy trail, so be careful as you cross. Not long afterward you will ski through a tamarack bog. It is bright here, a portent of things to come. After some more birch and aspen, you'll enter another wet area, this one vegetated by lots of black ash. Note the stubby branches and twigs. There are also some white cedar here, a couple close to the trail and then some off in the distance.

You will pass by some white pine, where the forest becomes three layered: small balsam fir, intermediate height aspen, and upper-layer white pine. Then you are in yet another wet area, this one full of speckled alder.

Just past the alder is a trail junction. If you want to visit the trail-side shelter, go left. You will see the vast, open expanse that the Turtle

River flows through. The Department of Natural Resources cuts back all the woody vegetation in the area. A pair of relocated trumpeter swans lives here in the summer, and the cleared landscape favors the survival of young swans.

There is a fast little downhill that leads you to a bridge over the Turtle River, then a climb on the other side. The shelter is on the left. It's a pleasant place, with a wood stove and plexiglass picture window. A sign above the door proclaims that it was constructed in 1985 by the Wisconsin Conservation Corps.

Head back over the bridge and go straight ahead at the junction. Ski into an aspen woods that have both white and red pine growing above. Stay straight past two trail junctions, then heed the caution sign before a downhill that takes you across the snowmobile trail.

You will come into an area that's more open, having been logged in the 1990s. You will note that since crossing the snowmobile trail there have been no more pine. The topography is also hillier. After you ski through a bowl-like area that has hills on all sides, you will climb a hill, then see the field near the parking area. After skiing along the edge of the woods, you'll reach the trail's first junction, where you have already been. Bear left and it's less then five minutes to the parking lot.

Montreal Nordic Trails

Directions: There are at least three access points to the Montreal Trails. This tour starts at the trailhead on Spring Camp Road. From the junction of Highways 77 and 51 in Hurley, go west on 77 approximately 4 miles to South Elm Street. Turn left on South Elm and take it about .3 mile until it dead ends at a T intersection with Iron Belt. Jog right on Iron Belt, then turn left onto Spring Camp Road. The trailhead is about .2 mile on the left.

Grooming: This is a diagonal stride trail. About half the system is double tracked. The rest is a comfortably narrow single track.

Total km: system, 11; this tour, 9

Fee: donation

Trailhead facilities: There are none. Hurley, a couple of miles east on Highway 77, is your best bet for supplies. The Belle Chalet between Silver (Highway 77) and Copper Streets on 5th Avenue in Hurley serves some great Italian food.

Contact: Iron County Development Zone Council, 100 Cary Rd., Box 97, Hurley, WI 54534; (715) 561-2922.

If you're interested in a little mining history while you ski, this is the trail for you. Back in the early 1900s the area west of Hurley bustled with iron mining. The Montreal ski trail not only winds its way through a historic mine site, it uses about 2 km of an old railroad grade built for the mine.

This is a fun and easy tour. The main loop is laid out around the base of a forested hill with a high point of 1,777 feet. The trail's high point is at about 1,750 feet; its low point is at about 1,600 feet.

Start at the parking area on Spring Camp Road. The railroad grade is nearly flat here. After about 200 m, turn left at the junction with Cloocky's Slide Trail. Although it's rated "more difficult," this part of the trail is quite easy. You will climb a bit then coast along a ridge. There is one of many informational signs on the right, this one marking the site of a former powerhouse; the stone foundation of the structure is still visible. The sign includes a picture of the structure when it was in use, and it's hard to imagine the large turbines occupying this site that's now a forest.

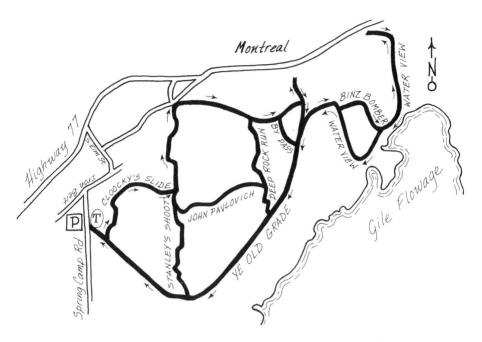

The trail then enters the edge of a small opening, with a view to the north. There are some old ramshackle buildings, and some apple trees in the open field. This was likely an old homestead. The view beyond the buildings is of a couple of hills that are part of the Penokee Range. (See the Uller Ski Trail later in this section for more on the Penokees.)

Leaving the opening you will encounter a bit of a downhill run before reaching a junction with Stanley's Shoot. Go left, and the next mining artifact is enclosed by a chain-link fence. The fence, on the left, protects you and others from an old mine shaft. There's a signboard that tells you more about the shaft.

Past the historic site, there's a downhill, then a road crossing. After the road, the trail enters some pine, and curves right. Highway 77 is off to the left, as is most of residential Montreal. The trail parallels "# 4 Street," running through several rows of pines, then reaches a junction with Deep Rock Run, an intermediate-level trail. Continue past this junction and in less than .5 km you will reach By Pass.

If you don't take By Pass and go straight you will reach another trailhead located behind an old mining building, now a warehouse for Rose Wreath Company. It's a nice .5 km downhill run to the parking area. You will need to return back up the downhill run and go left on By Pass. Then you will make another nice downhill run and reach Ye Old Grade Trail.

Take Ye Old Grade right, and you have embarked on a wonderful, slightly uphill stride that will last for almost 2 km. The grade is very gradual, as one would expect from a railroad. If you crave an aerobic experience, you can double pole the entire distance. But don't forget to take in the view, through the trees to the left, of the Gile Flowage.

When the grade starts cutting thought the basalt bedrock of the mountain, the trail is nearing its junction with Stanley's Shoot. If you turn right and take this trail, you climb more than 100 feet before you reach its junction with John Pavlovich Run, the only section of trail in this system that's rated "most difficult." Just 100 m farther is Cloocky's Slide, a junction you reached earlier on this ski. If you ski John Pavlovich Run you'll drop about 25 m in slightly more than .5 km before reaching a junction with Deep Rock Run. Turn right, and in a couple hundred meters you'll be back at Ye Old Grade.

If you choose to pass by Stanley's Shoot, continue up the grade—which is essentially flat by now—and in about 1 km you will reach the parking area where you left your vehicle.

Pattison State Park Trails

Directions: From Superior, Wisconsin, take Highway 35 approximately 16 miles south. The entrance to Pattison State Park is on the left (east). Follow the park road until you see the sign for the ski trail, which points to the parking area, a right turn off the park road.

Grooming: The trail is groomed for striding only.

Total km: system, 7; this tour, 7

Fee: Wisconsin State Park vehicle sticker

Trailhead facilities: none

Contact: Pattison State Park, 6294 S. State Road 35, Superior, WI 54880; (715) 399-3111.

Pattison State Park is the home of Big Manitou Falls, Wisconsin's highest falls, at 165 feet. This ski trail does not go near the falls, but does parallel the Black River for several kilometers. The Black River flows out Black Lake, which sits astride the Minnesota-Wisconsin border in a particularly inaccessible area, about 25 miles south of Lake Superior. Before it reaches the lake, but after Big Manitou Falls, the Black empties into the Nemadji River, another stream that arises in Minnesota and empties into Lake Superior in the southeast section of the city of Superior.

Start this ski from the south side of the parking area. The trail heads out a park service road, then makes a right turn, and skirts a split-log-fenced park storage area for about 25 m before it enters a conifer-filled woods.

You will ski across Springbrook Creek on a one-span wooden bridge. When there's a lot of snow, the creek is so buried that it's hardly visible. The woods here are comprised mostly of maple, basswood, and red oak. The trail is essentially flat. You will ski past a bench that overlooks an opening with the Black River, winding 50 feet below.

After a series of small hills you will reach a junction, complete with map board. The 2.4 km Red Loop heads left here and back to the parking lot. Go right and there's a longer, gradual downhill that ends at another junction. Bear left and you are off on Blue Loop. There's a

117

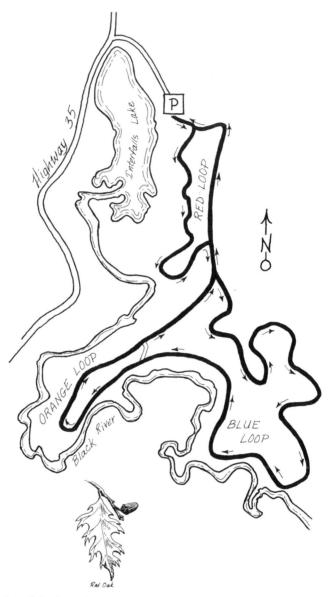

lot of climbing for the next .5 km. The trail takes you up onto the high ground that surrounds the river basin. There are three switchbacks that climb the hill. As you near the top, look ahead to the left and you will see the bluffs of Duluth through the trees.

There are some bigger trees here on the upland. The most obvious are the white pine, many of which have lost their leader some years ago. Some have trunk diameters of more than two feet. You will ski right past one yellow birch that's about three feet in diameter. Then there's a big white pine with three twisted leaders visible up the trail; such twistedness is unusual for a white pine. Some calamity must have occurred in this woods around 1900 that resulted in the wounded tops of those big white pines.

You'll ski a series of three uphills and downhills, before you crest one final hill. From this hilltop, you can see the river basin on the left. Then you shoot down the hill. It's lots of fun, but beware the right turn at the bottom. The river is now next to you on the left. Its cut banks and a flood plain are visible on the opposite side.

The trail snakes alongside the river for the next kilometer or so. You will pass a sign that says: "Site of Martin Pattison's Lumber Camp, 1880–1883." You will barely feel the climb that takes you up and away from the river. The woods become less impressive, with smaller sugar maple and aspen dominating.

A long downhill takes you to the next junction—this with the Orange Loop—which is about 1 km long. It's worth the trip. Initially you are on a bluff over looking the river, then you dip down a tricky hill, made so by the hard right turn near its bottom. After a couple of easy ups and downs, you will ski past an eight-by-six foot shelter and up a short hill. From the hilltop you can see the bluffs around Duluth again. Then it's a fun ride down the side of a ridge to the next junction.

Go left, and it's only a short stride to the next downhill, which is a fast one with a left turn midway. You will glide by the entrance to the Blue Loop, where you started that long climb up onto the highland around the river. Just continue straight; you can double pole all the way to the bridge over Springbrook Creek. Make a left turn past the bridge and then ski along an area where the park folks store their picnic tables, and you are back at the parking area.

If you want to see Wisconsin's highest waterfall, Big Manitou Falls, climb into your vehicle, go back to Highway 35, and turn left. Then go right at the first intersection (with County B), just past the highway bridge over the Black River. There's a parking area on the left. Hike back across B and follow the signs to an overlook of the falls.

Journal: I can remember the first time I saw Big Manitou Falls. I was writing Great Wisconsin Walks, and when I saw the falls I was disappointed. Sure they are more than 160 feet tall, but there just isn't much water. Perhaps in April, or May, when there's more runoff. Somehow I think that the dam just above the falls altered this natural feature so that it just isn't as impressive as it once was.

If you want to see a cool waterfall in Wisconsin, head for the Potato River Falls near Gurney. While only about a third of Big Manitou's height, the width of the falls and the volume of water over them combine to make a great sight and sound show.

Rock Lake Trail

Directions: From Cable, take County M east 7.5 miles to the parking area on the right. From the junction of Highway 77 and M in Clam Lake, take M west 12 miles to the parking area on the left.

Grooming: Rock Lake Trail is solely a diagonal striding trail. It is narrow, with a single track set, and the snow packed in a area about a ski length in width.

Total km: The outer loop of this system is 16, and if you add the four crossovers—one for each of the shorter loops—and the Rock Lake Loop, the total distance in the system is approximately 22; this tour, 18.

Fee: U.S. Forest Service seasonal parking permit required

Trailhead facilities: There is an outhouse. Lakewoods Resort, which has a nice restaurant and bar, is just a quarter mile east on the north side of County M.

Contact: Hayward District Ranger, Chequamegon National Forest, Route 10, Box 508, Hayward, WI 54843; (715) 634-4821.

Rock Lake is a well-designed trail, consisting of five one-way loops, each longer than the previous one. The topography is glacial, with little and big hills, and several backwoods lakes. Because the trail is designed for skiing, its difficulty level never really exceeds intermediate ("more difficult") ability. The hills are used well, with gradual climbs (no head walls) and sweeping downhills with no unkind turns. However, the frequency of the climbs and descents— plus the length of the outer loop—combine to earn that section and the short Rock Lake Loop a "most difficult" designation.

Rock Lake Trail is only a few miles from the Telemark Lodge and the fabled Birkebeiner trail; throughout the years it's been skied by just about everyone who has skied the Birke. Lots of folks love Rock Lake.

This tour will trace the 16 km loop, the longest at Rock Lake, and will take a side trip on the Rock Lake Loop. Ski out from the parking area to the left of the big signboard on the east side of the parking area. You will cross the return trail, then a snowmobile trail before reaching the first cutoff, this one for the 2 km loop. Stay right and you

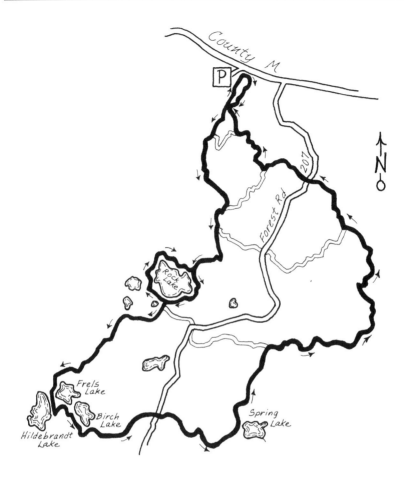

will do the first real climbing of this ski, then enjoy a three-dip downhill, followed by a little rise, and a fourth dip. Unless you slow yourself down, you'll sail past the junction with the next cutoff, this for the 4 km trail.

Until now you've been skiing through mostly northern hardwoods: oak, basswood, maple, along with some ash, and a smattering of understory balsam fir. Shortly after the 4 km cutoff, you will begin seeing big white pine. The first two near the trail are on the right and they are more than two feet in diameter. The pine here are beginning to form what's called a supercanopy. Although it will take another 50 to 100 years, you can see how they are already starting to tower over all the deciduous trees.

Past the cutoff for the 7.1 km loop, you will see some red pine, then you will see an open boggy area off to the right. This is just before you reach the junction with the return leg of the Rock Lake Loop. Continue left and you can see Rock Lake off to the right. The trail climbs up a hill via a series of three pitches that require herringbone technique, then slides downhill, making for perhaps the fastest ride of the day so far.

At the bottom of this hill is the junction with the Rock Lake Loop. Go right to circle the lake. The slide that began before the junction continues, then there's a climb, followed by a fast downhill into a little marshy area that connects a low spot on the left with Rock Lake. You'll climb, then descend, over and over; there isn't a level piece of trail the entire 1.8 km around the lake. On the northeast side of the lake, just before you reconnect with the main trail, you will ski through a thick pine forest. A slightly tricky downhill, with a hook to the right near the top, marks the last descent on the Rock Lake Loop.

Go right at the junction and you'll retrace your strides back up those three herringbone pitches and down that nice slide to the junction with the Rock Lake Loop. Go left this time and continue 50 or so meters to the last cutoff, this for the 11.5 km loop.

The trail climbs and drops over the glacial topography for the next kilometer or so. Sometimes you're in deciduous woods, sometimes among big pines. When the deciduous woods get younger—when the trees are noticeably smaller—you are nearing a ridge top. The trail will curve right and you will see several ridge lines off in the distance. If there's a wind, especially a southerly wind, you will hear it flow through the pines overhead. As you curve back south, Frels Lake is off to the left. When you see the little wooden sign that reads, "Frels Lake," get ready for a downhill ride—one of the more difficult on this trail, but still nothing to worry about. After you see Hildebrand Lake on the right, you are in for perhaps the longest climb on this tour. Your reward for the climb is a view of Birch Lake on the left.

For the next 2 km the trail rolls through a pure northern hardwood forest, one that isn't very old, with most trees about 30 to 40 years of age. You'll cross a snowmobile trail, Forest Road 207. Then, across from the little wooden sign that reads "8K," you can see an approximately 20-acre area that was clear-cut several years ago. If you keep a keen lookout, you may see the 15-foot-tall charred stump on the left just before you begin seeing big pines again. The pines signify that you are nearing Spring Lake, which will be on the right.

Yellow birch populate the forest near the junction with the 11.5 km loop. After this junction you will note that as it goes up hills the trail seems just a bit wider—not from grooming, but from more use, more skis hitting the edge and beating down the snow. Herringbone technique is easier up such hills. After a rollicking series of downhill pitches, the trail settles into long, gradual uphill and downhill grades again. If your grip is poor, you will tire your arms out, and you'll long for the parking lot.

At the next junction, with the 7.1 km loop, it is only 2.9 km to the lot, so take heart. Just past the junction, if you look left, you can see a huge valley, which the trail skirts as it crosses the snowmobile trail again. The last couple hundred meters to the junction with the 4 km loop are mostly downhill, a welcome change from the last couple of kilometers.

A right at this 4 km loop junction takes you to the 2 km loop junction, which is at the bottom of a nice easy downhill run. Caution is advised as you can't see someone on the cross trail coming until it's too late. The same is true of the next two junctions, first with a snowmobile trail, then with the ski trail shortly after it has left the parking lot.

A gentle downhill and a little rise bring you back to the beginning of the trail and the parking lot, on the left. You've now skied the famous Rock Lake Trail. Bring on the Birkebeiner!

Journal: Near the end of my 65-mile drive to ski Rock Lake, I ponder what grip wax I'll use. The temperature has gone from a chilly 7 degrees a couple of hours ago to 27 right now. Last night the weather guru in Rhinelander was predicting 38 for a high. Ten minutes ago the Duluth radio station was calling for a high of 45. I decide to go with Swix Blue Extra. Before I ski off, I also put some Violet Special and Red in my pocket. I figure I'm ready for the predicted warm-up.

From the start my grip is OK, but not great. About 5 km into my ski I decide that my grip has deteriorated and I need more Blue Extra; that a longer wax pocket should do the trick. When I ski off with my newly applied wax, it is quickly apparent that little has changed, my grip is still marginal.

I make do for another 4 km, until while climbing a hill just past Spring Lake, my right ski spurts backward and I almost do the splits. I apply some Violet Special and finish climbing the hill. Things are a bit better, but still not good.

Then I reach a couple kilometer section of trail that consists of long, gradual ups and downs. The downs are great, but the ups aren't. Without good grip, I use my arms a lot. They are getting very tired. So I stop one more time, in order to put on some Red, my last option. I only put it on my left ski, thinking that if it's better, I'll do the other ski when I'm a little farther down the trail. Well, the Red does help a little, but the trade-off is that it's really slow going down the easy grades. Rather fed up with my inability to find the right wax, I stubbornly ski the last 6 km without applying any more wax.

In my car and about to leave, a fellow double poles from the end of the trail into the parking lot, next to me. He wants to say something, so I put down my window. "Did you have any grip?" he asks. "Sure," I tell him, "my Universal klister worked great."

And it would have, too, if only I'd had it with me.

Superior Municipal Forest

Directions:	From Highway 2 just south of Barker's Island, take 18th Avenue east, which turns into 28th Street. Follow 28th to its end. The main trailhead is on the left. This ski begins from the Billings Drive trailhead, so you want to continue on 28th, which becomes Billings Drive just past the main trailhead. Go about 1.5 miles to the second trailhead, which is on the left.
Grooming:	These trails are well-groomed, for both skating and diagonal stride.
Total km:	system total, 26; this tour, 10
Fee:	Yes, you may pay at either trailhead.
Trailhead facilities:	There is a warming hut and chemical toilet at the 28th Street trailhead.
Contact:	Parks and Recreation Department, City of Superior, 1407 Hammond Ave., Superior, WI 54880; (715) 394-0270.

F ew cities can boast their own forest, and Superior boasts not only Wisconsin's largest, but also a wonderful ski trail nestled on fiordlike bluffs with impressive vistas. Your winding ride down Billings Drive to that trailhead allows you a couple of glimpses of fingerlike bays similar to those you will be skiing near on this tour.

This is a tour of the Yellow Trails. Although rated in the system's literature as "advanced," unless you are really afraid of downhill speed, Yellow Trails are no more than intermediate in difficulty.

Start across the road from the parking area and trail sign. The first .2 kilometer sweeps down through a wetland surrounded by pine-covered hillsides. The trail is wide, expansive, and inviting. Climb a long hill out of the wetland and turn right at the first junction, then right again. You will be skiing the Yellow Loop counterclockwise.

Large red and white pine invite you down the trail. When you see some white cedar trees, you are near the first of the five hills that earn this loop an "advanced" rating. This first hill and the next one are both steep but straight, and if the track is clean—that is, not pockmarked by other skiers who have fallen—they are easy rips.

If you look to the right after the second hill, you can begin seeing some of the ravines and bays that make this ski so scenic. The next kilometer or so takes you through aspen, birch, spruce, and other rep-

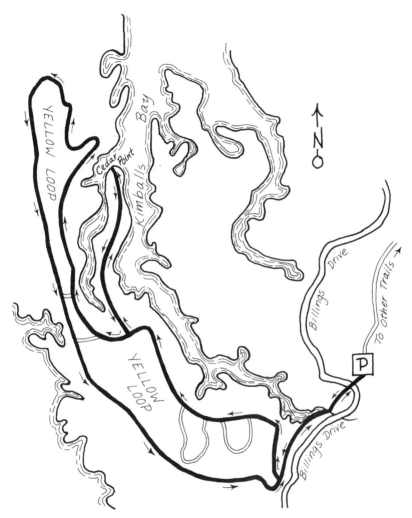

resentatives of a mixed northern forest. Sometimes the understory is a bit naked, perhaps because a large deer population prevents woody vegetation from getting much above snow level. When you arrive at the next junction, take the 1 km side trip out to Cedar Point. You'll ski through an almost pure, natural stand of red pine. Unfortunately, some of these trees are dying.

Kimballs Bay becomes increasingly visible on the right, as does another finger of water on the left. Both are 30 to 40 feet below the trail's elevation, so you'll get an impressive view. The cedar trees become ever more frequent and thick around the trail—a sign that you are near the downhill slide onto the bay. The hill isn't too bad, unless it's icy, or worse, has bare spots. Take the ride. Once out on the bay, you can ski around on the crust if there is one, or slog through the deep snow. In any event, check out the view of Duluth and the bluffs beyond. I counted 16 communication towers up on that bluff.

Climb back up onto the point and ski back to the junction with the main trail. Turn right and you'll encounter the third downhill. This one has a bit of a right curve near the bottom, but isn't difficult. Note the conglomeration of little three-foot-tall white spruce competing for space and light on the outside of the curve. Seed must germinate well here.

The fourth downhill is marked with a 10-foot-tall spruce sitting in the middle of the trail. It lends a Christmasy feel. This is the steepest hill on the tour, but it isn't as long as the others. If you just relax and manage the slide, you will be rewarded with a ride halfway up the other side. This area between hills four and five is noted for lots of wildlife sign; I saw fresh prints of rabbit, fox, coyote, and deer in the few hundred meters between the two hills.

Hill five is a lot like the others, nothing to worry about. Just let your momentum carry you up the other side as far as it can. The hills are now finished. The next kilometer is through gently rolling terrain. Cedar Point is visible on the right, as is some of the bay you skied out onto. When you reach a bench, resist taking the ungroomed path that leads behind it, and stay with the groomed trail, which will lead you to the same place.

You will reach a junction where the trail goes left or right. A yellow arrow points left, which is where the trail heads back to the parking lot, but if the trail is groomed right, take it. In less than .5 km, you will be back down to Kimballs Bay, only with a better view of Duluth.

Ski back to the junction with the yellow arrow and cruise past where you previously turned right. The trail for the next 4 km, back to where you entered the loop, is flat. There is a lot of alder and one section of attractive pine and cedar woods. One tree that you haven't seen yet on this tour, but that's well represented on the ski back, is black ash. It's a tree that likes wet ground. You will see one with wooden steps attached right next to the trail in about 2 km.

When you reach a T junction, it's where you started the Yellow Loop. Turn left, ski through the open wetland, up the hill, and you are back to the parking lot.

Teuton and Valkyrie Trail Systems

Directions: From the intersection of Highway 13 and County C in Washburn, take C northwest approximately 8 miles. The parking area is on the left.

Grooming: Teuton is groomed for both skating and striding, except Loop A. Valkyrie is a striding trail.

Total km: system, 20; this tour, 5 on Teuton, 9 on Valkyrie

Fee: Forest Service vehicle fee required

Trailhead facilities: There is a pleasant shelter farther back from the road, beyond the cross-country ski parking area. There are also outdoor toilets. Back toward Lake Superior, the city of Bayfield is home to Maggie's, an audacious bar and restaurant that serves great food amid many pink flamingos. Check it out.

Contact: Washburn Ranger District, 113 E. Bayfield St., P.O. Box 578, Washburn, WI, 54891; (715) 373-2667.

Since there are two quite different systems right next to one another, we will tour both. Access the Teuton system from the parking area. Bear right at the first opportunity. The trail is quite wide, with a skating area between two striding tracks.

When you reach the cutoff for Loop A, which is diagonal only, go left, on Loop B. Most of the ensuing kilometer is uphill, although not all at once. There are little hills, then some bigger ones. The forest is almost pure red oak in places. White birch compete here and there, as do some larger aspen. This is not a trail full of diverse timber. Unlike Valkyrie, conifers are few and far between.

By the time you reach the junction with Loop C, the climbing is almost over. You can see a ridge ahead and off to the right. Loop C climbs that ridge and plays along it. You want to go left and stay on Loop B. It is only about 30 m until you start heading downward. The trail is not really difficult, but the hill has a couple of twists in it that can be tough if it's icy. Then you must climb again, one last, long trudge up a ridge. The trail curves left over the ridge top; when you can see the snowmobile trail through the woods ahead of you, it's time to glide.

The trail heads down the other side of the ridge, angling along the ridge into a chute. A right curve keeps you from seeing what's ahead, so snowplow if you are worried. The downhill seems without end.

The end does come, but not before the Loop A merges from the left. As you whip down the last of the hill you might want to keep an eye out for other skiers merging on the trail. When you begin seeing some pines in the distance, you are near the trailhead and the parking lot.

A more demanding and perhaps more rewarding ski is on the Valkyrie system. The remote Loop C takes you to some wonderful places, with expansive vistas. But finding the trailhead can be as tricky as skiing Loop C. You have to carry your skis across County C, where the trail begins to the right of the snowmobile trail.

Besides lots of distance—about 10 km—Loop C offers some fast downhills. The first is just after Loop B cuts off to the left. The second is much later, just before you rejoin Loop B. Both curve slightly, which adds to their difficulty. In between are some gradual climbs and descents, plus a stride along a jack pine ridge that is beautiful and serene. There are some clear-cuts, which mar the overall effect somewhat, but it's a memorable ski.

Journal: It's one of those cloudy days that seem brighter than if the sun were out in full. I've been skiing for 40 minutes at Valkyrie, on Loop C. It's my first time here, and it seems like I haven't gotten very far. I've been climbing a lot, and negotiated one killer downhill that ended near a snowmobile trail. As I ski along a rare level area, through the 2 inches of powder that fell last night, I mistakenly plant my right pole too far right, off the packed trail. Before I can do anything else, I am listing 45 degrees right, and my pole is buried nearly to the grip.

I recover, and then climb yet another steep hill, this one a mandatory herringbone. Suddenly, at the top, I realize that the climb is finished and I see the trail snake along a ridge in front of me. On my left, through a cloudy haze, several ridges ripple off to the horizon. There is no sign of humanity, only conifer-steepled peaks. This could be the Black Hills, covered with ponderosa pine or the Cascades, blanketed with white fir. But it's Wisconsin, and those are jack pine, a much maligned, get-no-respect tree that looks magnificent here. I know that there's at least another 5 km left before I return to the trailhead, and I'm just a little disappointed that there isn't more.

Uller Ski Trail

Directions: Take Highway 77 southwest out of Pence, 2 miles to Hoyt Road. Go north on Hoyt .8 mile to the trailhead on the left. Since this is a point-to-point ski, leave a vehicle at the Weber Lake parking area. Get to Weber Lake by taking 77 to its intersection just west of Iron Belt with County E. Take E about 4 miles until just before the Whitecap Mountain Ski Area. The Weber Lake parking area is straight ahead at a 160-degree bend in E before the Whitecap entrance. You will see the west end trailhead for the Uller Ski Trail to the right of the parking area entrance road.

Grooming: This trail is pleasingly narrow and groomed for single-track diagonal striding.

Total km: system, 22; this tour, 12

Fee: donation

Trailhead facilities: None. Iron Belt is home to Sidekicks 77, a bar and restaurant featuring some fine Italian fare. Supplies are best found in either Hurley to the east or Mellen to the west.

Contact: Iron County Development Zone Council, 100 Cary Road, Box 97, Hurley, WI 54534; (715) 561-2922.

This is a great ski trail: scenic and remote. Unlike many trails that are a conglomeration of footpaths, woods roads, and logging trails, Uller was designed as a ski trail. It is a point-to-point trail, but with a cutoff and spur that almost make a loop. It has a reputation locally as a difficult, hilly ski and this is true to some extent. The climbs are long and the descents are fast. But there are no head walls, the kind you find on the Birkie trail. A couple of shelters, one a neat little cabin, add to this trail's charm.

From the Uller trailhead at Hoyt Road the trail is double tracked, straight, and flat. Out in the distance, near the place where perspective pulls the tree lines on each side of the trail together, there is a bluff face. Its white blanket of snow stands out against the blue ski. It's snowy and not tree covered because the steep slope and stony face afford tree roots precious little purchase. You will climb up and over that bluff, or one like it. This is going to be fun!

From the trailhead, the track leads you through a countryside cov-

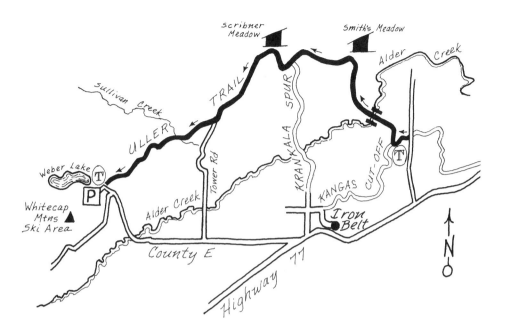

ered mostly with aspen, ash, and alder. It winds through a couple of small open areas of less than an acre. It is flat.

You'll reach the junction with Kangas Cut-off quickly. Bear right to continue this ski to Weber Lake. Soon a sign on a tree will announce you are entering the Iron County Forest. There will be signboards posted with forestry information here and there along the rest of the trail. They are educational, interesting, and frustrating to folks who argue that we have enough aspen stands and expertly managed timber, folks who long for old growth and wildness.

When you reach the wooden bridge that spans Alder Creek, stop on top and take a look around. This is the best view of the Penokee Range you will get from this trail, and it's a good one. There are "mountains" to the left and right of you, off in the distance. A million years ago (give or take a few hundred thousand), the Penokees were at least Alps-sized. But wind and rain and several glaciers have ground them down to what you see here—still an impressive expanse of rock.

Ski down off the bridge, through the remaining bottomland near the Creek and you will reach a snowmobile trail. Once you cross it, you will note a sign that declares you are now on the North Country Trail. You also will feel that you are gaining a little altitude. Approaching Smith's Meadow Shelter, you will notice an opening in the woods off to the right. The trees along the trail are almost all hardwoods. You will pass some large yellow birch near the trail.

When you arrive at the shelter, which is an unpretentious wooden shack, you may wish to rest a while. You are about a quarter of the way to Weber Lake.

When you leave the shelter, get ready for the trip's first real climb. Unless your grip is phenomenal, you will need to herringbone climb this long pitch. But you'll be rewarded with your first real downhill shortly after the climb, then there's another climb. During and just after the second climb you can see many large trees scattered about the forest. This area hasn't been cut in quite a while, and it looks wonderful.

The Krankkala Spur enters from the left. If you're tired and want to go back to your vehicle at Hoyt Road, you should just turn around. If you take the Krankkala Spur to the Kangas Spur, you'll travel about twice as far and have to ski or walk some roadways.

Continuing on from the Krankkala Spur, you'll ski over a barely noticeable Boomer Creek then gain more altitude before skiing along the northeast side of a large hill (one of the Penokee Mountains). You will notice another opening in the woods on the right, which is the beginning of Scribner Meadow. There's even a wood-duck house on a post, in what must be a wet spot in the meadow.

Scribner Meadow Shelter is really a cabin. Make sure you enter the place and check it out. Maybe that quarter-full vodka bottle is still setting above the door. There's a little wood stove, an ax and bow saw, old paper for starting a fire, and blankets—so if you're cold, warm up! There's also a diary, which makes fascinating reading: such as the 1996 entry that bemoans the 16-inch snowfall that made getting to the cabin almost impossible.

Be rested when you trek off again, because the longest climb of the trip is just ahead. After looping out into the meadow, you'll make a sharp left turn and begin a climb that lasts several minutes. Most of it requires herringbone technique. It is this climb and one other a bit farther along that make the trail best skied in an east-to-west direction. Although this is a long climb, imagine it as a downhill if you were coming from the west. Remember the sharp right turn at the bottom. Ouch!

The long uphill is rewarded with a small downhill run, then you ski through more northern hardwoods, although the sizes of the trees along this stretch aren't as impressive as on earlier stretches of the trail.

The trail uses a portion of Tower Road for about .5 km. You can tell you're on a road by noticing the ditch on the right, and later the left. The road leads up the hill to a fire tower. You're headed down. The trail leaves the road, and then begins dropping quickly down the hillside. You'll notice the trail's first caution sign. Heed it. The trail makes a sweeping loop to the right, and you will pick up lots of speed. The surprise and reason for the caution sign is that at the bottom of the hill the trail narrows and crosses little Sullivan Creek. There are rocks and open water on both sides of the couple-foot-wide trail where it crosses the creek. If you miss the little crossing, you're in trouble.

Having survived the creek crossing, you will ski along the creek bottom amid black ash and hemlock. This sheltered spot feels downright cozy, with a steep hillside on the left and a rock face on the right.

One more climb awaits you: the climb mentioned earlier, which would be an imposing downhill. Then you'll ski between hills for a while. The hill on the left has a gnarly stone-capped precipice topped by a white pine. There will be a shelter on the left, beyond the snowmobile trail that has unfortunately come into view. When you see another yellow caution sign, you are about to come down out of the Penokees. The downhill is long and fast, but there are no surprises at the bottom. You can see Whitecap Ski Area off to the left. The trail ends just off of County E, on the access road to the parking area for Weber Lake. This is where you left your vehicle.

Journal: For years I had wanted to explore the Penokees. I had seen them lots of times, most recently while running the Pavo Nurmi Marathon, which parallels them along Highway 77. Today I'm headed into them on skis, with friend Bob Kovar. The day is bright, and single-digit cold. We are standing on a little bridge over Alder Creek. The elevation of the bridge lifts us enough that we can see over the alder tops and view the magnificent snow-covered bluffs in front of us. I imagine I'm in Montana, facing the eastern foothills of the Rockies. And I'm going to ski up and through those. Wow! Maybe we aren't at 8,000 feet elevation, but I still feel a little breathless.

Mount Ashwabay Trails

Directions: From Bayfield head south on Highway 13 about 3 miles to Ski Hill Road. Go right (west) on Ski Hill Road about 1 mile until the road ends in the parking area.

Grooming: Most of this system is striding only. There are a couple of loops that are groomed for skating.

Total km: 25

Fee: Yes, it includes access to the T-bar lift and tow ropes that take you up the downhill ski slopes.

Trailhead facilities: There is a chalet that offers food and equipment rental. Food and alcohol are available in the lounge, which is in a separate building.

Contact: Mount Ashwabay, P.O. Box 928, Bayfield, WI 54814; (715) 799-3227 or (715) 779-5252.

I've skied at Mount Ashwabay many times and although I visited Ashwabay while writing this book, I was unable to ski there, hence there is no tour. Nonetheless, I recommend you give it a try. It's a small downhill operation, with a friendly feel. If you are a good cross-country skier, you can play on the downhill slopes without any problem. If you are looking for some downhill fun on an actual cross-country trail, try Seagull. Take the T-bar up the slopes, and then go right. The first 2 km are tame. Then things get exciting. The downhills are chutelike. The last one is about 300 m long and will test your snowplowing ability.

VII

The Duluth Area

Hartley Ski Trail

Directions: From the intersection of Superior Street and 21st Avenue, take 21st north up the hill until it turns into Woodland Avenue. Follow Woodland to Fairmont Street. Take Fairmont left a few blocks to the trailhead.

Grooming: The trail is groomed for diagonal stride only. It is narrow, and not a good place to ski in low-snow conditions due to exposed rocks in the trail.

Total km: system, 5; this tour, 5

Fee: Minnesota Ski Pass required

Trailhead facilities: none

Contact: City of Duluth, Parks and Recreation, 12 E. Fourth St., Duluth, MN 55805; (218) 723-3337. Or Duluth Cross County Ski Trail Hotline, (218) 723-3678.

There are two loops at Hartley. The outer loop is 3 km and probably the most difficult, with one or two downhills that rate expert in icy conditions. The inner loop is 2 km and pretty easy, save for one downhill. Enter either loop from one of three locations. Each location has a parking lot and then a small spur trail leading to the loops.

Starting at the Fairmont Street parking area, you'll ski up a short spur to reach the outer loop. Once at the outer loop, note where you are because it's easy to miss the spur to the parking area after you complete the loop.

Go left on the loop, and soon you'll be sliding down a gentle hill. The outer loop makes a 160-degree left turn near the bottom of this hill; it's tricky, but fun. If you travel 100 yards too far you'll hit the inner loop.

Continuing on the outer loop, you'll climb a few hills and arrive at a long, gradual downhill that looks more imposing than it is. Enjoy the ride and check out view of part of Duluth off to your left. Trees block much of the view, but since this is one of the high points on the trail, it's the best you'll get.

A steep, short downhill marks your exit from the trail's high point. The hill is not too difficult if the snow is soft, but if it's icy, you should

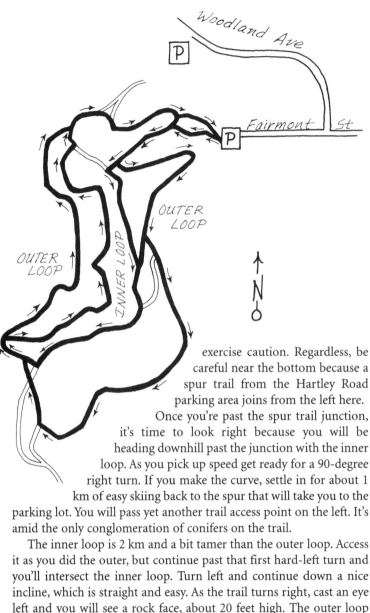

exercise caution. Regardless, be careful near the bottom because a spur trail from the Hartley Road parking area joins from the left here. Once you're past the spur trail junction, it's time to look right because you will be heading downhill past the junction with the inner loop. As you pick up speed get ready for a 90-degree right turn. If you make the curve, settle in for about 1 km of easy skiing back to the spur that will take you to the parking lot. You will pass yet another trail access point on the left. It's amid the only conglomeration of conifers on the trail.

The inner loop is 2 km and a bit tamer than the outer loop. Access it as you did the outer, but continue past that first hard-left turn and you'll intersect the inner loop. Turn left and continue down a nice incline, which is straight and easy. As the trail turns right, cast an eye left and you will see a rock face, about 20 feet high. The outer loop cuts across the top of this rock face. There are some interesting formations here that are worth a look.

You will reach a wooden sign that points you right, down a long hill. Care is required here because besides the hill, the trail joins with the outer loop for a bit and skiers may be coming from the left, also down a hill. Once the trails join, you will pick up speed, and then have to make an almost impossible 170-degree turn in order to stay on the inner loop. Control is recommended.

If you've avoided sliding onto and around the outer loop, you'll stride up a small hill, then glide down a short but fast little downhill before you enter a swampy section of trail. There are some small trees around, but the major constituent of the winter-visible plant community is the often impenetrable, speckled alder.

When you reach some jack pines and other conifers, you are close to an access point at the north end of the trail. Loop out around and past this access and you will approach the spur trail that leads to where you parked.

Journal: I stop at the top of a hill and notice a woman off to the right of the trail, picking her way between trees and big boulders. The hill doesn't look too bad, and I wonder why she's seeking an alternate route down. I find out shortly after launching myself downhill. Small pieces of rock are sticking up out of the hillside trail. I snow-plow hard to a stop, missing one sharp shard by a pole's thickness. Then I sidestep the rest of the way down the hill. When I meet the woman past the bottom of the hill, she gives me a wry smile before I ski on ahead.

Jay Cooke State Park Trails

Directions: From the intersection of I-35 and Highway 210 just south of Cloquet, take 210 approximately 6 miles east. After the road enters the park, go approximately 3 miles to the park headquarters and picnic area on the right. Or climb up into and through the park on 210 from Fond du Lac, which is east of the park.

Grooming: The trails are diagonal stride only.

Total km: system, 51; this tour, 10

Fee: Minnesota Ski Pass and State Park sticker required

Trailhead facilities: The state park headquarters is an interesting old stone building, with fireplace, vending machines, and bathrooms.

Contact: Jay Cooke State Park, 500 E. Highway 210, Carlton, MN 55718; (218) 384-4610.

Start your ski from the parking lot adjacent to the headquarters and picnic area. You had best carry your skis for a little ways. Head toward the river, which flows behind the park headquarters building. Although I skied over the swinging bridge that spans the St. Louis River, I suggest you walk, unless there is quite a bit of snow. The bridge does swing, and creak, and squeak. Halfway across you can see up and down the river quite well. Unless it is well below zero, there will be open water between slabs of ice and snow-covered rock. Although seemingly high off the river, a bridge at this spot was washed out by spring floods back in 1950. Standing there, it's difficult imagining such a torrent of water.

Once across the bridge continue walking up the hill on the other side. When you see some diagonal ski tracks, put on your skis, and take off. The Silver Creek Trail cuts left at an intersection near the top of the hill. The system is exceptionally well-marked, with trail maps at each junction.

The woods are full of small red and sugar maple, aspen, birch, cedar, and spruce. You will glide past a three-stemmed basswood on the left. Farther left is the St. Louis River and its broad valley, a valley carved 10,000 years ago by glacial-melt water, not by the current river. There will be opportunities for viewing both the river—with some open water coursing between patches of ice and snow—and the hill-

139

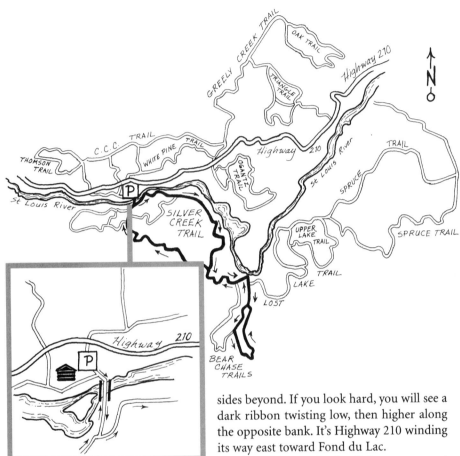

sides beyond. If you look hard, you will see a dark ribbon twisting low, then higher along the opposite bank. It's Highway 210 winding its way east toward Fond du Lac.

Along this stretch of trail there are several downhills, with occasional gentle curves. One downhill is posted with a caution sign. It is the most difficult, but unless conditions are icy or many skiers have fallen before you, the hills are nothing to worry about.

As you curve right, into a parklike, semiopen area dotted with spruce and birch, the trail divides. Take the left branch. It's only 10 m to a picnic table and log shelter on the edge of a precipice that drops off about 50 feet to Silver Creek. This is one of the loveliest views on the Silver Creek Trail. Directly below is the creek, meandering toward its confluence with the St. Louis River. The creek is often free of ice, its rippled sandy bottom visible from your vantage point. The river valley recedes in the distance, its hillsides dotted by conifers, spruce spires pointing skyward.

When you're ready, ski away from the creek and toward a bluff that rises behind where you'd been standing. The trail winds through some small, flagpole-sized aspen, then down to a junction in an aggregation of spruce. Silver Creek Trail goes right, but you want to head toward Lost Lake Trail, so go left. It's only 20 m down to an iron-railed bridge over Silver Creek. As you cross the bridge, note how open this creek bed is, with few alder or other woody shrubs. The deer probably keep the vegetation clipped off. The day I skied here, deer tracks crossed the bridge.

The trail takes you into the lowland creek bed. There are brown seed heads everywhere: stiff and showy goldenrod, tansy, and asters, plus lots of tan grasses that stick above the snow. Red-twig dogwood punctuates the landscape, although it's been heavily browsed by deer.

Aspen grow on the higher ground, on rounded hillsides softened even more by snow. You will gradually climb such a hillside, then curve around to another junction and trail-side shelter. Check out the overlook; a sign near the shelter points to it. The view is of the river valley and the bluffs beyond. Two towers associated with Minnesota Power's Thompson Hydro Electric Station peek out from behind one of the bluffs and are an intrusion on the scenic view. (The station, across the river along Highway 210, is really quite fascinating and worth a visit.)

Back to the trail, head left, to another junction and some—what else—overhead power lines. The Bear Chase Trails are to the right, Lost Lake to the left. Go right for this tour. After about 200 m of trail, take the East Bear Chase Trail right. It meanders up a small creek bed. The hills seem like they grow taller on each side as you make seven creek crossings on pierlike wooden bridges. The trees are lovely: cedar, spruce, and black ash near you and the creek; birch and aspen farther up the hillsides. There are even some ghosts along the creek. These almost white, barkless, dead-but-statuesque trees are all that remain of wonderful old American elms, victims of the imported Dutch elm disease.

You will pass some red oak trees, many of these dying because of either oak blight or chestnut borer. Then the trail curves left and begins a climb. Although only about 30 m, the climb is steep and will get you huffing after your leisurely cruise along the creek.

You will trace the narrow edge of a windswept ridge top, which drops off into a deep valley on both sides. The view right is of distant ridges and it's exceptional—one of the best on the tour.

It isn't long before you cash in the altitude. The first drop is steep and quick, then after a short up and down, you will descend a long ridge back to the junction with East Bear Chase.

You are now headed back over country you have already skied. Once you cross the Silver Creek bridge, bear left and you are back on the Silver Creek Trail, covering new ground. The trail hugs the bottom of a steep hill on the right, flirting with the edge of some wetlands near Silver Creek. After a large, marshy opening on the left, the trail goes up a little 3-m-high spine of land that comes off the hillside. From the top of this bump, which is really some surface bedrock, you can see a large open area ahead. Ski on down and across a bridge. To your right is a massive beaver dam and an equally impressive beaver pond beyond.

You will then begin a slow climb, which increases in steepness until you come to an open-sided shelter. The view here is good, but keep climbing and you will get a panoramic view of the entire river valley you've been skiing in up until this point. It's as if a giant bowl has been carved out of the Precambrian stone bedrock, covered with assorted vegetation and sprinkled with snow.

When you reach the next junction, go right, then straight at the next junction, which is within 200 m. There are some large trees through here: yellow birch, white pine, and one red oak right next to the trail that's three feet in diameter—the largest tree you've seen today.

When you can see the river ahead, turn right at the junction and you will ski back to the hill above the bridge. Don't ski down the hill. Rocks have a way of sneaking up to the top of the snow pack and wreaking havoc with your ski bases.

The swinging bridge is just ahead and your car beyond.

Journal: Perhaps Bear Chase Trail's name should be changed to Deer Chase. As I began dropping off the ridge top near the end of Bear Chase, I saw a deer ahead of me and below. It paralleled the trail for some way, then cut across in front of me as I plummeted toward it. I had hit two deer with vehicles the past summer, and was briefly afraid I might score another one. The deer disappeared over a ridge, and I relaxed.

42

Lester-Amity Ski Trail

Directions: From downtown Duluth, take Superior Street east to Lester River Road. Go left on Lester River Road one block. Parking area is on left.

Grooming: The trail is groomed for both diagonal and skate skiing, and is generally wide enough to accommodate both. The trail receives a lot of use, and can become hard-packed.

Total km: system, 15; this tour, 8; lighted, 5

Fee: Minnesota Ski Pass required

Trailhead facilities: Although Lester Park serves as the trailhead, there are no winter facilities there.

Contact: City of Duluth, Parks and Recreation, 12 East Fourth St., Duluth, MN 55805; (218) 723-3337. Or Duluth Cross County Ski Trail Hotline, (218) 723-3678.

Lester-Amity is a fun place to ski. There's something inviting about the terrain. Perhaps it's the playful loops or the sometimes surprising length of the downhills.

What isn't inviting is the hill climb that begins your ski. In order to reach the hill and trailhead, you have to cross a cute stone bridge from the parking area, head into the park, and walk right toward a large wooden sign that declares the trail name. Otherwise pleasant, with large pines forming a canopy at the trail's entrance, the hill ahead can be imposing. And if its a low-snow year—or late in the season when the sun's strength is returning—there will be bare spots.

Overcome this small obstacle, and climb the hill. Actually, you'll continue on a gentle uphill for almost a kilometer. When you reach Point A on the map, you have an option of turning left and heading back down to the park and parking area.

If you don't go left, you'll arrive at another junction. The trail to the right heads to the golf course. It's not always open, and unless you want to check it out, continue straight. You'll pass another junction, where the return trail from the golf course rejoins this trail. If you look through the trees to the right you will be able to see a ridge with some tall pine and spruce sticking up over the other trees. Soon you'll reach Junction B, another opportunity to turn back.

If you haven't been faint of heart, you will be rewarded with the trail's only official scenic overlook in about .5 km. The trail traces the

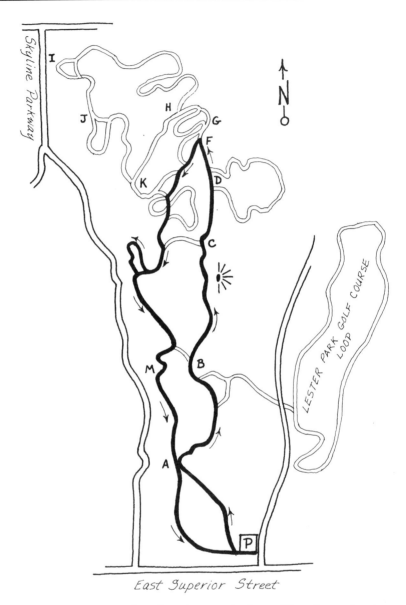

East Superior Street

edge of a sheer 50-foot drop down to the Lester River. Across the river valley you can see pine, spruce, and deciduous trees along the ridge. The river itself is below, usually ice covered, often with snowshoe and ski tracks imprinted on it. Slightly upstream from where you stand is a little frozen waterfall, sometimes shining a bubbly blue color.

As you continue your ski, you will reach Junction C. If you turn left here and begin your return journey, you will avoid a couple of fast downhills. If you go straight, you will reach another junction, D, from which a right turn will take you on a loop of slightly less than 1 km of intermediate difficulty. This loop rejoins the trail you've been skiing on and then reaches Junction F. Beyond F the main trail loops back and forth, avoiding the steepest hills but still providing some thrills. There are junctions, here at F and at G, I, and J where short spur trails loop out down and up hills. These are exciting excursions for thrill seekers. They are all rated advanced.

You may turn left here at F, negotiate a short, steep downhill, and rejoin the main trail—headed south now—back toward the park. This is an area of the trail where several junctions within an few hundred meters can get you confused. As long as you stop and look at the maps posted on trees and light poles along the way, you won't get too turned around. You will pass a trail joining from the left; this is the short trail connection to Junction C, which you passed on your way out. After crossing a snowmobile trail there will be a trail heading right. Take it if you want to get a nice view of some hills and see a hockey complex. Where the loop curves back on itself, there is a fine overlook of a deep valley and a pine-covered ridge beyond. There's also a road down below, but it isn't easily visible from your vantage point.

The hockey complex lies to the right as you scream down a great hill. The run is long and fast, but it's also straight. The only difficulty occurs when there isn't enough snow, which means that dirt, grass, and rocks threaten the bottoms of your skis.

Just after the downhill, you will rejoin the main trail. You'll pass a parking area some folk use to access the trail; it's on the right. Then it's about 1.5 km back to the park and parking area. Remember the climbing you did early in the excursion? It's payback time! You'll be gliding most of the way home.

When you reach the park, check out the large white pine off to the right, along the bank of Amity Creek. It's over three feet in diameter and probably around 200 years old.

43

Magney-Snively Ski Trail

Directions: From the Boundary Avenue exit of I-35, take Skyline Parkway toward Spirit Mountain. Go past the parking areas for the downhill and cross-country areas to where the plowed part of Skyline Parkway ends. The parking area is on the left, trailhead on the right.

Grooming: There have been attempts to groom this trail for both skating and striding. Unfortunately it's too narrow, and the day I skied it the striding track was so far left that I kept getting slapped in the face by saplings and brush. This should be a striding-only trail.

Total km: system, 14; this tour, 4

Fee: Minnesota Ski Pass required

Trailhead facilities: none

Contact: City of Duluth, Parks and Recreation, 12 E. Fourth St., Duluth, MN 55805; (218) 723-3337. Or Duluth Cross County Ski Trail Hotline, (218) 723-3678.

Although a city trail, Magney-Snively feels really remote. After walking across Skyline Parkway to the trailhead, you will have no further contact with man-made things except, of course, trail-related items such as signs and evidence of grooming (and the ubiquitous snowmobile trail). There is often a snowplow-created bank that you have to surmount before you reach the trail. Most people walk up the first hill from the road to where there's a sign announcing the trail name.

Once you clip on your skis, get ready to climb. The trail tilts gradually uphill for most of the first half kilometer to the initial junction where the returning loop rejoins the trail. Bear left here, and climb some more, to the next junction, this one with the Bardons Peak Loop. There's a large, routed wooden sign here that points the way. Take another left and you are headed for one of the finest overlooks on the North Shore.

There are some larger trees here, especially some nice yellow birch. There are also many rees with broken tops, testament to the wind-swept elevation. If you look around, you will get a feeling that you are up high. When you peer past the trees, there's nothing but sky.

The trail has been mostly uphill or flat so far, but now you will

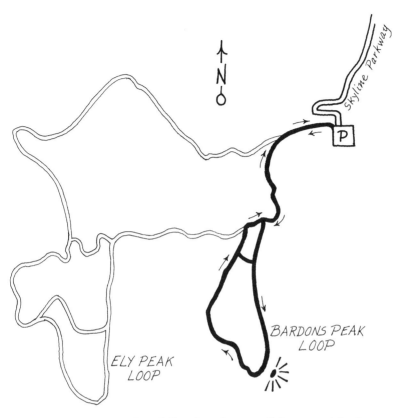

encounter some easy downhills. There is a cutoff that goes right. Just after this cutoff is a downhill that can be quite fast. Then there are two more downhills, each a bit easier than the previous one. It seems counterintuitive that you are skiing downhill in order to reach Bardons Peak. At the end of the third downhill, there's a lovely 18-inch-diameter basswood next to the trail on the left. Its trunk is straight and clear, without limbs to at least 30 feet above the ground.

As you ski on, you will note that the trees get smaller, more wizened. There are also more bedrock outcrops, although it can be difficult to see these because snow blankets them. Their south, sun-facing side is often visible, especially late in winter when warm March rays melt a season-long accumulation of cold crystals.

When the trees are hardly more than shrubs, you will begin seeing the vista. The hill slopes away gently, down to a precipice. In front of you is well over 100 square miles of two states, and one Great Lake. From the left, there is the North Shore, stretching up toward Two Harbors. Duluth looks tiny: puny buildings barely visible below. There's the harbor, both Duluth's and Superior's; giant ore boats are almost invisible against the urban jumble. The city of Superior is so spread out on the flat plain that you can't really see it. The South Shore curves off toward Squaw Bay and the Apostle Islands beyond. Perhaps most outstanding is the St. Louis River basin. This historic and geologically fascinating river twists below you, spilling into several lakes before reaching Superior. And the noise of two cities rumbles up the side of the bluff: trains, heavy machinery, and even a dog's plaintive wail. The experience here should not be missed.

After you leave the overlook, you will ski along the bluff edge for a bit. Before you leave the edge, look left and you can see Ely Peak in the distance. There's an overlook there, too, toward the southwest and Jay Cooke State Park.

The trail climbs up several small hills that are comparable to the downhills you skied coming out to Bardons Peak. Then there's a tricky downhill that cuts right near the bottom. Staying in the track is all but impossible, so be ready to jump out. You will pass the cutoff that would take you back out to Bardons Peak, then reach the junction with the main trail. A left would take you out on the main loop and toward the Ely Peak Loop. Go right and you are headed back to the parking area on the two-way trail. When you reach the next junction, which is within 50 meters, bear left and get ready for downhill fun. It's a short, fast ride to the next junction, where the full loop returns. Then the downhills continue as you glide your way back to the final downhill to the road. You might consider removing your skis up by the trailhead sign; the road, with its snowbank, can be daunting.

Journal: As I ski Magney-Snively I get more frustrated with each branch that slaps me in the face. Try as I might, I can't seem to miss all of them. I am in the striding track, but that track is way too far left. Sometimes the brush knocks my left pole off kilter, and I miss a pole plant. Sometimes I plant the pole, but it finds only soft snow, plunges deeper, and I almost tip over.

This is the worst grooming I've encountered all season. There are 12-inch-high snow walls across the trail from where the groomer lifted his drag, and the striding track is nonexistent up many hills, even though it isn't that steep and I could stride. Then, down a hill, I don't see a branch and it hits me full, across the face. Ouch! I resolve that this will be a short tour. Too bad, because this is a lovely place.

Snowflake Ski Center Trails

Directions: From the corner of 4th Avenue and Superior Street near the center of downtown Duluth, take 4th Avenue north five blocks to Mesaba Avenue. Enter the entrance ramp and head north to the stop-and-go light at Central Entrance Road. (There is a monolithic First United Methodist Church on the northeast corner). Turn left onto Central Entrance Road and go west several blocks until you reach another stop-and-go light at Arlington Avenue. Turn right here, and go north about 1 mile to an intersection with Arrowhead Road. Continue past Arrowhead, and you will be on Rice Lake Road. Snowflake will be on the right side of the road, in approximately a mile.

Grooming: Both skating and diagonal. There is a nice, wide skating lane and an intelligently placed striding track set to one side. The trail is well-groomed, in winter and in summer when brush cutting helps make a better trail come winter.

Total km: system, 13.5; this tour, 13.5; 5 lighted

Fee: yes

Trailhead facilities: The trailhead building is a log-sided chalet with two stories. On top, where you enter from the parking lot, is an area with chairs and a few tables next to a counter where trail passes and skiing accouterments are sold and rented. There is also a snack bar with packaged foods such as peanuts and chips, plus pop and juices. Downstairs is another open area leading to washrooms, showers, wax room, and sauna. There is even a piano and a ping-pong table in the open area.

Contact: Snowflake Cross Country Ski Center, 4348 Rice Lake Rd., Duluth, MN 55811; (218) 726-1550.

This is a complete Nordic center (unless you're a purist and need a ski jump to feel complete.) One cannot describe Snowflake without mentioning its creator/owner, George Hovland. George founded the center in 1992, after moving on from another local Nordic center at Spirit Mountain (see page 154). Hovland loves to ski and has been doing so since age 2. He represented the United States in the 1952 Olympics. As Hovland tells it, he was supposed to compete in Nordic combined, which includes ski jumping and cross-country. But when the folks in Europe saw him jump, they suggested he just ski cross-country. According to Hovland

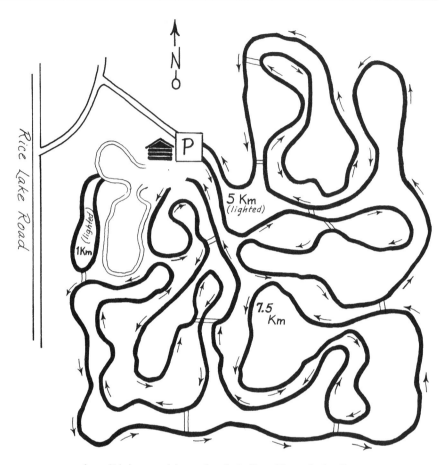

they didn't want him to be their first Olympic fatality.

Those who love cross-country skiing are especially glad Hovland didn't kill himself jumping. He's put together a wonderful Nordic system, and designed the trails here, which reflect his knowledge of how a trail should flow. All too often flow is ignored in favor of gut-wrenching climbs and butt-busting descents. If you want such anaerobic experiences, head for Wisconsin's Birkebeiner trail north of County OO, or the Alps at Nine-Mile Forest near Wausau, Wisconsin. What you get at Snowflake are roller-coaster-like hills, with a couple more abrupt climbs and downhills in between.

There are three segments at Snowflake. There's a 1 km lighted loop south and east of the chalet. This is an essentially flat trail, perfect for young kids, timid beginners, and parents pulling little kids in sleds. As a bonus, the trail is sheltered in the system's only coniferous forest, mostly balsam fir. There is a bit of a hill leading down to the loop from the parking area and topside entrance to the chalet. Consider hauling your gear down the hill and starting on the flat. Otherwise, give the hill a try; there is a lot of wide-open stopping room before you enter the woods.

The 5 km loop starts just north of the chalet. Most of it is lighted. Like the 7.5 km loop, it is packed onto the available acreage like a coiled snake and there are many opportunities to cross over onto a different section. Resist this if you can, because it will interfere with the flow of the ski, which is something that makes these trails special. About 1 km into your ski, the trail makes a gentle, 180-degree right turn. This will be the first of many such turns—all of which have just the right radius, permitting a quick tempo, outside ski-skate turn. If you're striding, you can execute an in-track, outside ski-skate turn and have just as much fun.

A couple of turns farther down the trail, you'll parallel a more open, farmlike field for half a kilometer. Sometimes you can observe planes as they land or take off from the Duluth airport, which is just a couple miles away. After looping around another wonderful corner, then a gentle climb and subsequent downhill, you will see a large metal building off in the distance through the trees. This is a tennis center. There's also a tall communications tower next to the building. After more rolling hills, you'll pass the building again, and curve down a gentle hill back to the chalet.

The 7.5 km trail exits the open area near where the 5 km trail started. It greets you with a nice, quick and easy downhill, then a couple of uphills. The first three-quarters of a kilometer is lighted, up to where a cutoff left takes you to the end of the 7.5 km trail and keeps you under the lights. Continuing past the cutoff you'll encounter the first significant downhill in the system. It's a gradual decline, and feels wonderful on good snow. In icy conditions it can be a bit tricky. After a curve left, and some climbing, you'll see a crumbling old log structure on your left, which dates back many decades—long before there was a ski trail here.

After the log structure, you'll curve right and begin a long descent with a sweeping curve right. There's a little bump at the end of the downhill, which when approached fast enough can get you airborne. There's also a cutoff left that will shorten your ski by about a kilometer if you choose it.

If you don't take the cutoff, you will ski up onto a ridge. The trail parallels Rice Lake Road for .5 km and then goes higher; you'll make one of the longest climbs on the trail. The reward is a nice long downhill. You will find yourself amid balsam fir near the bottom of the hill, and there's a cutoff right that leads you to the 1 km beginner's loop if you feel tired.

If you stay on the 7.5 km loop, you'll parallel the road again, heading back the way you came. You'll reach a high point in a clearing, from which you can see south across Rice Lake Road and off to the next ridgeline. From here, you'll start a descent that looks steeper than it is. There are four little knobs in the descent that slow you up, and make for a fun run.

The trail continues mostly north for more than a kilometer and turns when it reaches the edge of an open field. Because of some fruit-producing shrubs and trees growing in the edge between the field and forest, you may see some winter birds, perhaps waxwings, or maybe grosbeaks.

When the trail turns away from the field, you can see the 5 km trail occasionally off to the right. There's at least one cutoff if you want to go there. After more rolling trail and a couple of steeper, short climbs and descents, you will cruise by the old log cabin again, well above it on the hillside, then zip down a speedy hill to the chalet at the end of the 7.5 km trail.

Journal: When I ask George Hovland to name his favorite ski trail, he assumes a pained look. He asks, "In the world?" I respond, "No, in the U.S." He thinks for a while, then responds that here, at Snowflake, is perhaps his favorite, partly because it's convenient for him. But he qualifies that by saying, "Such a difficult question. You probably know, it's not so much the place you ski, it's the . . . skiing." Indeed.

Chester Bowl

Directions: From the intersection with Kenwood Avebue, take East Skyline Drive northeast to the Chester Bowl entrance on the left.

Grooming: This trail is groomed for skating.

Total km: 3

Fee: Minnesota Ski Pass required

Trailhead facilities: There's a chalet with bathrooms. There's also a ski jump here, and some downhill facilities located in the Chester Bowl.

Contact: City of Duluth, Parks and Recreation, 12 E. Fourth St., Duluth, MN 55805; (218) 723-3337. Or Duluth Cross County Ski Trail Hotline, (218) 723-3678.

I drove around central Duluth for more than half an hour looking for this trail. I never found it, and wasn't able to get back and try it. Hence, there's no tour.

Chester Bowl is reportedly a difficult ski, with steep hills and difficult corners. There's also a nice view of Lake Superior.

Piedmont Ski Trail

Directions: From the intersection of Highway 53 and Piedmont Avenue, take Piedmont north two blocks to Hutchinson Road. Go left on Hutchinson and go .7 mile to the parking area on the left. Adirondack Street will be on the right.

Grooming: The trail is double tracked, classic only.

Total km: 4

Fee: Minnesota Ski Pass required

Trailhead facilities: none

Contact: City of Duluth, Parks and Recreation, 12 E. Fourth St., Duluth, MN 55805; (218) 723-3337. Or Duluth Cross County Ski Trail Hotline, (218) 723-3678.

This is a short system that provides some scenic overlooks of the St. Louis River valley. I didn't ski here, so there is no tour.

Spirit Mountain Trails

Directions: From the I-35 Boundary Avenue exit, take Skyline Parkway toward Spirit Mountain. Go past the parking areas for the downhill, which are on the left, to a sign and short driveway for the cross-country trails, which are on the right.

Grooming: These are well-groomed trails that accommodate both striding and skating.

Total km: 22

Fee: yes

Trailhead facilities: There is an equipment rental/warming house at the trailhead. Pop and other snacks are sold.

Contact: Spirit Mountain, 9500 Spirit Mountain Pl., Duluth, MN 55810; (800) 642-6377.

Designed in a user-friendly loop system, the four loops offer all levels of difficulty. The "night skiing" 2 km loop meanders through a campground, affording some through-the-trees views of the St. Louis River valley.

I skied here and liked it. The flow of the trail is exceptional. The reason I didn't include my tour is that, as of press time, these trails are threatened by proposed development of a golf course. Make sure you call ahead if you plan to ski here.

VIII

The Near North Shore

Gooseberry Falls State Park

Directions: Park entrance is approximately 12 miles northeast of Two Harbors on the lake side of Highway 61. Take the park road to the parking lot by the Visitor Center.

Grooming: This is a well-groomed park. Two sets of diagonal tracks are laid down next to one another, facilitating skiing with a partner, or passing.

Total km: system, 21; this tour, 5.5

Fee: Minnesota Ski Pass, State Park sticker required

Trailhead facilities: Constructed in 1995 and 1996, the visitor center is almost as impressive as its surroundings. A cooperative effort between the Minnesota Departments of Transportation and Natural Resources, the building was constructed with many recycled materials, some from as far away as San Francisco. (Not surprisingly for such a nice, new building, you will find restrooms and other amenities, including vending machines in the center.) The displays and art-work are of museum quality. One exhibit is of a wolf; enclosed in a glass-walled case, the black-tipped, silver-haired creature comes alive. At 121 pounds, it's the largest wolf ever recovered in Minnesota. It was hit by a truck just a few miles down Highway 61 near the Split Rock River.

Contact: Gooseberry Falls State Park, 3206 Highway 61, Two Harbors, MN 55616; (218) 834-3855.

The ski trails are all accessible from a connector link that runs just to the right of the walkway up to the front door of the Visitor Center. Hop on the trail and head away from the parking lot. This will take you around the north side of the center and up toward Highway 61. Before you reach the highway, there's a massive stone wall on the left side. This is a retaining wall, built in the late 1930s by the Civilian Conservation Corps (CCC). It's 300 feet long, 15 to 25 feet high and 10 feet wide at its base. The suitcase-sized, mostly four-sided chunks of granite that comprise the wall weigh hundreds, perhaps thousands, of pounds each.

As you curve left around the wall, toward the road, you will see the river valley and another architectural wonder: the Highway 61 bridge that spans the river. Finished about the same time as the Visitor

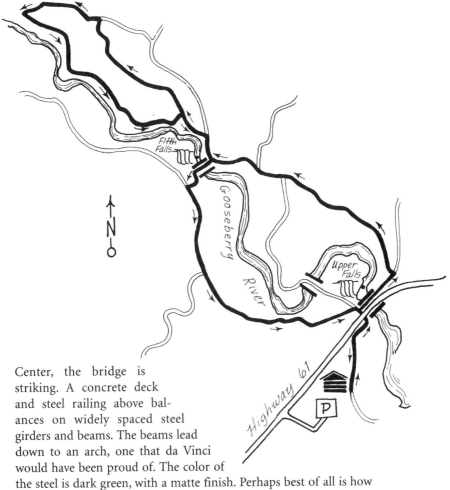

Center, the bridge is striking. A concrete deck and steel railing above balances on widely spaced steel girders and beams. The beams lead down to an arch, one that da Vinci would have been proud of. The color of the steel is dark green, with a matte finish. Perhaps best of all is how the designers blended the structure in with the surrounding stone. The supporting steel beams are grounded in surface bedrock on each side of the river so they look as though they grew there. And where the bridge deck leaves land near the old retaining wall, that wall goes right up to the deck, again making a smooth, visually satisfying transition.

Once you have crossed under the highway, go right at the junction and ski across the river on a subdeck of the bridge. The Upper Falls are visible on the left. Usually in winter all you can see is ice. The trail takes you by Falls View Shelter, another CCC rock-building project.

At the first junction go left, into some towering aspen. You will pass a deer exclosure on the right. The woods are comprised of aspen and birch, with some larger and smaller spruce. Then there are lots of dead birch that likely died of birch borer, which is a pest that burrows into the tree and girdles it. Past the next junction where you want to go straight, the grade is up, but very gradual. A ravine is visible off to the left. This is the Gooseberry River valley.

At the next junction bear left. The woods become dotted with cedar trees: short, stocky, conical crowns visible through the birch limbs. The next junction is very near the edge of the ravine and the river. As you ski with the river on your left, look right and see an intact birch woods. Although not dense, the stand is healthy, and the white trunks stand up from a carpet of brown grasses sticking above the snow. A few red-twig dogwood lend color.

The trail takes you through a stand of small, Christmas-tree-sized spruce, then a stand of 20-foot-tall aspen before you reach another junction. Bear left past some alder, then go right at the next junction. You will climb a bit, nothing difficult, then have your first free ride downhill in a long time. After another down, then up, get ready for a demanding downhill. What makes it difficult is the tightness of the left turn: You will twist about 120 degrees within 50 m.

When you coast to a stop, look on the side of the trail. You will see the park's largest tree, an impressive three-foot-diameter white spruce and just beyond it is a two-foot-diameter white cedar. The loggers missed this spot. Don't you wish they could have missed more.

Past the cedar, the river is only a couple of ski pole lengths away. This is a quiet place. For the next .7 km or so enjoy a gentle ski along a peaceful, ice-coated river. Look for animal prints. Beaver live here, and mink, and bigger creatures, too. Deer prints are frequently seen, as are fox and coyote, and even timber wolf. Enjoy the solitude.

Next is this tour's longest climb up out of the river valley and to a junction. Go right and retrace your ski back two more junctions to where the trail heads back down into the valley. A sign tells you that you should take off your skis and walk to the bridge, but if you are careful, you can ski it. The bridge crosses the river at Fifth Falls. Between the snow and the ice it's difficult to see a falls, but the view is lovely just the same. Downriver, rock ledge walls encase the riverbed. Brownish green cedar-bough pillows encase the rock ledges. And two scruffy white pine observe it all.

Climb up the other side of the river past where the trail levels out. Just beyond where the ski tracks begin again, there's a path left, back toward the river. This is the Fifth Falls Snowshoe Trail. I skied it, but must suggest you don't. It's a tough descent-ascent, and there's not that much to see, except a wooden Adirondack-type shelter that looks as though most of the population of Duluth have carved their initials on it.

Continue up the trail to the main trail and go left. You get to glide about 400 m until you reach a cedar woods. Although not very expansive, this woods have the dark, deep-woods feel of an authentic cedar swamp. Then the trail climbs just enough to afford you a final view of the river valley. It's a gradual slide down to another junction—this one with the snowmobile trail—just before you reach the final left turn and downhill that takes you back to the Highway 61 bridge. Go right, under the bridge, and follow the trail back the way you came out.

Journal: Paul Sundberg, the Park Manager at Gooseberry is a river skier. It seems there is a (fool?)hardy group of local North Shore skiers who get a kick out of skiing up and down some of the local rivers.

Paul suggested that I try the Devil Track River, just north of Grand Marais. He assured me it was a really safe river. When I went and checked out the river from the Highway 61 bridge, I wondered about his advice. Standing on the highway bridge looking upriver, I could see open water. There was a small spit of ice and snow that bent around both sides of the water, but I couldn't imagine skiing so close to a rushing torrent of ice water. I contemplated making the attempt, but remembered that old saw about discretion being the better part of valor. I got back in my car and called it a day.

46

Korkki Nordic Trail

Directions: Take Highway 61 north from Duluth to Homestead Road. Turn left (northwest) and go approximately 2 miles to Korkki Road. Turn left on Korkki and the trailhead is about .5 mile on the right.

Grooming: This is a difficult trail to groom because it is so narrow. It is generally well-groomed, with a single striding track.

Total km: system, 10, plus some short cutoff trails; this tour, 10

Fee: donation

Trailhead facilities: There is a very nice warming house. It is not always open, usually just on weekends and some weekdays.

Contact: Korkki Nordic Ski Center, 1711 Korrki Road, Duluth, MN 55804, (218) 525-7326.

This is a difficult trail. It's made so by its narrowness, not necessarily its hills. There is really not much vertical relief here, as the trail swings up and down lowland areas, only once climbing up onto much of a hill. But don't be fooled. A short downhill with a curve and nearby trees at the bottom can be tough—and Korkki is tough.

The trail was initially developed in 1955 by a renowned and revered local skier named Charlie Banks. It has a proud history, perhaps most notably being the site of the first women's National Cross-Country Ski Championships in 1967. The shelter was built in 1992.

When I skied Korkki, there were no maps available at the trailhead, but luckily a fellow named Scott Moore, a true aficionado of the trail system, drew me a map from memory. There was also a peculiar information sheet titled, "Course Rules and Protocol." Most striking was the following: "The trail is an advanced trail, designed for racers. The course will be extremely difficult for many skiers." It then goes on to list some alternative trails. It is a difficult ski—but rewarding.

Start at the parking area and go right. The first kilometer winds through a mixture of alder, aspen, spruce, and shrubs. The downhills are short but quick, and can be tricky when there's a curve at the bottom.

The first real downhill takes you into a black ash swamp, where the trail swings left and then climbs back up to higher ground. You will feel the narrowness of the trail here if you haven't already.

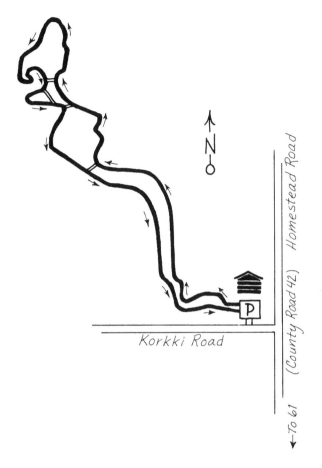

The 2 km cutoff is just after the first of several bridge crossings. Note that boughs have been laid across the bridge boards so snow will collect better on the bridge. Here and on all the ensuing bridge crossings, be careful not to get your pole caught between the boards.

The trail continues to the 4 km cutoff, crossing another bridge and providing some limited but attractive views of semiopen wetlands and of birch reaching above the conifers. There is a long, flat stretch that gradually begins up a hill. Before too long you are herringboning to the top of the biggest hill yet. Note there are red oak and sugar maple along the trail for the first time, a sure sign you are on higher, drier ground.

When you reach the 6 km cutoff, a sign warns you that proceeding on what's called Brian's Loop should only be attempted by advanced skiers. Past the cutoff about 100 m, the trail dips down the longest hill thus far. Although the runout at the bottom is straight, there are some serious moguls. After another climb, the trail bends right and drops.

This downhill wouldn't be difficult, except that the runout is over a narrow bridge. If you get nervous about such things, hike down.

After the trail crosses the bridge, there are three herringbone pitches before it traces an eskerlike ridge for .5 km. There's a large area of flooded trees on the right, then on the left. Beaver must be active here. As you loop left on the esker, there is a sudden downhill, not too steep, but with another bridge crossing at the bottom. Then it's up onto another snaking esker, this one identified with a sign, "Wolf Kill Ridge." The drop off this esker isn't as sharp or long as the last, and it takes you into a muskeg, something that hasn't been seen on this trail before. There's a large beaver house on the right.

From the muskeg, you start the longest herringbone climb on the trail. And after the climb, another 50 m of uphill striding awaits—if your wax is working. Your reward for the climb comes right after a sign that reads, "Caution, steep hills." Yes, hills, plural. I walked down the first one, psyched out by all the warnings. It really wasn't that bad. The next hill, which immediately follows, is the steepest of the bunch, but it isn't too long and the runout burns off your speed before you hit Fryberger's Curve, a hard left. When you see "Frank's Rest" on a sign, get ready for the last of this series of downhills.

The trail rises and falls like a roller coaster for the next couple hundred meters before it crosses another muskeg, this one without a beaver house. It's a short climb to another sign that announces, "Big Hill." There is a cutoff, and since Big Hill was closed when I skied here, I can't describe it for you. The cutoff climbs briefly, then begins a long, gradual, fun descent. There are a couple of 18-inch-diameter white spruce on the left, just before the 4 km cutoff joins the trail.

From here the trail's almost all a gradual downhill, which makes for a fun finish. Indeed, I didn't remember climbing enough on the way out to have earned this payback. Nice surprise!

Journal: Skiing for the first time at Korkki, I was just getting a feel for the trail's narrowness when I reached the first bridge. I strode across with confidence—until my right pole's basket caught between two bridge boards.

Since I was moving forward at a brisk pace, my right arm extended backward just as briskly, and when it could extend no farther, it yanked my entire body down into the snow. An instant replay would have been great.

Once down on the ground, I found myself unable to stand up. No, I wasn't hurt, but the pole was still stuck, and the pole strap was tight around my wrist so I couldn't get it off. The rest of my body was sprawled out prone, and I couldn't get my skis under me because my right arm was stuck in an outstretched position, toward the bridge. Then I started laughing. Never laugh if you are trying to stand up on skis, even if your arm and pole aren't stuck to a bridge. It took me at least two minutes before I finally wriggled my right arm out of the pole strap. I was still laughing.

47

Northwoods Ski Trail

Directions: From the intersection of Highway 61 and Outer Drive in Silver Bay, head inland 3 miles (Outer Drive becomes Penn Boulevard and Lake County Highway 5). The parking area and trailhead are on the right.

Grooming: The trail is packed by snowmobile and the narrow path is set with a striding track.

Total km: system, 19; this tour, 10

Fee: Minnesota Ski Pass required

Trailhead facilities: none

Contact: Northwoods Ski Touring Club, P.O. Box 52, Silver Bay, MN 55614; (218) 226-3803.

This is a cozy trail, but it also provides some of the best vistas on the North Shore. Ski off from the trailhead into an aspen woods thickly understoried by small balsam fir. The East Branch of the Beaver River bobs and weaves off to your left, and the trail follows. By the time you reach the first junction, the fir are larger, as are some of the spruce. Looking left, the river valley widens and is full of alder. Beyond the valley are hills, complete with some towering white pine.

At the next junction, you can record something for posterity in a guest book that you can find in a wooden box set on a post. Just beyond the guest book junction is the first real downhill—it's an easy one. The view to the left just gets better, with a vaster alder thicket and higher hills beyond. At one point the trail crosses part of that thicket, then runs beside Cedar Creek.

After the trail crosses a snowmobile trail it enters a more open low area. In the distance, yellow and rust colored aspen and birch branches paint a hillside, more subtle than the strokes of fall leaves, but just as lovely.

You cross an area of small trees, an area that was logged not long ago. Then you enter a completely treeless area, the size of a big yard; this is where the logs were stacked. The openness affords you a view to the east, where treed hillside meets naked bluff, covered in drifts of white.

163

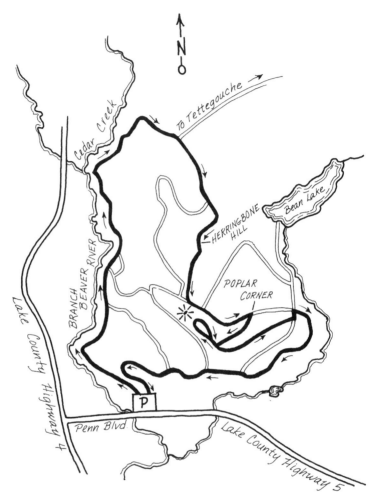

On the far side of the opening, the trail splits. This is Big Pine Corner, and indeed a large white pine sits on the left of the trail. That trail, where the white pine sits, goes to Mic Mac Lake and connects with the Tettegouche State Park system. A sign on a tree 50 meters toward the park reads, "You are now entering Palisade Valley, 4.8 kilometers to Tettagouche Trails." It's a lovely, unique ski because of the high bluffs on either side of the trail.

The trail that goes right is the one you want. You will climb up a broad valley for the next 600 m, to the next junction. Continue straight past the junction and you will be on the steepest climb of the tour. Two large white spruce on each side of the trail herald the climb's beginning. This isn't called Herringbone Hill for nothing: that's the only technique that works for the next couple hundred meters. The reward is the view off to the right, through birch trees that stand above small balsam fir. The ridgeline that you see is at least 4 miles away.

When the herringboneing is over, the striding is still uphill, until the land very quickly tips down. The downhill that follows is not unreasonable; it's fairly straight, and not as steep as the uphill grade. Other skier's sitzmarks might trip you up, but otherwise it's very ski-able—as long as it isn't icy. After you've glided to the next intersec-tion, look straight ahead. There's a gradual slope, then an abrupt vertical. The top is about 150 feet above you, which is where you are headed. Turn left and ski out into a clearing dotted with some aspen and past a junction that goes left. It's an uphill stride to the next junc-tion, where you want to go right. This is Poplar Corner.

There isn't much climbing, but you are gaining altitude as you ski through a birch woods. Then the trail divides again. Go right, sweep around a curve and uphill a bit until you reach one more junction. Although the trail trends straight, go left. You may see some sitzmarks near this junction. You will find out why in a minute.

After bearing left, it's only a few meters until you can see a view—and what a view. It gets better and better, and when you climb a little herringbone hill the entire valley stretches out beneath you. One more little herringbone maneuver and you are near the top of that rock wall you saw from the end of your long downhill slide a few min-utes ago. Wow! If it's clear and you look south you can see Lake Superior through a couple of notches in the hills. Even more amaz-ingly, beyond the lake, you can see Wisconsin.

There's a small, 15-foot-tall spruce tree in the center of the plateau you are on, and the groomer usually makes a circle around it. Close to the edge, make the trip around. You can see west, north, some east, and south. What more could you want? This is a cool place: wild and windswept, what a mountaintop should be.

If you are worried about the trip down, don't be. Somehow the person who designed this trail manages to get you back down a ser-pentine slide-way without a major drop. Still, remember those sitz marks near where the trail divided on the way here. Some folks crash, but the downhill isn't bad. The worst piece of downhill is farther on. Retrace your ski tracks back to the next trail division where the trail bears right. There's a short, but steep, little dip to the right as this overlook loop joins back up with the main trail.

Once back down and on the main trail, you'll ski into and through a birch woods that are old enough to have some character. When you reach the next junction, go past it a bit for a look up at the bare rock hillside ahead and the giant beaver pond below. The trail continues on to Bean Lake, but you want to go back to the junction and bear left. A long, somewhat steep downhill isn't far. This section of trail is rated expert, but the hill's not too bad.

After the downhill, you ski through alder and aspen, and there's a large open area on the left—another beaver pond from a dam on a small creek that runs there. A large ridge runs along on the other side of the creek, and the trail parallels it for a while.

Continue past the next junction, across the snowmobile trail, and see the sign that reads, "Trailhead, 1 mile." There's one more neat view from a clearing—this of the East Beaver River valley—then the trail dips down to the parking area.

Tettegouche State Park
Yellow Birch Trail

Directions: Travel 4.5 miles northeast from Silver Bay on Highway 61. The park entrance is on the right. To reach the trailhead take the park road to its end, where there is a large parking area.

Grooming: The trails are groomed for diagonal striding only.

Total km: system, 22 (including the connecting trail to Northwoods Ski Trail in Silver Bay); this tour, 7.5

Fee: Minnesota Ski Pass and State Park admission required

Trailhead facilities: Outhouses, although there's a visitor center at the park office, near the park entrance.

Contact: Tettegouche State Park, 5702 Highway 61 East, Silver Bay, MN 55614; (218) 226-6365.

The trailhead at Tettegouche isn't very pretty. The trees are scrubby and there's too much fencing visible. But the fence is for a good cause: The six-foot-high circles of welded wire surround pine seedlings that, without the protection, would be eaten by deer in a millisecond. The other fence, on the left side of the trail as you head up the hill from the parking area, is part of a deer exclosure. The University of Minnesota at Duluth is conducting some experiments on the germination and growth of white cedar when deer are kept away. Most deer exclosures that I have seen are at least eight feet high, sometimes 10 feet. This one seems too short. Any deer worth her salt could easily clear the top with one effortless bound.

At the top of the hill you've been climbing are some larger white pine. They are wonderfully picturesque and mark the beginning of a lovely landscape. A short downhill takes you into white cedar, then you'll make a gradual climb up to the High Falls Overlook cutoff, which goes right. If you are sure of your skiing ability and it isn't icy, try skiing down to the stairs at the overlook. Otherwise take a hike. The trail is a tricky ski because it's ungroomed, packed only by hikers, and less than two feet wide. Snowplowing for speed control is out of the question. The way to slow up is to keep one ski in the deeper, untrodden snow on either side of the packed stuff. Even then there will be some speed and given that there are a couple of tree-lined tight

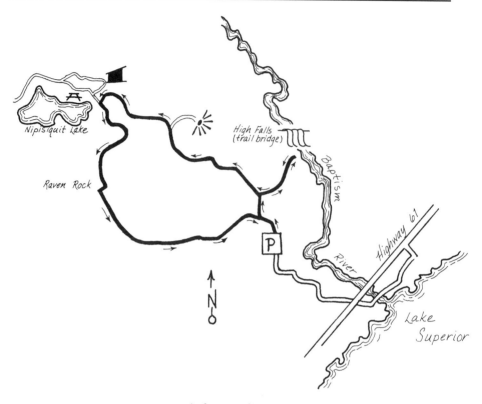

corners, you may wind up needing to bail out on your butt. The trickiest spot is preceded by a flat-to-slightly-uphill section followed by a 90-degree left. Conifers obscure the 8 m of relatively steep downhill just past the left turn, and then the 80-degree right turn. A tree stands ready to greet you at the outside of this last turn. I suggest sidestepping at least half of the 8 m downhill.

Your reward, at the bottom of some stairs that really must be walked, is an overlook of the highest falls in Minnesota. It's 70 feet from where the river begins its drop over the rock ledge down to the pool below. In winter you often see not water but ice, which freezes as the spray shoots out over the falls. There will usually be some water visible at the bottom of the falls. Ice climbers frequent the frozen falls.

When you are done viewing the falls, head back the way you came, being careful with the couple of downhill pitches. You will be surprised there are any, given the ride you had getting down here!

Go right at the junction with the main trail and you will glide down a gentle hill into a cedar stand. Listen for the chickadees that frequent this dense cover. They often provide a melodious serenade.

Then the trail winds through an open aspen, birch, and alder stand that is followed by a 20 m descent to a little bridge, an easy 30 m climb, and then a 15 m climb up the steepest grade so far on this tour.

It will test your wax and uphill technique. This climb levels off gradually and you will find yourself in an even more open woods, with few trees more than 20 feet high.

After a long, level stretch you will reach the cutoff to a Lake Superior overlook. I didn't ski this because it was untrodden and the snow was deep. If you choose to ski it, remember that it is uphill going out. It's the return ski that could present a problem.

From the overlook cutoff, continue down the main trail on a nice, easy grade surrounded by taller aspen and birch. Then climb again, into more conifers. If you look right, you will see a hillside with an almost vertical rock face close to the trail. A gradual downhill will take you away from the hill and across a snowmobile trail. The ski trail then becomes a multiuse one, which allows snowmobiles for the 50 m or so down to Nipisiquit Lake picnic area. Before you get to the lake you will cross a little bridge and off to the left is a three-acre wetland, complete with cattails and red-twig dogwood. It's a pretty site. So is Nipisiquit Lake, worth a ski down to it through the picnic area.

One leg of the ski trail here loops up and around the lake, and then goes on for several kilometers. As you stand with your back to the lake, the leg you want for this tour goes to the right. You will cross a bridge at the bottom of a short hill just after you leave the lake. The creek here is lovely, with beach-ball-sized rocks dolloped with snow sitting amid dark, cold, free-flowing water.

Some impressively large white spruce mark your entrance into an expanse of wonderful old-growth trees. The trail cuts through the middle of a spruce grove. One of the biggest, on the right, is more than two feet in diameter and about 100 feet high.

The trail climbs another hill at the top of which is a big white cedar leaning across the trail. Then you start seeing large yellow birch. These relatives of white or paper birch (both are genus Betula) are not unusual here on the North Shore, but a collection of trees of this size is rare anywhere. The trail leaves the old birch stand briefly, but then passes through an almost pure stand of younger yellow birch—another rarity here on the North Shore. Eventually the trail heads roller-coaster-like back into the big trees again before it reaches a junction with the Superior Hiking Trail.

The road to Raven Rock is to the right. You want to head left, staying on the ski trail. On the right, Raven Rock presents its jumbled rock face as you ski down the trail. After a very short climb you will notice that the earth to your left has disappeared. Actually, it's still there, but it drops off so steeply you can't see it. This is a hint that this ski is going to get exciting really soon.

The impending downhill can be lots of fun. It can also be dangerous, not because it is particularly steep, but because it goes on and on. As you start downhill, the rock face on the right is close by, but you soon leave it behind. Try looking up into the canopy. Notice the tree-sized limbs of big yellow birch as they arch and twist across the sky. It can be a view that makes you dizzy.

When you see a wall-like stand of cedar, white spruce, and a few white pine ahead, you are almost halfway down the hill. You will cross a 20 m level spot, and then continue going down. About the time you think your glissade has to be over, you'll see a yellow caution triangle posted on a cedar trunk. The trail will curve right and continue down, but less steeply than it did before. Finally, you will come to an uphill, which signals the end of your wonderful ride and almost the end of the trail. You will pass another deer exclosure fence on the right, then cross a snowmobile trail. There's one more little downhill, another deer fence, and then you will reach a junction. Turn right, and it is a mild downhill glide to the parking area.

Journal: Temperature, snow conditions, your skis, your wind resistance, and a few other things all combine with the steepness of a downhill slope to determine what your terminal velocity will be (sorry about the word terminal, but that's what it's called). Terminal velocity is the top speed you will reach going down the hill. If the slope here on the Yellow Birch Trail is icy and fast, your terminal velocity will be 30 or 40 mph. You probably don't want to go that fast. The day I skied the Yellow Birch loop it was 35 degrees, an inch of ungroomed snow sat on top of the snowpack, and the humidity was 100 percent. The snow was really slow. Making things slower still were my waxless skis. My ride down the hill was not fast at all. My terminal velocity wasn't more than 15 mph and I loved looking skyward as I passed below the giant limbs of the yellow birch.

IX

The Far North Shore

Bally Creek Trails

Directions:	From the intersection of Highway 61 and County 13 just southwest of Grand Marais, turn away from Lake Superior on 13. When 13 makes a T intersection with County 7, go left. Just past the intersection with County 6, go right at County 48. Stay on 48 until it turns left. Go straight at this turn, and you will be on Forest Service Road 158. Take this to where the snowplow stopped and you will be at the Bally Creek Trailhead. The parking area and trailhead sign are on the left. The cabins at Bally Creek Camp are on the right. The one visible from the trailhead is named Moose Lips Lodge (see photo).
Grooming:	The trail is packed by snowmobile and groomed with a Tid-Tech. Skiing is diagonal stride only.
Total km:	system, 18; this tour, 12
Fee:	Minnesota Ski Pass required
Trailhead facilities:	None, but rental cabins are available.
Contact:	Bear Track Outfitting Co., Box 937, Grand Marais, MN 55604; (218) 387-1162 or (800) 795-8068.

The Bally Creek system sits in the middle of some active forestry endeavors. That's euphemistic, for there has been a great deal of tree cutting in and around this trail system. This tour takes you through some planted red pine and white spruce—tree plantations. It also exposes you to clear-cut areas that were cut within a year of the publication of this book, with more planned in the future. Yet there are two features of the trail that make it a must ski. One is the frequent presence of moose, and the other is an incredible view of Eagle Mountain, the highest point in Minnesota.

From the parking area, ski down Forest Service Road 158, past where the snowplow stopped plowing. There's a wide, inviting track here, suitable for skate skiing, but the rest of this system is narrow single track. When the trail cuts right into the woods, follow it. There is a short section of trail through bigger trees, then the trail exits the woods into a large area that was clear-cut in the mid-1990s. Red pine have been planted on the right side of the trail. There's a view of a ridgeline farther to the right. The trail loops gently uphill and left to a junction in the middle of the clear-cut. If you head right, there's a long, gradual glide down to a cedar woods, then an narrow trail that leads back to the cabins and the parking area. This little trail comes complete with in-your-face cedar boughs.

Our tour takes us left, farther up the hill, toward a couple of lonely looking white pine saved by the forester. (Actually, they were saved by David Williams, owner of Bear Track Outfitting Co., the fellow who grooms these trails. He worked with the forest service people prior to the cut and made sure the pines were saved—this after a state harvest nearby cost the forest a couple of venerable old pine trees.) There are more white pine farther up the ridge. You will curve left, then hook back right, all the while in the clear-cut area and climbing. After the curve ends, you top out and start a long, quite gradual downhill. Look out on the horizon straight ahead: If it's clear you can see Eagle Mountain, the highest point in Minnesota, at 2,301 feet above sea level. You are at about 1,700 feet. There are actually two massive bluffs in the distance, the bigger one on the left is Eagle Mountain.

After a good look it's time to tend to your skiing, because there's a long downhill ahead; it's not difficult, but does need your attention. Moose can tear up the trail, and their tracks are not uncommon here. As you slide through an area of smaller, recently cut trees into another 60-acre-or-so clear-cut, you may see a moose.

Before the trail dips into a woods again, look back where you've been. There's nothing to see—the top of the hill you came over is hidden by a couple of intervening ridges.

There's a junction just inside the woods. A right turn takes you down about 10 vertical feet, out to Bally Creek, and into a large open area, likely

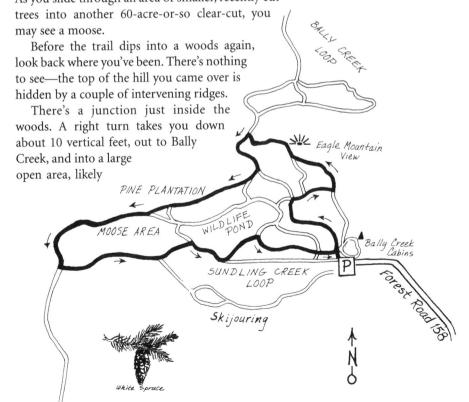

a big beaver pond. Go left and you will ski to Forest Service Road 158. Go left when you reach it, and climb up past the clear-cut area to a junction. You want to go right. Notice the white pine near here and along the trail for a little way. They are just teenagers, 30 to 50 feet tall. It's good to see some younger pine; they should grace this trail for hundreds of years. A humbling thought.

There's a nice stretch of double-pole downhill to the next intersection. Don't go left, but head straight. The trail here is roadlike, with obviously cleared shoulders. It is pretty flat. Continue straight at the next junction, too, and you will see the tip of a dead cedar far up the trail. As you near it, you can see four live cedar near the dead one. They look soft, rounded in form, especially compared to the nearby balsam fir with razor-sharp outlines and narrow spires that cut an edge into the sky. Once you reach the cedar, notice that they are quite large, maybe two feet in diameter. They are also tall for cedar, perhaps 60 or even 70 feet.

The trail curves left, cuts through an open area, then circles back to the right. It enters an area where red pine have been planted on the left, and white spruce on the right. Snowshoe hare love it here, under the dense canopy of 20-to-30-foot-tall pine and spruce. There will be tracks all over.

Don't take the next left, which is a cutoff and connects with the trail after it loops around up ahead. Instead, go straight until you see the trail bend left into a conifer tunnel. Balsam fir line the trail, making a dense wall. Red pine close in overhead, making a ceiling. Snow dripping from every branch caulks up the open areas between trees and branches, making for a cozy, cavelike feeling.

As you emerge from your cave, you will reach the Big Cedar, which is indeed large, about 30 inches in diameter. If you look up, note that it isn't as tall as those you saw earlier. The big cedar marks the end of the pines for a while. It's about 30 m to a junction. If you go right, you will be on your way to Cascade State Park. Go left and ski past a pond on the right, and then into an unfortunate scene. The clear-cut is bad enough, but the forestry people at the Minnesota DNR have butchered the landscape. They have had a bulldozer scrape all the slash, brush, and stumps (plus an untold amount of precious topsoil) into long, 10-foot-high rows with football-field-sized flat areas between. Pine have been planted in the football fields. It would seem a travesty anywhere, but here it seems even worse.

Steel your eyes to the ugliness and ski on; you will put the awfulness behind you soon enough. Go right at the next junction, near the edge of the clear-cut, and you will ski into a birch-aspen woods and encounter a gradual downhill. Then you'll have to negotiate a real downhill, the first one since just after your view of Eagle Mountain. It's up a little hill and you are at another junction. If you go right you will connect up with a skijor trail that uses a logging road through the middle of a clear-cut. Go left and you will climb, needing to herring-bone a bit. At the next junction go right, then left at the next.

The trail curves around a beaver pond on the left. As the curve straightens out, look left and you can see the beaver lodge out in the pond. You can ski over to the pond and you will see brownish green cedar that ring the pond. There are even some small cedar, which are rare many places due to an excessive deer population and the attendant overbrowsing. At the next junction bear right, then go straight at the next and you will be back to your car.

Journal: I can see the big lake out my window. I can see the wind whip water and create a froth against a distant rock outcrop. I figure 20 mph gusts and the television says 21. The temperature is nine degrees Fahrenheit. At least the sun is out.

This is my first day in Grand Marais and I'm set to ski some remote trails. As I exit the motel, the wind is so strong it requires a shoulder against the door to open it. Adding insult, the wind takes my breath away as I walk into it toward my car.

Once I'm at the Bally Creek trailhead the woods lend some shelter, but the car rocks as the wind rakes over it. Then I'm out on the trail, a long stretch of road skiing—cold, but tolerable. By the time I hit the clear-cut area, I am too warm and strip off my windbreaker. That's why, when the snow devil swept past, I felt not a chill, but awe. A 30-foot-high pillar of snow, twisting tornadolike, bounced down the hill-side, traveling a couple hundred yards before flinging itself apart, billions of snow crystals glistening in the late morning sunlight. How could I feel cold?

50

Cascade River State Park

Directions: Approximately 21 miles northeast of Tofte, at mile marker 101 on Highway 61.

Grooming: Trails are groomed for diagonal stride only.

Total km: system, 11; this tour 4

Fee: Minnesota Ski Pass and State Park sticker required

Trailhead facilities: None, but the park office has a restroom and someone who can tell you about the trail conditions.

Contact: Cascade River State Park, 3481 W. Highway 61, Lutsen, MN 55612; (218) 387-3053.

This tour takes you to the cascades of the Cascade River. It involves some walking, and involves removing your skis at least once.

Finding the parking area may be the most difficult part of this ski. From the park entrance, follow the signs to the campground. When you reach the entrance (this is the tricky part), turn right. You will pass the ski trailhead on the right, then park immediately beyond. If, as I did, you miss the right turn and find yourself driving by Campsites A-2, A-4, etc., just keep on driving; you will reach the same parking area, just from the other direction.

Head out on your skis and bear left at the first junction, less than 100 meters into your ski. Although the woods are thin—understocked as foresters say—the spruce are all the more striking. They are tall and narrow, with branches bunched into enormous needle pom-poms. While the trunks are not big in diameter—less than two feet—the trees are notable for their height. Stop and crane your neck up at one. I almost fell because as I leaned back, my skis slid out from under me.

When the trail reaches another junction, about 120 m farther, you have reached the cutoff to the cascades. If you like, you can ski the first three-quarters of the way down. You really should stop at the top of some stairs. There's a green circle ahead with a wavy white line through it denoting an "easy" trail, but don't believe it! Hike down to the bridge, only 20 m, and look upriver (right). Depending on the conditions, water flow, temperature, and accumulated snowfall, there

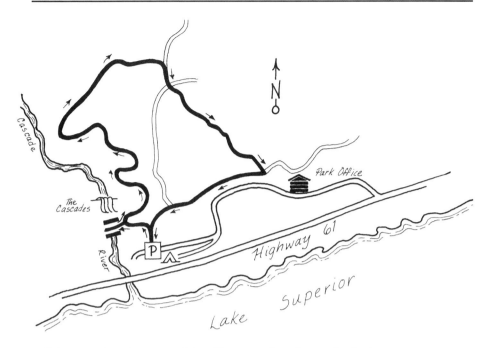

will be cascades of water and ice. There are four drops, the farthest upriver may be difficult to see.

Get back to the main ski trail however you would like—with or without skis—then with skis attached, go left. Within the next 400 m there are several opportunities to remove your skis and head left in order to see the river gorge, as the Superior Hiking Trail parallels the river below you. In the next .4 km the trail takes you higher; you will gain about 100 feet of elevation. You will also pass through an area where 70 percent of the trees blew down some years past. There are still some of the tall spruce, but most of the wood is on the ground. A very common small tree in this area, sometimes shrublike because it's a favorite deer and moose browse, is mountain maple (*Acer spicatum*). Also called moose maple, this tree often colonizes an area after disturbance.

The trail has moved away from the edge of the Cascade River ravine, but if you look straight ahead and slightly left, you will see the outline of Lookout Mountain. Skiing toward it you will reach a point that overlooks the river gorge. This point of land harbors several large white pine, remnants of vast tracts that covered this and other river basins along the North Shore before the 1900s. Lookout Mountain is also visible across the river.

The trail curves right at the point, changing direction by 90 degrees. A new landform that you will be following for the next kilometer or so is on your left. It's a deep ravine, as deep as the one which the Cascade River courses through. The little creek at the bottom is known locally as Trout Creek, a name someone on the park crew gave it while building the bridge used by the Superior Hiking Trail.

The trail proceeds along the edge of the Trout Creek ravine and enters an old-growth cedar stand. Many of the cedar are over two feet in diameter, which is large for a tree with growth rings that are often only a millimeter apart. Toward the end of the cedar grove you will encounter some large aspen. The bark of these trees is very dark; perhaps a lichen has taken hold on the outside of the tree and colors it.

When the trail reaches a junction, go right, then straight in about 50 m where you reach another junction (a right turn will cut off about .4 m of this tour and take you down the steepest trail in the park). Even if you go straight, be ready to glide; you are in for about .7 km of downhill. There are several little jogs in the trail that can be difficult at high speed, so control your speed while descending. There's also a little mogul formed by a tree root about halfway down, that, with the help of a sun-thawed soft spot, sent my upper half down the trail ahead of my bottom half—at full speed! I think I slid about 10 m before enough snow built up under my chin to stop me.

When you reach the next junction, turn right. It's about .5 km of mostly level skiing back to the parking area.

51

Deer Yard Lake Trails

Directions: From either Grand Marais or Highway 61, 8 miles southwest of Grand Marais, take County 7 to County 45. Go west on 45 to Forest Road. Continue straight on Forest Road when 45 goes right. The parking area is about 1 mile on the left.

Grooming: The trails are groomed for diagonal stride.

Total km: system, 18; this tour, 14.3

Fee: Minnesota Ski Pass required

Trailhead facilities: none

Contact: Cascade Lodge, HC3, Box 445, Lutsen, MN 55612; (218) 387-1112.

This ski starts through a mixed bag of small pine, spruce, and shrubs. There are some plantation pine on the right. Look hard and you can see some seedling cedar hiding on the edge of the pine.

You'll reach a junction where you go right, then climb a bit, into bigger trees, mostly birch and maple. A deep ravine develops on the right, and you will pass a big old white pine growing downslope, just over the edge of the ravine. It lost its top some years ago in a windstorm, but looks healthy today.

There's an easy downhill, then some fairly level skiing through mostly maple. A very large cedar sits a couple of ski pole lengths to the right of the trail. When you reach the short spur that takes you out onto Deer Yard Lake, head on down; the slide is short and easy. Once out on the ice, take a look toward the opposite shore. Cedar hug the lakeshore, climbing only a short way up the hillside. There's an impressive (for the North Shore) stand of white pine on this end of the lake, above the cedar. While it's possible to ski along the lake, it can be difficult hacking your way back to the groomed trail, so go on back up the way you came down. Go right when you reach the trail.

For most of the next kilometer the trail stays down close to the lake, and cuts through some magnificent lowland forest. The cedar are big—some more than 18 inches in diameter—and some of the yellow birch are more than two feet in diameter. There are a lot of blown-over trees, too. When windstorms cross the lake these trees are the forest's first line of defense. Where the trail traverses slightly higher ground, you'll pass by some incredible white spruce that are up to 100 feet tall. And they are verdant: thick, with dense needles on tightly packed branches.

Soon after you see the spruce, you will see a big white pine down the trail. This tree and others that follow, are more than 100 feet tall, two to three feet in diameter, and well over 125 years old. Some of the pines have dead tops, probably the result of lightning strikes. A big white pine can endure much hardship, living 10, 20, or even more years with major damage.

Once the trail curves left almost 90 degrees and climbs a bit, you are skiing through an almost pure maple woods. You have rounded the trail corner south of the lake and are headed away from it. Soon there's the first downhill of any significance, and it has a sharp curve at the bottom. There's also a signpost to the right side of the trail, and a big yellow birch on the left.

The trail is level for about a 100 m, while it winds through a birch forest. Then it makes a sharp left and begins to climb. The maple trees get bigger as you get higher. As you curve right near the top of the hill, get ready for a long downhill that is gentle at first, steeper later. It ends at an extraordinary spot. A wooden sign is posted on a little spruce near a ribbon of water eight feet below. The sign reads, "Water." A quart cooking pan and a white cup hang from the sign on nails. The water ribbon below is only about a foot wide, but you can see water flowing briskly. Somehow it emerges from underneath the trail you are standing on. Drink if you like, but from what I'd read about the threat of Giardia microorganisms, I passed.

The trail climbs a bit from the little spring back into maple woods. A rock face appears on the left. It's about 30 to 40 feet high and sheer. It would be a likely spot for a bear den. Then there's a sudden downhill, not too steep, but you'll get going fast enough that you may miss the biggest maple of the tour, on the left. It's well over two feet in diameter.

The trail curves left after the big maple, passes an almost three-foot-diameter cedar, and then reaches two junctions. The first is with a trail that goes right. Keep going to the next junction, which is with a trail that goes left. This trail takes you up to the highest point on this trail, 1,881 feet above sea level. It's the highest point on any North Shore trail in this book.

The trail is actually an old road that used to lead to a fire tower. It's groomed shoulder to shoulder. A striding track is set on each side, with lots of room in between for snowplowing on the way down. The climb is significant, about 200 feet. The view is of Deer Yard Lake, which is a band of white through a lot of maple branches. A little slice of Lake Superior is also visible. The ride down is fun. It took me 15 minutes to climb up, and two minutes getting down. There are two

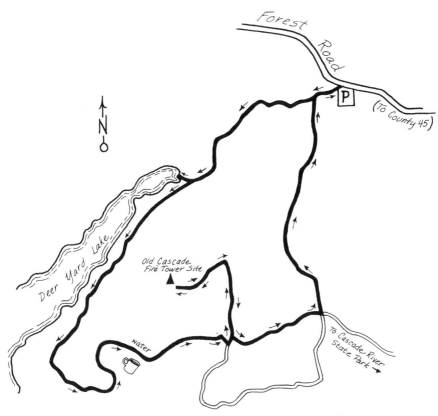

level sections so it's not impossible to control your speed. But if it's icy, I would think twice before making the climb.

Once back at the bottom, turn left, and continue toward the next junction, which you can glide all the way to, about 800 m. Make sure you turn left at the junction and don't slide past, or you will be heading for Cascade River State Park about 5 km away, and about four times as far from where you parked your car.

Once you've gone left, the trail dips, then climbs to a view of the hill you were just up on top of. Be impressed with your accomplishment. After another little dip into an alder-filled valley, then a little climb out, the trail enters an alleylike chute lined with 10-foot-high spruce that look like they were hand-planted. This long, mostly straight and flat stretch is a great place for practicing your diagonal stride. Set a good pace—maybe 80 percent of your maximum speed—then stick with it regardless of the terrain. It will entertain you on what can seem like an interminable piece of trail. When the spruce end and red pine appear, you are nearing the end. Remember to head right at the junction, and it's less than 200 m to the parking area.

Judge C. R. Magney State Park

Directions: From Grand Marais, take Highway 61 for 14 miles northeast to the park entrance on the left.

Grooming: Odd but effective. There is no track set here, just a packed trail that is ski-pole wide. Why not track? Since most of the trail is uphill going out, it's downhill coming back. With no track, it's easier negotiating the narrow path when heading downhill: There are no grooves to catch your edges on.

Total km: system, 5.5; this tour, 5.5

Fee: Minnesota Ski Pass, State Park sticker required

Trailhead facilities: none

Contact: Judge C. R. Magney State Park, 4051 E. Highway 61, Grand Marais, MN 55604; (218) 387-3039.

There are two separate trails here, and we will tour both of them. Let's do the longer one first. Head out from the parking lot through an open field. Go right and you will reach where the trails start. There is a signboard there. Go left from the sign, then turn right, and you are off on the trail.

The hill goes down for a few meters, then starts up. There is quite a bit of balsam fir on this section of trail, some of which are fairly large. There are virtually no downhills the entire 1.5 kilometers until you reach Gauthier Creek, save a few undulations. Although the general lay of the land is uphill, the ski is not difficult.

The river valley lies to your right, and there are occasional glimpses out across it, but nothing really down into it until later in this tour. Not far from the trailhead you will begin seeing large aspen. You will pass one on your left that is almost on the trail. It is more than 20 inches in diameter. Then climb two steeper bumps and you will have a good view of more big, towering aspen ahead. If there aren't any clouds, you will see the lovely contrast of the light, almost white trunks and branches of aspen against the brazenly blue sky.

Ski on into and past some spruce. If you haven't noticed yet, look at the mosslike material that hangs down from the lower branches. This is actually lichen. Lichen are a combination of fungi and algae that grow symbiotically. The local name for these lichen is old man's beard.

Just before the trail makes one of its infrequent dips, into a little ravine, there is a white pine on the right. You will see more of these later. As you climb up out of the ravine, there are more big aspen. One of these, right next to the trail on the left, is about 30 inches in diameter. The largest aspen in the country is only 36 inches. This would be a good place to search for championship-sized aspen as there are a lot of big specimens around you. They are more than 75 feet tall, and some don't have any branches until 50 feet up their trunk. Their tops look stiff and strikingly broomlike, as limbs reach upward, sweeping the sky.

The approach to Gauthier Creek is downhill, with a curve right. The day I skied here it looked as if the groomer had missed the curve recently. Snowmobile tracks lead into a tangle of alder behind the trail sign on the left. The alder were broken and laying in all directions, and there were lots of people tracks in the snow around the area. You want to ski on down to the bridge and cross the creek.

At the trail junction across the bridge, go right. You will return on the left. The aspen are younger here, and soon you should start seeing deer signs.

One leapt across the trail in front of me. Interestingly, you will also begin seeing six-foot-high circles of two-by-four-inch welded wire fencing. These are put over individual pine seedlings to protect them from deer. Just a bit farther, a fenced deer exclosure begins. A sign on the right reads, "White Pine Restoration Project 2000."

You will come to a three-sided shelter. The trail loops back and begins its return here. But before you follow it, continue on down the sometimes ungroomed trail you've been on. It's just about 100 m until you reach a bench. Looking right you can see the river valley below you. It is several hundred feet down to the river. If you look downriver (south) on a clear day, you can even see a bit of Lake Superior.

Head back to the shelter and junction, then bear right. There's a quick little downhill, the first in a long time. It takes you into a dense spruce and fir woods. There should be plenty of deer signs here, and perhaps some wolf prints. Another downhill—the best one of the tour thus far—and then an uphill takes you out of the dense trees, back into aspen.

You will ski about .5 km along a rock face on the right, across a wet area. You are skiing along Gauthier Creek. It's a lovely little ski, which takes you across a bridge and under some black ash trees. You will reach the junction where the trail split before. Go right, cross the bridge, climb the hill up from the creek, and get set to glide. Save for a couple of short, flat-to-uphill grades, the way home is all downhill. And it's a pleasant ride that goes down gradually. Zip up your jacket if it's cold, and enjoy an exhilarating trip.

If you want to ski some more when you get back, head up the steep hill to the right of the trailhead sign. (This is actually straight as you return from skiing the long loop.) Go left at the hilltop junction. The woods are full of young birch and the trail may be peppered with birch seed. These fleur-de-lis–shaped seeds disperse from the trees all winter. If you look up you may be able to see the long catkins, which are made up of the seeds before they break apart. When you begin to see a deep chasm on the left, Gauthier Creek is below, near its confluence with the Brule River. There will be a large, open area on the right with two enormous aspen standing tall, and several others broken off high in the air. A big wind must have come in here and made the clearing.

When you can see the ravine again, check it out. It's a short ski or hike to the edge. The Brule River is below, and the view is great. If there's a strong south wind, you will hear Lake Superior waves crashing against the shore about a kilometer away.

Back on the trail, you will hug the ravine edge for a couple hundred meters, then curve right, back to the junction near the top of the hill. Go left, and be ready for the steep downhill back to the trailhead. The parking lot is left at the trailhead sign, but you may need to runout straight as you zip downhill. Then just head back toward the hill and turn right.

Journal: I don't believe in intuition. But my senses and their interaction with my environment do leave me wondering sometimes. As I skied at Magney, I became increasingly sure that there was a deer nearby. There were fresh tracks on the trail, and lots of old ones, too. Just as I was concluding that there must be deer nearby, one jumped across the trail in front of me, about 40 meters distant.

I stopped, watched her disappear into the thick spruce, and then skied on. Not long afterward, I was skiing through that dense spruce as I took the return loop. That's when I began seeing wolf prints, many of them fresh. And then I felt watched. Perhaps a wolf was nearby, looking at me as I skied past. I will never know for sure. But I like to think so.

Lookout Mountain/ Upper Ridge Run

Directions: Find Cascade Lodge on the north side of Highway 61, at mile 99. The trailhead is located straight up the entrance road, past the office building and cabins.

Grooming: The first section of this ski accommodates both skating and striding, but the trail narrows down a bit after the cutoff to Lookout Mountain. It's best to diagonal the whole thing. The Lookout Mountain section may not be groomed as often as the rest of the system.

Total km: system, 14; this tour, 7

Fee: Minnesota Ski Pass required; Cascade Lodge charges $3.50 for parking.

Trailhead facilities: The lodge offers full facilities.

Contact: Lutsen Tofte Tourism Association, P.O. Box 2248, Tofte, MN 55615; (888) 616-6784.

The trail goes out to the left from the parking area, elevation approximately 700 feet above sea level. It traverses an open area below a power line, then turns into the woods and begins climbing. For the first 600 m of trail you will gain about 10 m of elevation for every 100 m of trail length

The woods on this early section of trail are a mix: aspen, birch, balsam fir, and white spruce. Many of the birch are yellow birch, and, indeed, their silvery bark and odd exfoliation may indicate that they are hybrids of white and yellow birch.

When you reach the first junction, head right, then right again 100 m farther up the trail. Left at either of these two junctions takes you 6 km to the Hall Loop. As you ski gradually up hill, Cascade Creek is close on the right, but it isn't generally visible. You will get a better view of it on the way back.

More obvious is Lookout Mountain, seen straight ahead as you near the junction with Upper Ridge Run, where you want to bear left. As you continue toward the Lookout Mountain cutoff, check out the bare mountain rock faces, now on your left. Look at the skinny white

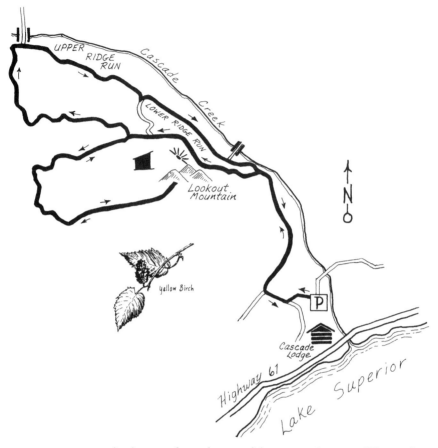

spruce jutting out above the top of the mountain. You will be up there in just a few minutes.

When you reach the junction, go left and begin a long, moderately steep climb. This is a two-way trail, so keep your eyes open for skiers coming downhill at you. By far the steepest climbing is in the first 300 m; even so, there's only one pitch that requires herringbone (depending, of course, on the snow conditions, your technique, and wax). While you climb, notice the series of little ravines off to your right. It also is possible to see the ridge that leads to the top of the mountain if you look through the treetops to the left.

Once the trail flattens out, there are several large white pine on the right. One is dead, and another leans sideways at a 30-degree angle.

The trail makes a hard left into a stand of birch, mixed with some fir and spruce. Look at the birch trunks. They are not white. They are covered with a lichen of some kind that looks almost black. Because so much of the trunk is covered, each tree appears more like a dark-barked sugar maple than a birch. If you look up at the branches, though, you will confirm that these are indeed birch.

Once in the black birch, you begin another climb, although this one is not as long or as steep as the initial pitch up the mountain. Then the trail dips twice in little drops that let you change pace and relax. Next it climbs one more time. Look around. There isn't much to see when you look out through the treetops. You are nearing the summit, which at slightly more than 1,200 feet puts you about 500 feet higher than when you started. Feeling dizzy?

It is actually slightly downhill to the shelter, then farther downhill to the overlook. Be careful if you ski this. It's best to take your skis off and walk over to the benches near the precipice. Also watch where you take off your skis. You don't want them sliding downhill and shooting off the edge of the mountain. Make sure you sign the register. Most importantly, drink in the view. Lake Superior is off to the right, but surprisingly not much of it is visible because it disappears behind highlands north of Terrace Point. Note the different hues cast by each type of treetop below: Even without leaves the poplar are yellow-green, and the evergreen cedar have a decidedly brown hue.

The trip back down is faster. It took me 35 minutes going up and 10 coming down. There aren't any technically difficult parts to the descent, but if the snow is fast—or worse, icy—you'll have to control your speed, especially when you reach the junction with Pioneer Trail/Upper Ridge Run.

Go left at the junction, and begin another climb. One pitch on this stretch is steeper than anything on the way to Lookout Mountain's summit. There are dense stands of small, four-to-six-foot-tall balsam firs through here, which lend the trail a tunnel feel. It's a good place for snowshoe hare and their friends, the foxes. Tracks of both should be evident.

When the trail makes a strong right curve and you see two gigantic aspen that are more than two feet in diameter, you will be at the end of nearly all your climbing for this tour. A junction is just past the aspen. Go left across Cascade Creek, and you are headed either for Deer Yard Lake, or the rest of Pioneer Loop. You want to go straight on Upper Ridge Run. And a run it is!

It is all downhill for the next 700 m. The trail essentially follows the same drop in elevation as does Cascade Creek, which flows off to your left. It cuts across elevation lines at about 10 m of vertical for every 100 m of trail—similar to the early climbing you did—but downhill this time. Again, there's nothing of great technical difficulty, but control your speed so you are comfortable.

If you don't look quickly, you will slide right by the junction with Lower Ridge Trail, but that's OK because you are headed in the correct direction. There is one steep drop on Lower Ridge Trail, so you may want to be looking for it.

You also will slide quickly by another junction, this one headed left—again with a trail across Cascade Creek—is where the Pioneer Loop rejoins the system. The next junction is where we took a left heading out, before we reached Lookout Mountain Trail. Retrace your path; the pitch is mostly downhill, and the left turn at the next junction can be tricky at full speed. Make that turn and another quick left, and you are finished with this tour.

54

Massie and Hall Loops

Directions: From Hansen Hjemstad Road in Lutsen, go 1 mile northeast on Highway 61 to County 41 (Hall Road). Turn left (northwest) on Hall Road, and the parking area and trailhead are on the left in about .4 mile.

Grooming: Groomed for diagonal striding with two sets of tracks, one on each side of the trail. Skating is also possible, depending on how the trail has been groomed.

Total km: system, 11.6; this tour, 10.1

Fee: Minnesota Ski Pass required

Trailhead facilities: None, but Solbakken's Nordic Resort, at mile marker 94, offers whatever you'd need.

Contact: Lutsen Tofte Tourism Association, P.O. Box 2248, Tofte, MN 55615; (8880 616-6784.

From the trailhead, head out to the west, toward Lutsen. We're going to ski the Massie and Hall Loops clockwise. Initially the forest is mostly alder, cedar, and shrubby birch. The first couple hundred meters is easy downhill. When I skied here there were lots of wolf signs: prints and scat. Deer winter in this area, leaving the higher elevations where the snow is deeper; wolves follow. Soon you will see some larger white pine scattered in the woods, then a somewhat open area; perhaps a blowdown occurred here some years ago.

It's about a 75 m climb to the first junction, where you will make a right and go a short way to another junction, this one with a sign proclaiming, "Massie Loop." Bear right and start the climb. Although not terrifically steep, the climb is steady. Two majestic white spruce on each side of the trail announce the top of this hill. Then the trail is fairly flat for a while. The area looks cut over, but may just be blown down. If you look left, you will see an old road that is now used for skijoring. The road ends at an old homestead where this trail's namesakes, the Massies, lived. You can see the homestead's open field ahead and off to the left, as the trail makes a sharp right turn and begins heading northeast.

After a couple of ups and downs the trail makes a long, maybe 150 m gradual dip. You will note that there are more and more cedar. Deer

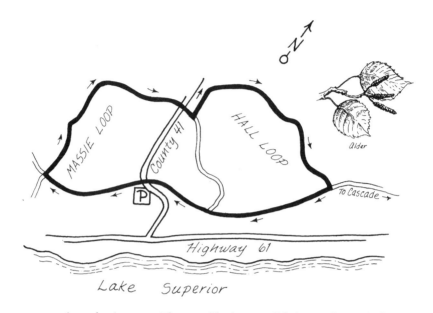

signs also increase. Then, suddenly, you glide into a dense, dark stand of cedar. This is the real thing, with a primeval feel to it. Big, two-foot-diameter trees cant upward at odd angles. The sky is gone, and you see nothing but cedar boughs above you. You are sliding through a stand of pure white cedar—Thuja occidentalis in botanical parlance.

Then you glide by a place where there is more light. The wind has knocked over some of the trees, tipping them on their sides. One's tipped over the trail, its still-green branches grace the air above your head as you slip by. If you're lucky, a raven will rasp for you as one did for me. It sent a little chill down my spine. I loved it.

As the cedar thin out and more light returns, the trail is still headed down. Then it crosses a cleared path that runs perpendicular. This is actually the unplowed continuation of Hall Road. Looking right you can see Lake Superior; left is the bluff top. Less than 100 m farther is the junction with Hall Loop.

Bear left, and climb again. If it's cold the climb will be appreciated because that last long downhill through the cedar cooled you down. The woods here are scrubby and open. The bluff is visible ahead, but don't worry, the trail bends to the right before you get there. You will pass some large individual cedar and one little copse of them that contains trees of more than 20 inches in diameter.

When the trail finally makes a strong right turn get ready for fun. There is a 100-m-long straightaway downhill that is just right if the conditions aren't icy. If it is icy, watch out. Remember: Sometimes others fall ahead of you and make big dents in the snow. This down-hill takes you out of the cedar area and into a deciduous woods. The trail flattens out for a while, then dips for 35 or so meters, curving right. A big white pine is visible on the left, about 10 m off the trail. There are a lot of alder along the trail and the snowshoe hare like it here. Their tracks should be everywhere.

The trail continues downhill, somewhat abruptly the last 100 m, to the next junction. A left takes you to the Cascade River Trail system. You want to go right and cruise along a trail that's been cut into the side of the hill. Soon there is a fairly thick cedar forest on the right, and scrub trees left. The latter area has been logged. The last 50 m before the next junction is a fairly steep downhill.

Past this junction—which is the segment of trail that makes up the northeast side of Massie Loop and southwest side of Hall Loop—there is a nice long slide. Try getting in the tracks and staying there. A bit of a squiggle in the middle of the downhill will test your resolve.

There's a brief climb after the downhill and you are back at the parking area.

Journal: No matter how hard I try not to be, I am always saddened (sometimes angered) by the results of logging, especially here on the North Shore. These thin-soiled, highly erodible ridges do not recover well from having their trees stripped from them; the last kilometer of this ski illustrates that. On the right side of the trail the woods are dense, dark, and full of bigger cedar, birch, and aspen. The left side is sparsely wooded, with few large trees. I don't like thinking about how much soil washed off the hillside when the area was logged. To be sad or angry, that is the only question.

Moose Fence Ski Loop

Directions: From the junction of Highway 61 and County 2 (Sawbill Trail) go north (away from Lake Superior) approximately 7 miles to the parking area and trailhead on the right.

Grooming: The trail is groomed one to two times a week. If there's been a big snowfall it may take a couple of days before Moose Fence Ski Loop is groomed. The trail is groomed for both skating and striding.

Total km: system 8.4; this tour, 6

Fee: Minnesota Ski Pass required

Trailhead facilities: none

Contact: Lutsen Tofte Tourism Association, P.O. Box 2248, Tofte, MN 55615; (888) 616-6784.

Your first thrill happens before you even set a ski on the Moose Fence Loop. The drive up Sawbill Road is breathtaking. The road hugs the Temperance River gorge on the left, and the view is expansive. As you near the trailhead, you will cross a bridge over Sixmile Creek. This is the same creek you will ski down to in the middle of this tour.

Before starting, read the sign at the trailhead. It explains that the 20-foot-high white pine hugging the trail on the first leg of this tour were planted by the U.S. Forest Service in an effort to find a strain resistant to the imported white pine blister rust, a disease that weakens and kills native white pine. These trails got their name from the moose-proof fence that had been erected around the perimeter of the pine. Moose love white pine seedlings and would have eaten all the trees long before the Forest Service could have determined if any trees had resistance. The study is ongoing, but the fence is gone.

Head off down the trail, which is left from where the sign sits. You'll loop around some trees and then dive into the woods around a right curve and past a steel gate. There is a long, grinding climb ahead. It took me four minutes before I got to the first downhill—an all-too-short drop of about 20 m. Then it's more climbing.

If you look off to the left, it's obvious that you are up higher than when you started. Through the treetops you can see a distant ridge. At least all the climbing wasn't for nothing. You will pass the junction

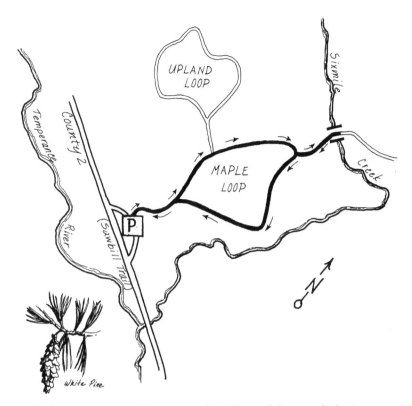

with the returning Maple Loop, on the right, and then reach the junction with Upland Loop. The Upland Loop is very flat, and cuts through 10-to-15-year-old plantations of balsam fir and white spruce.

Continuing on the Maple Loop, there is yet more climbing. The woods are mostly hardwoods, with some larger maple. This is a lovely hike in fall when the sugar maple are blazing. You may also see a large white cedar amid the maple. These occasional "upland cedar" were part of the original forest but are rare today because deer have prevented new seedlings from establishing.

When you see the cedar on the right, rejoice because there's a wonderful long, gradual downhill ahead. There aren't any tricky turns, so relax and enjoy the ride. It was along this section of trail that I saw several wolf prints. The animals had followed the trail for at least 100 meters, and there were two sets of prints. I kept hoping to see a wolf around the next curve, but didn't.

You don't need to interrupt your downhill slide when you get to the next junction; just slip on by and continue down to the bridge over Sixmile Creek. You will notice that the forest changes quite a bit as you get closer to the bridge, and into the creek bottom. From the bridge you can see lots of black spruce, a wet-loving bog tree. Cedar tolerate wet also, and there's a small one growing in the middle of the creek by the bridge. Sometimes you can see critter tracks in the snow along the creek. Otter are not unusual here.

Once you've taken in the scene, head back up the hill to the junction you flew by on the way down. Go left at the junction, and you will be pleased to find that there is more downhill. The woods—flagpole-sized aspen, birch, and some conifers—are smaller here. There is one notable exception: An ancient white pine stands out on the left.

As you approach a hard-right turn in the trail, you will be able to see a ridge in the distance straight ahead. This is the ridge on the other side of Sixmile Creek. The trail parallels this ridge and the creek for some time. If you look from several of the vantage points permitted through the trees, you will see the outline of a huge old white pine above all else on the ridge. It would be interesting to go measure this behemoth and see just how big it is; but that's for another trip—one on snowshoes.

Our loop curves right and climbs again. The climb is more gradual than the one near the trailhead, but it does go on for a while. When you notice that the woods are full of big maple again, you are almost done climbing on this tour. Also, look for the giant old yellow birch on the right. It's mostly dead, but still impressively large.

As the trail turns away from the creek, you can begin seeing another distant ridge on the left, this one on the other side of the Temperance River. It is a lot more distant than the ridge on the opposite side of Sixmile Creek. At the same time, the trail begins a descent that hardly stops until you reach the parking lot. Just make sure you bear left at the last junction, and then enjoy the return trip down the hill you climbed on your way out.

Journal: It's late afternoon, I've been driving since before noon, and I am anxious to ski. The drive up the Sawbill Trail to Moose Fence is exhilarating. The view, the anticipation of almost wilderness skiing, and the slightly slippery, snow-packed road all add to the excitement. As I don my ski boots I wonder if there's enough time left for this ski. I decide, yes there is, especially since there's a full moon tonight. I am off.

The ski goes well, I am back at the car before it's dark, and now I'm a bit disappointed because I didn't get to see the moon, which should be rising on the other side of the high ground east of the parking area.

As I drive back down the Sawbill, near where it dips into Sixmile Creek's valley, a glance left, to the east, lets me see a sublime white globe hanging amid the tree branches. It's like an exclamation point at the end of a wonderful ski.

Oberg Loop

Directions: Southwest of Lutsen take Onion River Road west and north from Highway 61 approximately 2 miles. The road is not plowed beyond the parking area, which is on the left.

Grooming: Two sets of diagonal tracks are laid down on each side of a 3 m wide trail.

Total km: system, 12.4; this tour, 10.4

Fee: Minnesota Ski Pass required

Trailhead facilities: A very chilly looking outhouse.

Contact: Lutsen Tofte Tourism Association, P.O. Box 2248, Tofte, MN 55615; (888) 616-6784.

Although there's some disagreement with my peers, I feel this trail is best skied in a clockwise direction. Either clockwise or counterclockwise, the climbing has to be equal, but clockwise seems less difficult.

Start from the northwest end (far side on the right from the entrance) of the parking lot. You will ski mostly downhill about .3 km to a junction. Go right and you will enter a flatland, which is part of the marshy bottomland along the Onion River. There's plenty of shrubby vegetation: alder, willow, and some mountain maple, but there aren't any hills. If you ski the Sawtooth area often, you will find this section of trail unique in its levelness. Make sure you look back down the trail after you're out a few hundred meters because there are some wonderful views of Leveaux Mountain.

About the time you start climbing a little, you may notice that the trees begin getting taller, then more diverse. By the time you hit a real climb, you can see a 60-foot-tall white spruce up ahead, near the top of the hill. It heralds your arrival at where the trail divides. If you head left, it's at least 5 km to a trailhead, and it is on the Sawbill Road, at least 20 miles from where you parked your car for this loop. You want to head right, but it's worth a small detour left and down the hill to the little bridge over the Onion River. The river is small here, and sometimes you can hear it rush around the rocks and under the bridge.

Go back to the junction, turn left, and climb the rest of the way up to Onion River Road. Cross over the road and begin climbing again. A large spruce and equally large cedar stand on each side of the trail near the bottom of the hill you will be climbing. If you look ahead, up the hill, you can see another tall white spruce. It is near the top of the hill. Enjoy the climb.

Past the hilltop, the trail turns right. There's a stand of 25-foot-tall, pole-sized maple on the outside of this turn. As you look down the trail, which is pretty flat right here, you can see many small birch, its new reddish tan bark blazing. Notice how the birch are only along the trail, not deeper into the woods. This is because they need more light than maple, and the trail you are skiing allows that light. There also are some upland cedar visible along this section of trail.

The trail undulates, gaining some altitude, then losing it, for the next .5 km or so. If you look right toward the end of this section you will get a glimpse of Lake Superior. Then get ready to rock! The first of three long downhills is ahead. The first is the best (read: steepest). One problem may be the sitzmarks left by those before you. The hill literally looked as if it'd been shelled with small-caliber artillery the day I skied it. And since folks were moving pretty fast when they tumbled, the craters were deep. I left one myself.

On one of these three downhills you will encounter a snowmobile-trail crossing. I went by it so fast I can't remember which hill it's near the end of. The woods through here, if you can discern them as you whip past, are full of smaller trees.

After a brief flat stretch, another downhill appears. Watch out for this one because there is a curve left at the bottom. After this down-hill, Lake Superior is visible on the left and then Oberg Mountain comes into view ahead and left. Once you cross the snowmobile trail again, and are near the next junction, look toward Oberg. You can see a rock outcrop that juts out from near the mountaintop. It must be one of the overlooks on the mountaintop hiking loop because you can see a round metal pipe that looks like a handrail.

Go right at the next junction or you will be headed for Lutsen, not as far as the Sawbill Road, but still not where you want to go. There are no more difficult hills on the rest of the trail. You will pass Oberg Lake on the right, a striking feature in the otherwise treed landscape. It isn't very big, perhaps eight acres, and looks more like a beaver pond than a lake. The dark green conifers that ring it make a lovely winter scene.

There's one last climb up and over a spine of land that leads left up Oberg Mountain. Then it's a long glide down the other side, all the way back to the parking lot.

Journal: I had seen a lot of wolf signs during these three days of North Shore skiing. Almost every trail I skied had wolf prints in the snow somewhere along the way. Yesterday, at Lookout Mountain, I'd seen some fur and a hunk of deer hide on the trail, along with lots of wolf and raven prints. Today, at Oberg, I saw another spot where wolves and ravens had eaten.

Not far from Oberg Lake the trail had been pounded by wolf; there were prints everywhere. Then I saw fur scattered along the trail. Finally, I came upon an area right on the trail that was covered so thickly with shredded fur that my skis wouldn't glide. I stopped. The fur's color made me wonder about what animal it had come from. Deer seemed an obvious choice, but there were some shreds of black fur in the mix.

I could see a large depression in the snow, off one side of the trail. There was blood splattered there, covered by a light dusting of snow that had fallen a couple of days earlier. There was also what I recognized as the contents of a stomach, frozen in the shape of the organ before varmints had eaten all but the contents. There was a lot of scat also, but it seemed too small to be wolf. I picked up some of the fur, especially some black pieces, and stuffed them into my fanny pack.

Later that day I stopped in at the Superior Forest Headquarters in Tofte. The helpful woman at the desk looked at the fur and without hesitation identified it as deer. When I asked about the black, she suggested it had come from the tail. Thinking about the deer I had seen, and especially those I'd seen close up while skinning them, I remembered such black fur, surrounding the white underside hair of the "white-tail."

I had been witness to the remnants of a brutally real North Woods drama. I counted myself lucky, and waited to see a wolf around every remaining curve on each trail I skied on my Sawtooth Mountains excursions.

Pincushion Mountain Trails

Directions: From its junction with Highway 61 in Grand Marais, take County 12, the Gunflint Trail, 1.7 miles north to the trail sign that points you right. It's a short drive down County 53 (certainly one of the shortest county roads in the world) to the trailhead parking area.

Grooming: The entire system is groomed for both striding and skating, with a wide skating area and a nicely maintained diagonal track.

Total km: system, 25; this tour, 7

Fee: Minnesota Ski Pass required

Trailhead facilities: There is a large trailhead shelter house, complete with bathrooms. Grand Marais is home of the Gunflint Tavern, a smoke-free place that serves wonderful food, as well as lots of great brews. Right next door is the Cuppa Diem, a place for morning coffee and some bakery goods.

Contact: Grand Marais Chamber of Commerce, P.O. Box 1048, Grand Marais, MN 55604; (888) 922-5000.

If you're skiing the Pincushion Mountain Trails, you'd better ski to Pincushion Mountain, which is where this tour leads. Head out north from the shelter, across the wide, open field that covers several acres. Once in the woods, the trail stays really wide for the first 200 m or so. It climbs, then dips down to Junction 2 (each trail junction is numbered, and we'll use those numbers in describing this tour.)

Go right at 2 and ski through some tall aspen that are up to 15 inches in diameter down to Junction 4. Take a left here, dip into a little ravine and cross a bridge, then climb up to Junction 5. Go right, and don't worry about the caution sign posted on a big aspen. A long downhill follows, but it isn't difficult, just fun. A long, level stretch is followed by a bit of a climb up through a mixed birch, aspen, and spruce woods. Go right at Junction 6, but then head straight or you will take the Short Cut Trail and miss Pincushion Mountain.

Ski down into a ravine, along some water on the left side of the trail—water that hardly ever freezes. Now you're skiing on a flat trail that winds through a lovely stand of white birch. It's a good spot to practice your open field skate. About the time you've got your rhythm, there's a short, steep downhill, then a similar uphill. As the

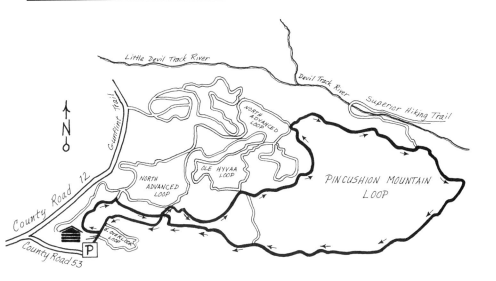

trail curves left, look ahead: An anomalous white spruce sits looking lonely, amid the birch.

A long climb begins here, past the spruce curve. It gets steeper as you go, eventually ending at Junction 7. Turn right and look through the treetops to a ridge beyond. Then start down the trail. Soon you will be tracing the top of a deep ravine. The Devil Track River flows through that ravine, and the trail comes up to the edge several times. By now you are flying down this long, gradual descent. You may zip by the little trail-side shelter as the downhill continues. It doesn't level off for more than .7 km, somewhat after it joins (and begins using) the Superior Hiking Trail. Two little undulations, up, then down, presage a longer uphill. Notice the lack of conifers.

You can see the first part of Pincushion Mountain's summit through the trees on the left. A trail sign posted on a tree lets you know it's time to remove your skis and walk up to the mountaintop. The walk up is almost as exciting as the ski to it.

The best directions are to follow those before you. There are no signs. If there has been no one before you, walk left off the trail and climb until you can't go any higher. Your climb up the head wall—which is about a third of the way up—may require you to kick a few toeholds into the snow for your slick, plastic-soled ski boots.

As you near the summit, the snow will be thin, except for a few drifts. The wind whips across here and takes most of the snow with it. The summit is solid rock, almost no soil. There are a couple of fist-sized patches of tiny grass, brown but proud, sticking above the bit of snow that collects around them. And there are lichens, those odd, symbiotic amalgamations of fungi and algae. Look for them anywhere the snow has swept the rockface clean. Somehow there also are some trees here. They are dwarf, wizened, bonsai-like imitations of their species: aspen and jack pine.

But you came here for the view, and except for a few trees lakeside, it is a 360-degree one. While the lake is dominant along the shore, the bluffs and valleys inland grab attention here. Rivers of trees course down off hillsides, slip into valleys, and flow to the lakeside. Dark conifers contrast with yellow branched aspen, each river contrasting subtlety with the other. Brownish green cedar form ripples in the conifer stream, as reddish birch buds swirl inside the aspen.

If it's sunset, you can watch the golden glow deepen after the sun has dipped behind the Sawtooth Mountains. And you will see in a graphic way why the range is called the Sawtooths.

Back from the summit, clip on your skis and shoot down the next hill, which may require some snowplowing. The downhill ride ends in a wet area, where lots of birch are dying and alder seem at home. Ski this flat area and then you'll enter a deep, dark spruce/fir woods. There are usually lots of deer signs here, their deeply trodden paths crossing the ski trail every hundred meters or less. It's also a wolf hang-out since they are attracted to venison, one of their favorite winter foods.

The trail climbs out of the spruce/fir woods, back into birch/aspen, then hits Junction 19. After an all-too-brief downhill, it climbs some more, hitting Junction 4. Another little downhill teases you, but then more climbing bonks you on the head. A downhill finishes your tour and takes you into the several-acre clearing. The shelter is straight ahead, the parking lot on your left.

Sugarbush Loop

Directions: From Highway 61 in Tofte, take the Sawbill Trail 2.7 miles northwest to the Britton Peak trailhead on the right.

Grooming: These trails are skate and diagonal.

Total km: system, 15; this tour, 12

Fee: Minnesota Ski Pass required

Trailhead facilities: There's an outhouse. In Tofte, there's a general store, a great bakery, and award-winning lodging.

Contact: Lutsen Tofte Tourism Association, P.O. Box 2248, Tofte, MN 55615; (888) 616-6784.

Your excursion onto the Sugarbush Loop begins with a short 30 m climb from the left side of the parking area into a forest thick with sugar maple. Then there are a couple of pleasant downhill pitches to the first of many junctions. This one has a giant sugar maple behind the junction sign. Go left here and then left again at the next two junctions, which are near one another.

If you made all those left turns you are now on the Wood Duck Loop, named for the spring and summer occupants of a less-than-one-acre cattail marsh on the left.

It's a short ski to the figure-eight junction, where Piece of Cake Loop meets Wood Duck. Go left again and it's a 20-meter herringbone climb to a beautiful large white birch near the top of the hill. Just beyond is the junction with Hogback Loop. For a change, go right, and you will glide all the way to the next junction, marked with an "F" on the sign post. Turn left (what else) here and it's a short climb up to the junction where Hogback Loop returns. Go right and you will slide down to a bridge crossing. The little creek that the bridge crosses starts in a meadow off to the left. You can view some of the opening and its flatness by looking up the creek bed. Imagine a moose feeding.

Just a short climb beyond the bridge is the Homestead Loop. Head left from this junction and you won't have to deal with any more junctions for the next 7 km. You will gradually climb into a hard maple woods. The trail cuts through the middle of a little patch of 10-foot-high spruce. Just ahead and to the right are a couple of victims of the fierce wind that can whip across these ridges. The white spruce

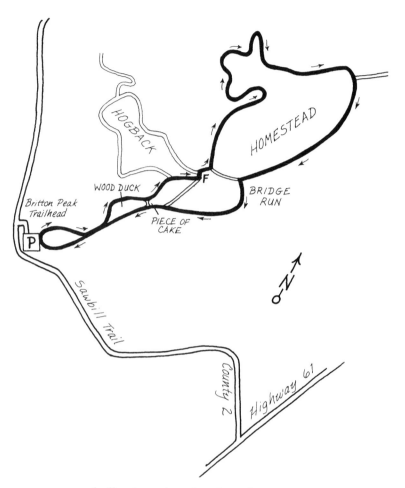

snapped off at about three feet above the ground and nearly fell across the trail. The big old yellow birch broke off 20 feet above the ground and its top fell the same way as the spruce. Behind these two fallen giants is another tall white spruce, its spire still skyward, defying whatever wild wind may come. It or its fallen comrade are likely the father and mother to the little patch of spruce along the trail (father and mother because white spruce are monoecious and produce pollen and seed on the same plant).

As you continue the tour you will wind through more maple woods—woods with lots of young sugar maples, which means the forest is regenerating itself well here. Sugar maples tolerate lots of shade, so generally will grow in under older trees.

The trail loops generally right and a steep slope develops on the left. You will climb and descend several times until you slip down into the head of a ravine that falls off steeply to the left. Three hundred feet below, invisible to you because of the trees and brush, the west branch of the Onion River begins. You will climb out of the ravine and curve left, paralleling the gulch for a bit, then curving right. On this curve you are at 1,450 feet. Look around: There's nothing but sky out beyond the treetops. The actual top of this landform is 12 feet higher, shown on topographical maps at 1,462 feet, and it is to your right.

Being at the peak, you know what comes next! There are five downhill pitches, each with a short break between. The second and fourth are the trickiest—the second because it's the steepest and the fourth because it hooks to the right near the end. The last pitch is marked with a caution sign, because there's a junction at the bottom. The junction is with the trail that connects the Sugarbush system with the Oberg Loop and others north and east. You want to bear right and ski out of the maple woods you've been in for so long into a birch and cedar woods. For the next kilometer the trail is uncharacteristically flat, staying at the 1,300-foot-elevation gradient. Then there's a short climb, and an easy downhill run to the next junction, this one with Bridge Run.

Go left at this junction and enjoy the short, steep drop down to the bridge. The bridge spans the same little creek that you crossed just before you started on the Homestead Loop.

If you look ahead, you will see the steepest, longest grade you will encounter on this entire tour. Steel yourself for the climb and head on up. You will gain 30 meters of vertical in about 200 meters of horizontal distance.

Go left at the next junction and you will be on Piece of Cake Loop briefly before reaching the figure-eight junction. There is a tricky little curve on a downhill near the end of Piece of Cake.

Stay left at the figure-eight junction and ski the flat south side of Wood Duck Loop until a gradual downhill slides you past the last junction and toward the trailhead. When you see the rocky base of Britton Peak on the right and then ski into some row-planted red pine, the parking area is just ahead.

Journal: I really enjoyed skiing the hills on the south side of the Homestead Loop. As I mention in writing the tour, there are five downhill pitches, one after the other. I had never skied here before, and had no idea what was next as I shot down off the trail's high point. There were two inches of ungroomed snow on top of the groomed base, but I still flew down those hills. And I loved it!

Lutsen Nordic Area

Directions: From the intersection of Highways 61 and 36, take 36 north about 3 miles into the general area. Tickets are sold in the main chalet area.

Grooming: These trails are groomed for both skating and striding.

Total km: 31

Fee: yes

Trailhead Facilities: This is a downhill area, one of the larger ones in the Midwest. There is a lot of activity and plenty of amenities are available.

Contact: Lutsen Mountains, P.O. Box 129, Lutsen, MN 55612; (218) 663-7281.

Much of the cross-country skiing here is up on the mountains, access is by a chairlift. And the terrain is challenging. The social scene is decidedly Alpine.

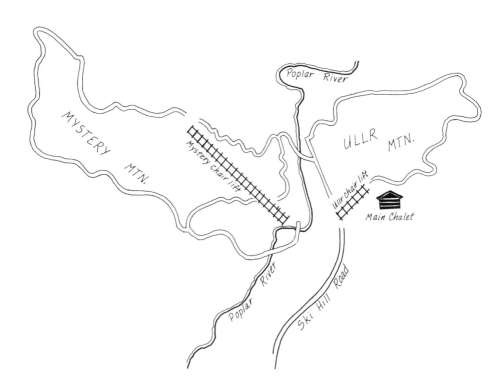

X

The
Thunder Bay
Area

59

Kamview Nordic Centre

Directions: From the intersection of Highway 61 and 20th Side Road, which is 5 km south of Thunder Bay Airport, turn left on 20th Side Road. Go .8 km to the entrance on the left.

Grooming: Tracked and packed, both skate and diagonal. These trails are groomed both well and often. I skied here in the midst of a snowstorm and a big-tracked groomer was out on the trail with me.

Total km: system, 28 (5.8 lighted); this tour, 6.5

Fee: yes

Trailhead facilities: Kamview's trail map touts its "beautiful chalet." When you see its tongue and grove cedar, the vaulted ceiling, and bank of south facing windows, you will agree with the description. Plus, there are some high-tech things thrown in for effect: There's a digital outdoor waxing thermometer (those Swix outdoor dial-types are always way off). There's also a computer terminal out in the public area, which is for keeping track of the Kamview Distance Log. Any member can enter his or her membership number and then key in the kilometers skied that day. Those with the most distance at the end of the season get plaques and other goodies. There's also a concession area with lots of food choices. The cookies are baked on-site and smell really good.

Contact: Thunder Bay Nordic Trails, R.R. #3, Site 2-Box 9, Thunder Bay, Ontario, Canada P7C 4V2; (807) 475-7081.

This tour heads out on Roadway Ramble, then around the Aspen Trail, and returns on Sundown. Stay left from the chalet to enter Roadway Ramble, a broad connector trail. It dips down to where a little creek flows under it. If you look left you can see an open wetland area. Then the trail gets steeper as it climbs. It ends at a kiosk that is comprised of a post with a roof that shelters what's below. Hanging from the post is a trail map, marked to tell you where you are. Under the map is an advertisement (this one was was for "investment executives" when I saw it, but the ads probably change). Under the ad is a rectangular box with a hinged top. Inside are trail maps and a box of tissues. Great idea for those of you who never learned how to blow your nose the "outdoors way." Below the rectangular box is a trash bag, hung in a wire-sided rack. These folks know how to set up a ski kiosk!

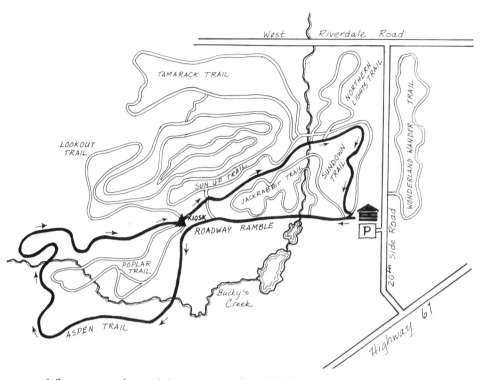

When you are done wiping your nose, bear left from the kiosk onto the Aspen Trail. You will ski down a gentle grade, through aspen that are 30 to 40 feet tall, then cross Bucky's Creek. In the lowlands, speckled alder, balsam fir, and some type of willow join the aspen. The rest of the trail to the next junction is flat, a great spot for practicing your V2 (a skate skiing technique that requires double polling to each side).

The junction is really a shortcut to Poplar Trail. There's another kiosk there if you need a tissue. This tour goes straight. You will see some bigger fir, then an open wetland area ringed on the left with balsam. About this time you can see some black ash, especially on the right, where it looks as though many of them are dead or dying. Perhaps there was a change in soil moisture; too much or too little will kill most trees. Beaver are often to blame.

Climb a little ridge and the trees are aspen again. The trail dips and climbs several times until it treats you to a nice downhill, curve left. If the snow's right, it's a great telemark-turn curve. At the bottom there are more black ash visible on the right, in a large wetland of about 80 acres. The trail flows nicely here. It dips, climbs, and curves, with one more nice telemark downhill, until it swings around the end of the black ash stand.

You are now back at the first kiosk you saw, and at the end of Aspen Trail. Make your way left, up a hill, toward some wooden structures and to Sundown Trail. Two of the structures are outhouses, overrated on the official trail map and each called a "washroom." The other wooden structure looks like four sides of an octagon. There are benches and a sort of roof. It's an interesting architectural piece.

Head off down Sundown—not to be confused with Sun Up, which is one-way the other way and parallels Sundown. This divided highway approach is one way to double your kilometers under lights. About now you should notice the cliff on the other side of Sun Up. The view of it gets better down the trail a bit. There's one nice down-hill on this section of Sundown.

When you reach the junction with Northern Lights Trail, the bluff is almost behind you and worth a look. Two white pine are conspicuous as they stick up over the left edge of the bluff.

Ski straight through an open area, up a steep little bump, bear left and you will see an odd little building along the trail. It looks as if someone might have misplaced an ice-fishing house, but actually it's the security and first-aid shed. Ski past it, and on into some bigger balsam fir, even some bigger aspen. The trail is snug between lots of conifers, then bends out into more open territory. The chalet is on the left.

Journal: You meet a lot of folks while writing a book. Sometimes one of them impresses you, leaves you thinking, "Wow, there's someone who really knows his or her stuff." I met a guy like that today at Kamview. Never having skied there, or anywhere else in or around Thunder Bay, I asked one of the women working in the concession area if there was someone I could talk to about Kamview, and she found Peter Crooks.

He's an intense-looking fellow: lean, thin of face, with the kind of eyes that latch onto you and don't let go until ready. After I introduced myself, he found us a place to sit and proceeded to tell me about not only Kamview but about the Thunder Bay Nordic Trails Association, of which he is the "manager." I suspect his title could be executive director, but he said "manager." He probably doesn't care much for titles, he cares that things get done, and done well.

Established in 1984, the nonprofit Trails Association is governed by an 11-member board of directors. It has grooming responsibility for Kamview, Kakabeka Falls Provincial Park Cross-Country Trails, and Sleeping Giant Provincial Park Ski Trails. That's about 100 km of trail, in three locations with more than 70 km of Canada between them. Crooks makes it work.

60

Kakabeka Falls Trails

Directions: From the intersection of Highways 61 and 11/17 in Thunder Bay, take 11/17 west approximately 30 km to Highway 590, just past the entrance to Kakabeka Falls Provincial Park. Go left on 590, .8 km to Luckens Road. Go left 100 meters on Luckens and the trailhead entrance is on the left.

Grooming: The trails are striding and skating.

Total km: system, 15; this tour, 11

Fee: yes

Trailhead facilities: There is a little house at the trailhead where you can register and pick up a map. It is unheated, but tastefully decorated with all manner of foot, hand, human, and animal prints. You have to see it to understand.

Contact: Ministry of Natural Resources, P.O. Box 5000, 435 James S. St., Thunder Bay, Ontario, Canada, Suite 221 P73 6S8; (807) 475-1261. Or Thunder Bay Nordic Trails, R.R. #3, Site 2-Box 9, Thunder Bay, Ontario, Canada P7C 4V2; (807) 475-7081.

Kakabeka Falls is on the Kaministiquia River. Creating alliterative tongue twisters is an Canadian hobby. Actually, Kakabeka is an Ojibwe word that means "thundering water." You cannot see the falls on this ski tour. They are best observed from the park viewing platforms. Find these by turning into the park off Highway 11/17 about a half-mile south of Highway 590. The falls are 39 meters (128 feet) high and 71 meters (234 feet) wide.

Start this ski due south of the shelter building. The trail goes straight south, past some park buildings. There are lots of aspen and some jack pine along the trail.

The first junction is with Poplar Point Trail, which goes left. There is a sign there that reads, "Narrow winding road. Travel by trailer or RV is not recommended." Sounds like fun, but we are headed right, on the Beaver Meadows Trail. You'll go down a long, gradual grade, followed by a climb, then another gradual descent into—what else— a beaver meadow. Actually, there is a large beaver pond on the left. The dam is immediately in front of you and the beaver lodge farther back in the pond. Beaver tend to stay in their lodges in the winter and chew on aspen they have cached nearby. If it's late winter, you may see some

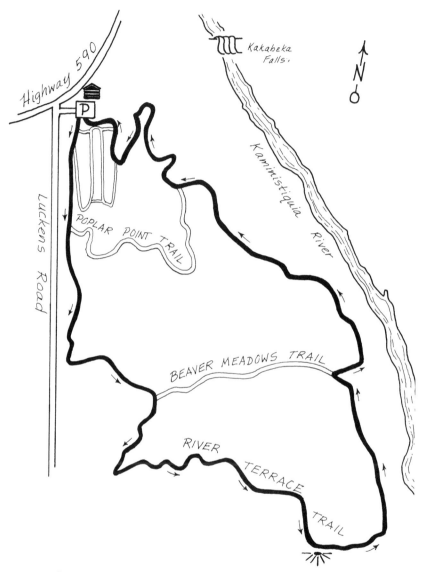

beaver trails out on the ice near the lodge. There is a nice stand of tamarack on the left of the pond. Looking down the creek, to the right, the view is very northern, with alder down low and spruce, tamarack, and fir spires lining the banks.

Ski on up from the creek and around a bend into the group camp area. The open area looks inviting and bright. As you ski back into the woods, look at the brown stems and seed heads sticking above the snow nearby the trail on the left. These are goldenrod. Dark-brown stems with curled lance-shaped leaves rise above the snow. The pyramidal seed heads atop the stems are tan to white; little bits of snow cling to them, creating a soft and fluffy effect. Close by are two small, 25-foot-tall tamarack.

When you see the first "Steep Hill" sign don't worry, the grade is easy. You will glide into another beaver meadow. This time there are ponds on both sides of you, plus an extensive stand of cattails on the right.

Cross between the two ponds, climb a bit, and you will be at the junction of River Terrace Trail. Take it right and regain some more lost altitude in a dense stand of small fir and spruce, then into a more open aspen stand. If you look on the edge of the trail, near where one stand of trees changes into the other, you will see the stalks and dried flower/seed heads of big leafed (woodland) aster. This very shade-tolerant aster maintains large ground-cover-type leaves, then when more sun becomes available, perhaps after a blowdown, it blooms. The spent blooms you see are technically called corymbs. What you see now, in the late fall and winter, are little puffs of seed at the end of each stalk. The puffs are a gathering of individual seeds, each seed having 10 to 20 very small, fine hairs.

The trail ahead twists and turns around easy curves, and up and down a few short hills. Notable plants include some red-twig dogwood, lots of mountain maple, and a bristly bramble that may be raspberry. Eventually you will be in an area of parallel ridges. The ski trail dips and climbs over these odd landscape features several times. Sometimes the trail traces the top of one ridge, then dips down off it, and up onto another. Finally, after a downhill caution sign, the trail dips down, then dips again, taking you out of the ridge area.

Not far from this double downhill are the spent seed heads of fireweed. They have unmistakable twisting tan fibers around a conical head, held on a stalk three or four feet high. The woods are pure aspen.

As the trail curves left, you will begin seeing more sky ahead. You are nearing an overlook. The groomer takes a little detour here, out to the edge. The most distant bluff is Mt. McKay, the one that overlooks Thunder Bay. You are overlooking the broad Kaministiquia River valley. Looking left from Mt. McKay you can see the serrated edge of plantation pines against the sky. Looking right from McKay you can see the Norwester Mountain Range as it stretches toward the U.S. border. Almost directly in front of you is a flat-topped butte, which is Candy Mountain. There are several ski runs on the other side.

Before you leave the overlook, note a couple of plants that you see here and nowhere else on this tour. Directly in front of you, within touching distance, is a hawthorn. Take note of the large thorns. A little farther down the hill are some bur oak. As you ski away, there are several larger bur oak on your right.

The trail now hugs the river ravine on the right. It's about 150 feet down to the river here. Trees block most of the view, some of them white pine growing down in the ravine. There is one steep hill warning sign as the trail curves down into a ravine that branches off the main river ravine. It's a nice run down and a steep climb up.

The trail you are on meets Beaver Meadow Trail not long after this down-up hill. Stay right and you'll have a nice long ride down into another feeder ravine. Stop at the bottom and look right. The river is visible here as a dark ribbon of open water surrounded by white. The river ravine has narrowed, and the river is swifter here than where you saw it at the overlook.

Now it's time for some climbing. Near the top of what is the longest climb so far, you will see a big jack pine on the left. It used to have two stems but one snapped off. A lighting-struck spruce sits close by. The trees on this segment of trail are larger than those anywhere else. There are even some large paper birch.

After a nice, long, nontechnical downhill the trail passes some cedar, the first on this tour, then curves left into some big hills that have towered above you for a while. Eventually you have to climb into and over those hills. It isn't an easy climb, and it's the trail's longest and steepest. I used the sighting of a couple of pine grosbeaks as an excuse to stop halfway and rest. They were eye-catching with their buff-red heads and upper bodies. It was a good excuse.

At the top of the hill is the junction with Poplar Point Trail. Go right and follow it approximately 1.5 km through mostly aspen to its end just east of the trailhead. If you end up in the campground, which is easy to do because the trail is a bit confusing here, just follow the campground exit signs and you will end up where you started at the trailhead.

Journal: Oh, Canada. I love the Canadian national anthem. The CBC plays it every night when it signs off the air. And now I'm here, ensconced in a Canadian motel. Who cares that it's a Best Western. I had some Canadian Coke today and bought some Canadian Citco gas. I haven't had to get any Canadian money; I'm using an American credit card.

So where haven't all-too-familiar multinational corporations usurped national identity? Beer, that's where.

Tonight I discovered two wonderful Canadian brews, one from BC (that's what Canadians call British Columbia) and the other from Guelph. I have to research where that is, but I'm sure it's in Canada, because the bottle cap had a beaver eating a maple leaf pictured on it. So if you're looking for something untainted by international commerce, I'd suggest you start with beer.

Sleeping Giant Provincial Park

Directions: From Thunder Bay, take Highway 11/17 east for 42 km to Highway 587, turn right on 587, and go south approximately 35 km to a sign that will direct you right toward the Visitor Centre in the Marie Louise Lake campground. Follow the signs to parking areas and trailhead.

Grooming: The trails are groomed for both skating and striding, and the skating area is wide.

Total km: system, 50; this tour, 18

Fee: yes

Trailhead facilities: The Visitor Centre is open on weekends, January through March, from 10 a.m. until 4 p.m. There are restrooms, a pleasant fireplace, a pop vending machine, and the Friends of Sleeping Giant may be selling food. It's a good idea to bring whatever food or other items you may feel you will need. There are also some very interesting displays at the Visitor Centre, including one on what was once the richest silver mine in the world. It flourished in the mid-1800s at Silver Islet, just off the tip of the peninsula where Sleeping Giant is located.

Contact: Sleeping Giant Provincial Park, General Delivery, Pass Lake, Ontario, Canada P0T 2M0; (807) 977-2526. Or Thunder Bay Nordic Trails, R.R. #3, Site 2-Box 9, Thunder Bay, Ontario, Canada P7C 4V2; (807) 475-7081.

The Sleeping Giant trails are the site of the annual, early March, Sibley Ski Tour, a tour and race over several distances that attract around a thousand skiers. Our tour for this book will be of the 18 km trail. It is rated intermediate to advanced in the park literature, but if you have the stamina for 18 km, the technical difficulty of the trail is certainly not beyond intermediate, and because of its wide nature even beginners would not be in danger.

The trailhead is between the Visitor Centre and the main parking area. About 100 meters down the trail there is a blue sign that indicates all trails, 2, 10, 18, and 48, go right. You will cross the Visitor Centre entrance road and then see a Sibley Creek Nature Trail sign.

As you ski the broad trail, the trees around you look tall. There are a lot of aspen, but some conifers and birch manage well here, also. When you start seeing speckled alder, and feel the trail drop a bit, you are nearing a bridge crossing. It you look right just before you reach the bridge, you will get your first view of Sleeping Giant. There is an outstanding view of this geological wonder about 5 km from the end of this ski, so don't gawk here too long since you have a lot of skiing ahead of you. From the bridge you can see Marie Louise Lake to the right. The lake's near shore is lined with a dense cedar stand.

After the bridge, the trail dips and climbs, with the climbs increasing in both length and steepness. Finally, after the longest climb, you will see a sign that pictures a skier in a racing tuck, aimed down the side of a triangle. The only words on the sign are, "Steep Hill." If you're a good skate skier you can skate down the entire length of the hill, so it isn't really that steep. Alternately, a good in-track skier will get in the same tuck position as the guy on the sign and zoom down hill in the track.

The next couple of kilometers trend generally downhill. There is one especially nice, half kilometer or so gradual downhill that's a fun, no-pole skate or stride. As you curve left at the end of this long downhill there is a spot where you can see the lake. If you look to the other side of the lake, which is over a kilometer away, you can see some buildings. These are at the campground, near where you started.

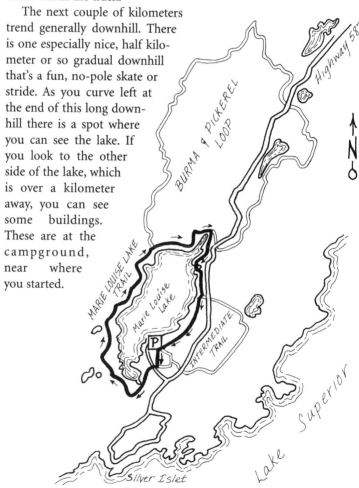

The trail cuts through a stand of large cedar, which is so thick that it's difficult to see into it more than a few meters. Then you will see a sign that announces, "Campsites, 500 meters." If you like, get in a racing mode and time yourself to the first campsite. I made it in 1 minute 15 seconds, which makes me wonder if it really is 500 m and not half that distance. The campsites are unoccupied, and your ski trail here is the road to them in the summer. The sites afford you more views of the big lake on the right.

Just past the camping area but on the left, is a three-acre area of dead spruce. It's likely that some beaver set up camp here, flooding and killing the trees.

You will ski approximately another kilometer, through some pretty woods with occasional tall, verdant white spruce trees standing out above all else, then reach a junction. This is where the 48 km trail joins the 18 km trail. There's a sign just off the 18 km trail, up the 48 km trail, that says it's 9 km back to the Visitor Centre. You've come halfway!

The trail continues on close by lake, and there are a number of good lake views, especially when the trail crosses a bridge. After the bridge, there's a stand of black spruce on the right, between the trail and the lake. These spruce frequently grow in wet areas and bogs. They never get as big as white spruce and are very narrow in habit. There also are some large mountain maple along the trail here, more than 30 feet high. One other tree that you haven't seen yet on the tour is red, or Norway pine; there are some of them on the right.

When you see a tall white pine ahead, you are nearing some impressive hills that will need to be climbed. The pine is big, one of several supercanopy white pine that you will see in the next kilometer. They are remnants of the vast virgin stand that stood here before we cut them all down. These were left, and we can be thankful for that.

There is a long, moderately steep climb starting from that first white pine, then an equally steep downhill. Then comes the steepest, longest climb on the tour. The trail curves left up the hill, and there are more big pine nearby. When you reach the top, there's a junction. The 48 km trail goes straight, and a sign says it's 6 km to the Visitor Centre, right. Unless you want to tackle the long tour, which has a lot more climbing, go right.

The next 3 km are probably the most fun on this loop. There are some hills, but no head walls like those you just climbed. The trail winds around, demanding a bit more control if you ski at higher speed. Plus, there are more large trees here: cedar and even birch that are two feet in diameter.

You will ski into an open area, near the park road on the left. The lake is on the right, and Sleeping Giant beyond. This is the best view of Sleeping Giant on this tour, and one of the better ones in the park.

The massive rock formation, which lies near the very tip of the Sibley Peninsula, inspired a legend of a giant named Nanabosho (The Giant) by the Ojibwe. He was said to have led them north to this area in order that they could avoid their enemy, the Sioux. Accidently discovering silver, Nanabosho buried it on an islet at the tip of the peninsula. He knew that silver would attract white men, who would take the Ojibwe land. The secret of the silver was revealed when an Ojibwe chief made himself ornaments from the silver and was then killed in a battle with the Sioux. Later, Nanabosho saw a Sioux warrior canoeing across Lake Superior. The warrior was showing two white men where the silver was buried. Nanabosho broke a promise he had made to the Great Spirit, in order that the secret hiding place of the silver not be discovered. He caused a storm that capsized the canoe and killed the men. To punish Nanabosho, the Great Spirit turned Nanabosho to stone, and he lies in front of you now, his head on the right, his Adam's apple, his chest, and his lower body. Never mess with the Great Spirit!

Besides looking at the giant, gaze at the big lake. You skied all around that! It's not often that you can see so much of an area that you skied, and it's an expansive accomplishment.

The last few kilometers of trail are essentially flat, and take you through areas where almost all the aspen blew down in a storm. The horizontal tree trunks lay in the same direction, the wind having blown in off the lake. New trees are sprouting in the openness and light.

After skiing through a small grove of large cedar (many with diameters of 15 or more inches), you will reach a junction and a sign that points right and reads, "200 meters to Visitor Centre." You are back to the trailhead.

Journal: I met some fine people here at Sibley. They shared their water, soup, (thank you Iris Renolds), and some wonderful smoked Gouda cheese. The cheese was made at Thunder Oak Cheese, south of Thunder Bay.

And then there was Jim Dyson. He's a fisherman and the son of a fisherman. Dyson lives in Silver Islet, near the end of the Sibley Peninsula. Most of the year he braves the scary waters of Lake Superior in search of whitefish and trout. This time of year he tends to plowing and caring for the Visitor Centre. He shared his knowledge of the place with me.

Silver Islet once held the richest vein of silver in the world, most of it was below Lake Superior. Miners actually dug below the lake bottom, piling the stone and mining debris above the lake, creating a larger and larger island upon which they built a small town. The story is told here at the Visitor Centre.

Lappe Nordic Ski Centre

Directions: From the intersection of Highways 11/17 and 102 (Dawson Road) go west on 102, 6.4 km to Highway 589 (Dog Lake Road). Go north (right) on Dog Lake Road 9.8 kilometers to 4th Concession Road. Go west (left) on 4th Concession 3.8 kilometers to Lappe, which will be on the right.

Grooming: The trails are groomed for striding and diagonal.

Total km: 13

Fee: yes

Trailhead facilities: There is a chalet, complete with food, showers, and sauna.

Contact: Lappe Nordic Centre, West 4th Concession Road, Thunder Bay, Ontario, Canada; (807) 623-3735.

Lappe is a well-run Nordic center that is a favorite of many Thunder Bay residents. Owned and operated by Reijo Puiras, the place has a racer's edge to it. Many races are held here, and it's utilized by local racers and teams. As I write this on March 31, there are two races underway at Lappe. One is a 24-hour endurance race and the other is a 10 km double-pole only, striding race with no kick wax allowed. Feel those triceps burn!

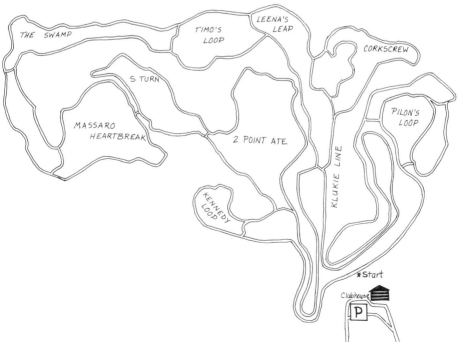

217

List of Web Sites

General Sites

www.norwiski.com
www.north-stars.org
www.skinnyski.com
www.silentsports.net

Sault St. Marie, Ontario, and the Eastern Upper Peninsula

Algonquin: www.skiontario.on.ca
Stokley Creek: www.stokleycreek.com

The Munising/Pictured Rocks/Newberry Area

McKeever Hills: www.uptravel.com
Pictured Rocks—Grand Marais: www.grandmaraismichigan.com
Pictured Rocks—Munising: www.algercounty.com
Tahquamenon Falls State.Park: www.dnr.state.mi.us
Valley Spur: www.uptravel.com

The Marquette Area

Al Quaal Recreation Area: www.marquettecountry.org
Anderson Lake: www.marquettecountry.org
Blueberry Ridge: www.marquettecountry.org
Kivela Road: www.marquettecountry.org
Marquette City Fit Strip: www.marquettecountry.org

The Keweenaw Area

Chassell Classic: www.keweenaw.org
Copper Harbor Pathway: www.uptravel.com
Maasto Hiihto: www.lauriummanorinn.com
Michigan Tech: www.uptravel.com
Swedetown: www.lauriummanorinn.com/swedetown

The Western Upper Peninsula

ABR Trails: www.michiweb.com/abrski
Milje's Ski Trails: www.uptravel.com
Porcupine Mountains Wilderness State Park: www.porkies.com
Watersmeet: www.sylvaniaoutfitters.com
Wolverine Nordic: www.wolverinenordic.com

NorthernWisconsin

Brule River State Forest: www.dnr.state.wi.us
Copper Falls State Park: www.dnr.state.wi.us
Drummond: www.travelbayfieldcounty.com
Pattison State Park: www.dnr.state.wi.us
Rock Lake: www.travelbayfieldcounty.com
Superior Municipal Forest: www.norwiski.com
Teuton and Valkyrie Trail Systems: www.norwiski.com
Uller Ski Trail: www.north-stars.org

The Near North Shore

Korkki Nordic: www.skinnyski.com
Tettegouche State Park: www.dnr.state.mn.us

The Far North Shore

Cascade River State Park: www.cascadelodgemn.com
Deer Yard Lake: www.cascadelodgemn.com
Judge C. R. Magney State Park: www.dnr.state.mn.us
Lookout Mountain: www.cascadelodgemn.com
Moose Fence: www.61north.com
Oberg Mountain: www.skinnyski.com
Pincushion Mountain: www.pincushionbb.com
Lutsen: www.lutsenresort.com

The Thunder Bay Area

Kamview: www.a1trails.com
Kakabeka Falls: www.a1trails.com
Sleeping Giant Provincial Park: www.ontarioparks.com/wint.html
Lappe Nordic Ski Centre: www.lappenordic2000.com

More Great Titles from Trails Books and Prairie Oak Press

Activity Guides

Great Wisconsin Walks:
45 Strolls, Rambles, Hikes, and Treks
Wm. Chad McGrath

Great Minnesota Walks:
49 Strolls, Rambles, Hikes, and Treks
Wm. Chad McGrath

Wisconsin's Outdoor Treasures:
A Guide to 150 Natural Destinations
Tim Bewer

Acorn Guide to Northwest Wisconsin
Tim Bewer

Paddling Southern Wisconsin:
82 Great Trips by Canoe and Kayak
Mike Svob

Paddling Northern Wisconsin:
82 Great Trips by Canoe and Kayak
Mike Svob

Wisconsin Golf Getaways:
A Guide to More Than 200 Great Courses
and Fun Things to Do
Jeff Mayers and Jerry Poling

Wisconsin Underground: A Guide to Caves,
Mines, and Tunnels in and around the Badger State
Doris Green

Best Wisconsin Bike Trips
Phil Van Valkenberg

Travel Guides

Great Minnesota Weekend Adventures
Beth Gauper

Tastes of Minnesota: A Food Lover's Tour
Donna Tabbert Long

Historical Wisconsin Getaways:
Touring the Badger State's Past
Sharyn Alden

The Great Wisconsin Touring Book:
30 Spectacular Auto Tours
Gary Knowles

Wisconsin Family Weekends:
20 Fun Trips for You and the Kids
Susan Lampert Smith

County Parks of Wisconsin, Revised Edition
Jeannette and Chet Bell

Up North Wisconsin:
A Region for All Seasons
Sharyn Alden

Great Wisconsin Taverns:
101 Distinctive Badger Bars
Dennis Boyer

Great Wisconsin Restaurants
Dennis Getto

Great Weekend Adventures
the Editors of Wisconsin Trails

The Wisconsin Traveler's Companion:
A Guide to Country Sights
Jerry Apps and Julie Sutter-Blair

Photo Essays

The Spirit of Door County:
A Photographic Essay
Darryl R. Beers

Wisconsin Lighthouses:
A Photographic and Historical Guide
Ken and Barb Wardius

Wisconsin Waterfalls
Patrick Lisi

Nature Essays

Wild Wisconsin Notebook
James Buchholz

Northern Passages:
Reflections from Lake Superior Country
Michael Van Stappen

Trails Books
P.O. Box 317, Black Earth, WI 53515
(800) 236-8088 • e-mail: books@wistrails.com
www.trailsbooks.com